Cyber-Physical Systems

Scrivener Publishing
100 Cummings Center, Suite 541J
Beverly, MA 01915-6106

Publishers at Scrivener
Martin Scrivener (martin@scrivenerpublishing.com)
Phillip Carmical (pcarmical@scrivenerpublishing.com)

Cyber-Physical Systems

Foundations and Techniques

Edited by

**Uzzal Sharma, Parma Nand,
Jyotir Moy Chatterjee, Vishal Jain,
Noor Zaman Jhanjhi**
and
R. Sujatha

Scrivener
Publishing

WILEY

This edition first published 2022 by John Wiley & Sons, Inc., 111 River Street, Hoboken, NJ 07030, USA
and Scrivener Publishing LLC, 100 Cummings Center, Suite 541J, Beverly, MA 01915, USA
© 2022 Scrivener Publishing LLC
For more information about Scrivener publications please visit www.scrivenerpublishing.com.

Wiley Global Headquarters
111 River Street, Hoboken, NJ 07030, USA

For details of our global editorial offices, customer services, and more information about Wiley products visit us at www.wiley.com.

Limit of Liability/Disclaimer of Warranty
While the publisher and authors have used their best efforts in preparing this work, they make no rep-
resentations or warranties with respect to the accuracy or completeness of the contents of this work and
specifically disclaim all warranties, including without limitation any implied warranties of merchant-
ability or fitness for a particular purpose. No warranty may be created or extended by sales representatives, written sales materials, or promotional statements for this work. The fact that an organization,
website, or product is referred to in this work as a citation and/or potential source of further information does not mean that the publisher and authors endorse the information or services the organization, website, or product may provide or recommendations it may make. This work is sold with the
understanding that the publisher is not engaged in rendering professional services. The advice and
strategies contained herein may not be suitable for your situation. You should consult with a specialist
where appropriate. Neither the publisher nor authors shall be liable for any loss of profit or any other
commercial damages, including but not limited to special, incidental, consequential, or other damages.
Further, readers should be aware that websites listed in this work may have changed or disappeared
between when this work was written and when it is read.

Library of Congress Cataloging-in-Publication Data

ISBN 978-1-119-83619-3

Cover image: Pixabay.Com
Cover design by Russell Richardson

Set in size of 11pt and Minion Pro by Manila Typesetting Company, Makati, Philippines

Printed in the USA

10 9 8 7 6 5 4 3 2 1

Contents

Preface

Cyber-Physical Systems (CPS) is the interconnection of the virtual or cyber and the physical system. It is realized by combining three well-known technologies namely "Embedded Systems", "Sensors and Actuators" and "Network and Communication System". These technologies combine to form a system known as CPS. In CPS the physical process and information processing are so tightly connected that it is hard to distinguish the individual contribution of each process from the output. Some of the exciting innovations such as autonomous cars, quadcopter, space ships, sophisticated medical devices fall under CPS. The scope of CPS is tremendous. In CPS, we can see the applications of various emerging technologies such as artificial intelligence, Internet of Things (IoT), machine learning (ML), deep learning (DL), big data (BD), robotics, quantum technology, etc. Almost in all the sectors whether it is education, health, human resource development, skill improvement, startup strategy, etc., we see an enhancement in the quality output, which is because of the emergence of CPS into the field. The CPS is considered the upcoming industry revolution.

This book is covering the different aspects associated with the CPS, such as algorithms, application areas, improvement of existing technology to name a few. The book has 13 quality chapters written by experts in their field. The details of each chapter are as follows:

Chapter 1 presents a systematic literature review on cyber security threats of the industrial Internet of Things (IIoT). In recent years, the IIoT has become one of the popular technologies among Internet users for transportation, business, education, and communication development.

Chapter 2 explains the integration of big data analytics into CPS. The evolving CPS technology advances BD analytics and processing. The control and management of BD are aided by the architecture of CPS with cyber layer, physical layer, and communication layer is designed which not only integrates but also helps CPS in decision-making.

Chapter 3 deals with the basics of machine learning techniques. Embedding these techniques in a CPS can make the system intelligent and user-friendly. ML aims to develop computer programs, that not only process the data to generate output, but also gain information from that data simultaneously, to improve its performance in every next run.

Chapter 4 presents a precise risk assessment and management strategy.

Chapter 5 presents a detailed review on security issues in layered architectures and distributed denial service of attacks over the IoT environment: As a part of evolution, the current trend is the IoT, which brings automation to the next level via connecting the devices through the Internet, and its benefits are tremendous. Meanwhile, the threats and attacks are also evolving and become an unstoppable menace to IoT users and applications. This chapter addresses critical challenges and future research directions concerning IoT security that gives insights to the new researchers in this domain.

Chapter 6 presents ML and DL (deep learning) techniques for phishing threats and challenges: Internet security threats keep on rising due to the vulnerabilities and numerous attacking techniques. The swindlers who take skills over the vulnerable online services and get admission to the information of genuine people through these virtual features continue to expand. Security should prevent phishing attacks and to offer availability and confidentiality. The phishing attack using AI is discussed in this chapter.

Chapter 7 presents a novel defending and prevention technique for the man in the middle of attacks in cyber-physical networks: Man in the Middle Attack is a type of cyber-attack in which an unauthorized person enters the online network between the two users, avoiding the sight of both users. The scripts developed successfully defended the deployed virtual machines from the Man in the Middle Attacks. The main purpose behind this topic is to make readers beware of cyber-attacks.

Chapter 8 presents the fourth-order interleaved Boost Converter with PID, Type II and Type III controller for smart grid applications: Switched-mode power converters are an important component in interfacing renewable energy sources to smart grids and microgrids. The voltage obtained from power conversion is usually full of ripples. To minimize the ripple in the output, certain topological developments are made. This is made possible by controlling the converters using Type II and Type III controllers and the results are compared with PID controller. The performance is analyzed and compared in the Simulink environment. The transient and steady-state analysis is done for a better understanding of the system.

Chapter 9 presents Industry 4.0 in HealthCare IoT for inventory and supply chain management. Industry 4.0 is a setup reality that fulfills various necessities of the clinical field with expansive assessment. Radio Frequency Identification (RFID) advancement does not simply offer the capacity to discover stuff, supplies, and people persistently, but it also gives capable and exact permission to clinical data for prosperity specialists.

Chapter 10 presents a systematic literature review on the security aspects of the Industrial IoT.

Chapter 11 acts as a readymade guide to researchers who want to know how to lay foundations towards a privacy-aware CPS architecture.

Chapter 12 explains the possible privacy and security issues of CPS.

Chapter 13 presents a review of the various application of the CPS.

Uzzal Sharma, Assam, India
Parma Nand, Greater Noida, India
Jyotir Moy Chatterjee, Kathmandu, Nepal
Vishal Jain, Greater Noida, India
Noor Zaman Jhanjhi, Subang Jaya, Malaysia
R. Sujatha, Vellore, India
April 2022

Acknowledgement

I would like to acknowledge the most important people in my life, i.e., my grandfather Late Shri. Gopal Chatterjee, grandmother Late Smt. Subhankori Chatterjee, my father Shri. Aloke Moy Chatterjee, my Late mother Ms. Nomita Chatterjee & my uncle Shri Moni Moy Chatterjee. The is book has been my long-cherished dream which would not have been turned into reality without the support and love of these amazing people. They have continuously encouraged me despite my failure to give them the proper time and attention. I am also grateful to my friends, who have encouraged and blessed this work with their unconditional love and patient.

Jyotir Moy Chatterjee
Department of IT
Lord Buddha Education Foundation
(Asia Pacific University of Technology & Innovation)
Kathmandu, Nepal-44600

A Systematic Literature Review on Cyber Security Threats of Industrial Internet of Things

Ravi Gedam* and Surendra Rahamatkar[†]

Amity University Chhattisgarh, Raipur, India

Abstract

In recent years, the Industrial Internet of Things (IIoT) has become one of the popular technology among Internet users for transportation, business, education, and communication development. With the rapid adoption of IoT technology, individuals and organizations easily communicate with each other without great effort from the remote location. Although, IoT technology often confronts unauthorized access to sensitive data, personal safety risks, and different types of attacks. Hence, it is essential to model the IoT technology with proper security measures to cope up with the rapid increase of IoT-enabled devices in the real-time market. In particular, predicting security threats is significant in the Industrial IoT applications due to the huge impact on production, financial loss, or injuries. Also, the heterogeneity of the IoT environment necessitates the inherent analysis to detect or prevent the attacks over the voluminous IoT-generated data. Even though the IoT network employs machine learning and deep learning-based security mechanisms, the resource constraints create a set-back in the security provisioning especially, in maintaining the trade-off between the IoT devices' capability and the security level. Hence, in-depth analysis of the IoT data along with the time efficiency is crucial to proactively predict the cyber-threats. Despite this, relearning the new environment from the scratch leads to the time-consuming process in the large-scale IoT environment when there are minor changes in the learning environment while applying the static machine learning or deep learning models. To cope up with this constraint, incrementally updating the learning environment is essential after learning the partially changed environment with the knowledge

*Corresponding author: gedam.hemraj@s.amity.edu
†Corresponding author: srahamatkar@rpr.amity.edu

Uzzal Sharma, Parma Nand, Jyotir Moy Chatterjee, Vishal Jain, Noor Zaman Jhanjhi and R. Sujatha (eds.)
Cyber-Physical Systems: Foundations and Techniques, (1–18) © 2022 Scrivener Publishing LLC

of previously learned data. Hence, to provide security to the resource-constrained IoT environment, selecting the potential input data for the incremental learning model and fine-tuning the parameters of the deep learning model for the input data is vital, which assists towards the proactive prediction of the security threats by the time-efficient learning of the dynamically arriving input data.

Keywords: Industrial IoT, smart manufacturing, industry 4.0, interoperability, deep learning, incremental learning

1.1 Introduction

In recent years, Industrial Internet of Things (IIoT) technology [1] has gained significant attention among the internet users in the real-world with the increased advantage of the ubiquitous connectivity and interaction between the physical and cyber worlds. With the enormously interconnected IoT devices, IIoT devices have been used in various applications such as smart homes, smart cars, smart healthcare, smart agriculture, and smart retail. The exponential rise of IoT technology often confronts security and privacy concerns [2]. Nowadays, cyber-attacks such as ransomware and malware have increasingly targeted IoT applications to impact the distributed network. Even though the existing security measures are adopted in the IoT environment, IIoT applications are still vulnerable to different attacks due to the massive attack surface [3, 4]. Hence, it is essential to design the defense mechanisms to detect and predict the attacks in the IIoT platform. Applying the traditional security models or mechanisms is inadequate for the IIoT environment due to the intrinsic resource and computational constraints. Intrusion detection models dynamically monitor abnormal behaviors or patterns in the system to detect malicious activity. The existing intrusion detection researches have mainly focused on rule-based detection techniques, which lack to support the detection of anomalies in the emerging IIoT platform [5]. To detect anomalies without false alarms, artificial intelligence methods have been widely used by security researchers. For the most part, in order to deal with the massive amount of data generated by IoT devices, machine learning and deep learning algorithms have been used to perform automated data analysis as well as to provide meaningful interpretations [6, 7]. Several research works have employed machine learning and deep learning techniques to detect malicious activity in the IIoT environment. Despite the combination of intrusion detection and artificial intelligence-based research, it still confronts the precise detection of anomalies in IIoT networks.

Owing to the dynamic arrival of the new malware classes and instances in the IIoT platform, traditional machine learning, and deep learning-based security models deal with the catastrophic forgetting problems. Catastrophic forgetting is the ignorance of the knowledge about previous significant classes while performing the classification for the new classes. The security experts have widely utilized incremental learning models [8, 9]. The incremental learning model continuously learns the new data with the knowledge of the previous learning results. It plays a significant role in improving the detection or prediction performance in developing the security models for the detection of known and unknown attacks. The incremental learning model often confronts the stability-plasticity problem: previous data retaining and new data preserving [10]. Hence, harvesting useful insights from the enormous amount of data are crucial to improve the learning performance. In essence, preprocessing the continuously arriving data streams to augment the training data is crucial for the incremental learning model. Thus, this work focuses on modeling the security mechanism for the IIoT application with the contextual preprocessing and the enhanced deep incremental learning model. With the target of improving the detection performance, it employs the incremental feature selection with optimization for the contextual preprocessing and fine-tunes the learning parameters for the proactive prediction of the malicious activities in the IIoT environment.

1.2 Background of Industrial Internet of Things

The Fourth Industrial Revolution (4.0) paradigm can be thought of as a road map that takes us through the four industrial revolutions in the development of manual-to-market industrial production processes. Figure 1.1 illustrates the process of creation. With the beginning of the First Industrial Revolution in the 1800s came the development of mechanization and electric power generation [11]. When mechanical and mechanical power were introduced in the 1800s, the very first Industrial Revolution was launched (Figure 1.2). This resulted in the transition away from physical labor toward the very first methods of production, which was particularly noticeable in the textile industry [12]. The improved overall quality of life played a significant role in the transition process, according to the researchers. Because of the electrification of the world, millions of people were able to industrialize and develop, sparking the Second Industrial Revolution [13]. To illustrate this point, consider the following quote from Henry Ford, which refers to the Ford T-Model automobile: "You can have

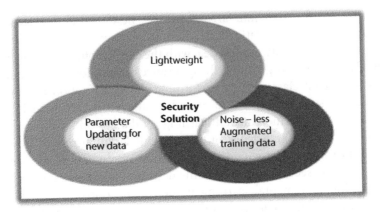

Figure 1.1 Challenges in artificial intelligence-based IIoT security model.

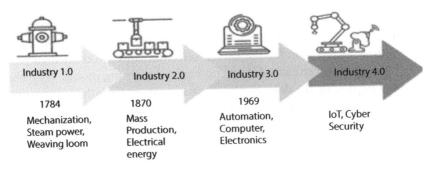

Figure 1.2 The industrial revolutions.

any colour as long as it is black." Although mass production is becoming increasingly popular, there is still room for product customization if mass production is not used. It is the third industrial revolution, which began with the introduction of microelectronics and automation and has continued to the present day [14]. Module manufacturing is encouraged as a result of this, in which a variety of items is created on flexible production lines by employing programmable machines as well as various materials [15].

These manufacturing processes, on the other hand, are limited in their ability to accommodate varying output volumes, which is a disadvantage. The fourth industrial revolution has begun as a result of the advancement of information and communications technology (ICT). Intelligent automation of cyber-physical systems with decentralized control and advanced networking is the technological foundation for artificial intelligence-based systems. Intelligent automation of cyber-physical systems with decentralized control and advanced networking is based on decentralized control and advanced networking (IoT functionalities) [25, 26]. A self-organizing cyber-physical production structure was created by reorienting this new industrial production technology using classical hierarchical automation systems. As a result of this new manufacturing technology, scalable mass-customized production as well as flexibility in terms of production volume are now possible.

Research Gap

The existing security researchers have handled the different types of attacks on the IIoT network by adopting the deep learning and incremental learning models; however, the incremental learning-based security models have been confronted with several shortcomings particularly, in the IIoT network, which are discussed as follows.

- Applying the available existing IIoT security solutions is critical due to the primary concern of the resource constraints in the IIoT network.
- Owing to the need for cross-layer design and optimization algorithms for the security mechanisms, the available security solutions are inappropriate for the IIoT model.
- The DDoS or intrusion detection models often confront the increased probability of false positives, leading to ineffective attack detection [16].
- Lack of modification in the machine learning model while adopting the security solution leads to an increased number of false positives and true negatives.
- Traditional deep learning models lack the development of a reliable, robust, and intelligent security mechanism over the massive scale deployment of the IIoT.
- Static machine learning and deep learning models lead to inaccurate decision-making due to the continuously arriving data streams from different IIoT data sources [17].
- Incrementally identifying the potential features and making the decisions from the extracted set of features over the continuously arriving data streams is critical.
- Traditional preprocessing methods lack to support the effective incremental learning results due to the variations in the inherent relationships of the arriving data [18].
- Incremental learning models lead to inaccurate decision-making without handling the drift data in the

IIoT applications due to the enormous availability of the continuously changing data.

- Modeling the deep learning algorithm with the appropriate parameter values is quite critical for detecting known and unknown attacks in the dynamic IIoT environment.

Challenges in IIoT Security

In the real-world, the IIoT applications often demand both the speed and accuracy ensured data stream mining methods. The IIoT platform confronts major security issues due to the ever-increasing complexity of the attacks, zero-day vulnerabilities, the nature of connected IIoT devices, and the lack of detection of new threats. The existing IIoT security models lack in providing suitable security solutions over the continuous arrival of the IIoT data. Owing to the resource-constrained IIoT environment, modeling the heavy-weight security solution is inappropriate. Even though traditional machine learning and deep learning techniques have been adopted to model the IIoT security solutions, effectively detecting over the continuously arriving IIoT data and developing the lightweight security solution is challenging [19]. The continuous arrival of IIoT data leads to the inaccurate detection or classification of the malicious activities due to the existence of the noisy data, which also leads to the increased computational time. Besides, detecting the new malware or attacks in the IIoT environment with a large number of training samples by the traditional learning model is ineffective [20]. To overcome this obstacle, the incremental learning models have been utilized by the IIoT security researchers. However, training the massive amount of arriving data streams and detecting both the known and unknown malware without selecting the potential features is critical. Hence, there is an essential need to preprocess the massive data streams and protect the IIoT environment from both the known and unknown malware-based attacks [21].

1.3   Literature Review

Several progressive and online algorithms have been written, mostly adapting the existing batch techniques to the progressive environment. Massive theoretical work was done in the stationary environment to test their capacity for generalization and convergence speed, often followed by assumptions such as the linear details. While progress and online learning are well developed and well founded, some publications are only generally aimed at the elder, especially in the context of big data or the Internet of Things technology. Most of these are surveys that classify available methods and certain fields of application.

The principle of progressive learning with a certain motivation for incremental learning is included in Giraud-Carrier and Christophe [15]. They promote progressive learning approaches to incremental projects and also illustrate problems such as e-effects ordering or a trustworthiness query. Gepperth and Hammer recently conducted a survey. Usually, the number of measurements and the number of incoming data instances can be approximated. It can also be presumed how critical the rapid response of the system is. It can also be guessed if a linear classifier is suitable for such tasks.

Challenges in the Environment

An overview of commonly used algorithms with relevant implementation of the real world is also given see Table 1.1.

Incremental learning is done more broadly in streaming environments, but much of the work is geared towards drifting ideas.

Main Properties for Incremental Algorithms for Domingos and Hulten To sustain the increasingly growing data rate, production, they emphasize the importance of combining models with theoretical performance guarantees, which are strictly limited in time and space processing.

Batch-incremental methods were contrasted and evaluated with examples-incremental methods. The inference is, for example, that incremental algorithms are equally effective, but use less energy and that the lazy strategies function especially well with a slider.

Fernandez *et al.* conducted a big test of 179 batch classes on 121 datasets. This comprehensive analysis also included several implementations trendy various toolboxes and languages. The best results were achieved with the Random Forest algorithm [24] and the Gaussian supporting kernel vector Machine (SVM) [25]. However, for incremental algorithms such work is still desperately missing. In this chapter, we take a qualitative approach and examine in depth the main approaches in stationary settings, instead of a broad comparison. We also track the complexity of the model, which takes time and space to draw the required resources, in addition to accuracy. Our analysis ends with some unknown considerations, such as convergence speed and HPO.

In machine learning, deep learning is a subfield that is concerned with learning a hierarchy of data inputs. Many areas such as image detection, speech recognition, signal processing, and natural language processing

Table 1.1 Comparison charts.

Author name and year	Methodology	Techniques	Security type	Application area	Limitations
Ullah, F. *et al.* (2019)	Detects the malware affected files and software piracy in the IoT through source code plagiarism and color image visualization	TensorFlow deep convolutional neural network	Software piracy and malware detection	IoT software source code	Fails to support the detection of unknown malware
Shafiq, M., *et al.* (2020)	Effectively selects the machine learning algorithm and identifies the Bot-IoT attacks traffic	Bijective soft set approach	Malicious and anomaly traffic	Smart city	Lacks to select the potential features for the continuous arrival of data

(Continued)

Table 1.1 Comparison charts. (*Continued*)

Author name and year	Methodology	Techniques	Security type	Application area	Limitations
Qiu, H., *et al.* (2020)	Eliminates the adversarial perturbations by utilizing the pixel drop operation and employs the sparse signal recovery method and wavelet-based denoising method	Deep neural network	Adversarial attacks	Image classification in smart applications	Lack of consideration on the parameter tuning leads to inaccurate detection over the dynamic data
Parra, G.D.L.T., *et al.* (2020)	Detects the URL attacks, SQL injection, phishing, and DDoS attacks in the IoT through cloud-based distributed deep learning	Convolutional neural network and Long short-term memory	Phishing and Botnet attacks	IoT applications	Training the massively arriving input data leads to time inefficiency

(*Continued*)

Table 1.1 Comparison charts. (*Continued*)

Author name and year	Methodology	Techniques	Security type	Application area	Limitations
Deshmukh, R. and Hwang, I. (2019)	Detects different types of aviation anomalies over air traffic variations by recursively updating the learning model with the mini-batch of surveillance data	DBSCAN-based clustering and Temporal-logic-based anomaly detection	Anomaly Detection	Terminal Airspace Operations	Fails to detect the surface anomalies in the airspace
Constantinides, C., *et al.* (2019)	Efficiently as well as effectively mitigates both the known and unknown attacks regardless of the signatures or rules	Self-Organizing Incremental Neural Network and Support Vector Machine	Known and unknown intrusion prevention	Internet of Things and Industrial Applications	Leads to increased false positives
Fan, X., *et al.* (2019)	Combines the unsupervised learning with the visualization technology to identify the network behavior patterns in real-time	Deep auto-encoder and Self Organizing Incremental Neural Network	Anomaly detection in a big market	Real-time network traffic	Fails to select the significant features and consider the variations in the features

(*Continued*)

Table 1.1 Comparison charts. (*Continued*)

Author name and year	Methodology	Techniques	Security type	Application area	Limitations
Reis, L.H.A., et al. (2020)	Integrates the incremental learning and unsupervised learning and detects the threats that affect the control loops in the plant	One-class support vector machine	Zero-day attacks and threats	Water treatment plants	Fails to reduce the false positive rate
Li, J., et al. (2020)	Performs opcode sequence extraction and selection to detect malware samples	Multiclass support vector machine	Known and unknown malware	Information security in small scale data	Fails to support the large-scale imbalanced data
Zhao, W., et al. (2020)	Identifies the changes in the flight operations by detecting the outliers through incremental clustering	Gaussian Mixture Model and Expectation-maximization algorithm	Anomaly detection	Flight Security	Fails to assign the number of clusters and fails to update the parameters

have now been enriched by deep learning algorithms, which have been learned by researchers in order to solve problems.

Deep learning methods are a category of learning methods that can hierarchically learn characteristics from the lower to higher level by constructing a deep architecture. The deep learning methods are able to learn features on several levels automatically, which enable the algorithm to learn complex mapping functions directly from data without human characteristics.

The key characteristic of profound methods of learning is that their models are all profoundly architectured. A deep architecture means that the network has many secret layers. A shallow architecture, in comparison, has only few hidden layers (one to two layers).

Deep neural networks are effectively implemented in different fields: regression, classification, size reduction, movement modeling, texture modeling, information retrieval, processing of natural languages, robotics, error diagnosis and road cracks.

In the ML model, a set of 21 feed profound neural networks was created, which included a variety of DNN values, such as the number of hidden layers, the number of processing units per layer, the triggering of functions, and methods of optimization and regulation. The permutation method [22] has been used to determine the relative value in the ensemble's accuracy of the various biochemical markers. Standardization batch [23] was used to minimize overfit effects and improve the stability of the model's convergence. The best results were obtained by using a DNN with five hidden layers and the regularised mean squared error (MES) function for loss estimation in the loss estimation, the activation PReLU function (PReLU) [24] for each layer and the loss optimization AdaGrad [25] for each layer. The highest DNN score with 82% accuracy was $\beta = 10$, i.e. when the predicted age was ± 10 years of true age, it found the sample to be correctly accepted, exceeding many groups of the competing ML models. Several models were evaluated for the combination of each DNN into an ensemble (stacking), and the elastic net model was most successful [26]. Albumin, glucose, alkaline phosphatase, urea and erythrocyte have been the most effective blood markers.

This model should be incremental learning as well deep learning in industrial IoT.

1.4 The Proposed Methodology

In recent years, the Industrial Internet of Things (IIoT) has become a popular technology among Internet users for transportation, business, education, and communication development. With the rapid adoption of IIoT technology, individuals and organizations easily communicate with each other without great effort from the remote location. However, the IIoT technology often confronts the unauthorized access of sensitive data, personal safety risks, and different types of attacks. Hence, it is essential to model the IIoT technology with proper security measures to cope with the rapid increase of IIoT-enabled devices in the real-time market. In particular, predicting security threats is significant in the Industrial IIoT applications due to the huge impact on production, financial loss, or injuries. Also, the heterogeneity of the IIoT environment necessitates the inherent analysis to detect or prevent the attacks over the voluminous IIoT-generated data. Even though the IIoT network employs machine learning and deep learning-based security mechanisms, the resource constraints create a setback in the security provisioning especially, in maintaining the trade-off between the IIoT device's capability and the security level. Hence, in-depth analysis of the IIoT data along with the time efficiency is crucial to predict the cyber-threats proactively. Despite, relearning the new environment from scratch leads to the time-consuming process in the large-scale IIoT environment when there are minor changes in the learning environment while applying the static machine learning or deep learning models. To cope with this constraint, incrementally updating the learning environment is essential after learning the partially changed environment with the knowledge of previously learned data. Hence, to provide security to the resource-constrained IIoT environment, selecting the potential input data for the incremental learning model and fine-tuning the parameters of the deep learning model for the input data is vital, which assists towards the proactive prediction of the security threats by the time-efficient learning of the dynamically arriving input data.

Figure 1.3 illustrates the processes involved in the proposed IIoT security methodology. The proposed approach incorporates the contextual preprocessing and the proactive prediction processes with the help of the deep incremental learning model and the optimization method. Initially, to effectively clean the continuously arriving data streams, the proposed approach explores the noisy and misclassified instances in the arrival of data and then incrementally selects the features within a particular timeframe based on the impact on the classification performance. In subsequence, it optimizes

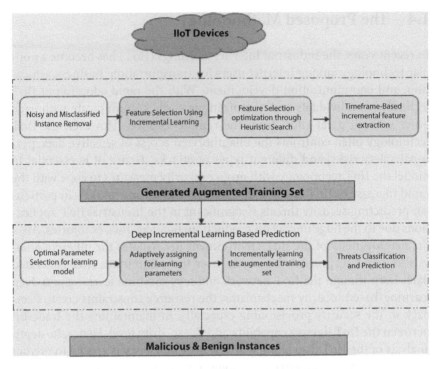

Figure 1.3 Deep incremental learning-based IIoT security model.

the feature selection process through the heuristic search strategy that targets improving the time efficiency in the attack detection process. Moreover, it assists in augmenting training data generation with the optimal features alone, which leverages the improved classification performance. The proposed approach applies the deep incremental learning model with the fine-tuning of the learning parameters for the input data in the IIoT environment. The adaptive updating of the learning parameters associated deep incremental learning model ensures the classification or prediction of the malicious instances in the IIoT platform based on the learning knowledge from the augmented training set. Thus, the proposed approach effectively protects the IIoT environment with improved time efficiency with the help of the deep incremental learning model along with the heuristic model.

1.5   Experimental Requirements

It is necessary to have an i7 processor with 32 GB or extended memory and a 500 GB hard drive in order to run the experimental framework on

Ubuntu 18.04 LTE. The experimental model makes use of the IIoT dataset, which combines the normal data with the data collected during the attack release. Furthermore, in order to run the deep incremental learning algorithm, the experimental framework makes use of the python libraries, which are running on the Python 3.6.8 platform.

Evaluation Metrics

Detection Rate: It is the ratio of the number of correctly detected attacks to the total number of attacks in the IIoT environment. It is also termed as the recall.

Accuracy: It measures the overall detection accuracy of the IIoT security model, which considers the accurate detection performance on both the attacks and normal activities.

Both true positive and true negative refer to the number of malicious activities that were correctly classified or predicted as attacks, as well as the number of normal activities that were correctly classified or predicted as normal. A false positive represents a malicious activity that was incorrectly classified or predicted as normal, while a false negative represents a legitimate activity that was incorrectly classified or predicted as an attack.

1.6   Conclusion

This work presented the incremental learning-based security model for the IIoT environment. The proposed IIoT security mechanism has focused on the classification and prediction of the cyber threats through contextual preprocessing and the deep incremental learning-based prediction. With the target of proactively predicting the malicious instances or activities in the IIoT, this work has outlined the processes of the generation of the augmented training set for the deep increment learning model. The contextual preprocessing involves removing the noisy and misclassified instances, incremental feature selection, and heuristic search-based feature selection optimization. The deep incremental learning-based prediction involves the optimal and adaptive learning parameters selection, learning the augmented training data with the fine-tuned values, and incremental classification and prediction. Thus, the proposed security mechanism proactively protects the IIoT environment from malicious activities through the lightweight and time-efficient intelligence model.

References

1. Alaba, F.A., Othman, M., Hashem, I.A.T., Alotaibi, F., Internet of Things security: A survey. *J. Netw. Comput. Appl.*, 88, 10–28, 2017.
2. Van Oorschot, P.C. and Smith, S.W., The Internet of Things: Security Challenges. *IEEE Secur. Priv.*, 17, 5, 7–9, 2019.
3. Haddadpajouh, H. and Parizi, R., A Survey on Internet of Things Security: Requirements, Challenges, and Solutions. *Internet of Things*, 14, 100129, 2019. doi: 10.1016/j.iot.2019.100129
4. Khraisat, A., Gondal, I., Vamplew, P., Kamruzzaman, J., Survey of intrusion detection systems: techniques, datasets and challenges. *J. Cybersecur.*, 2, 1, 20, 2019.
5. Hussain, F., Hussain, R., Hassan, S.A., Hossain, E., Machine learning in IoT security: Current solutions and future challenges. *IEEE Commun. Surv. Tutor.*, 22, 3, 1686–1721, thirdquarter 2020, doi: 10.1109/COMST.2020.2986444.
6. Al-Garadi, M.A., Mohamed, A., Al-Ali, A., Du, X., Ali, I., Guizani, M., A survey of machine and deep learning methods for Internet of Things (IoT) security. *IEEE Commun. Surv. Tutor.*, 22, 3, 1646–1685, 2020, doi: 10.1109/comst.2020.2988293.
7. Losing, V., Hammer, B., Wersing, H., Incremental on-line learning: A review and comparison of state of the art algorithms. *Neurocomputing*, 275, 1261–1274, 2018.
8. Bhuyan, M.H., Bhattacharyya, D.K., Kalita, J.K., Survey on incremental approaches for network anomaly detection. *Int. J. Commun. Netw. Inf. Sec. (KUST)*, 3, 3, 226–239, 2011, 2012. arXiv preprint arXiv:1211.4493.
9. Gepperth, A. and Hammer, B., Incremental learning algorithms and applications. European Symposium on Artificial Neural Networks (ESANN), Bruges, Belgium, ffhal-01418129f, 2016.
10. Dawoud, A., Shahristani, S., Raun, C., Deep learning and software-defined networks: Towards secure IoT architecture. *Internet Things J.*, 3, 82–89, 2018.
11. Guo, W., Mu, D., Xu, J., Su, P., Wang, G., Xing, X., Lemna: Explaining deep learning-based security applications, in: *Proceedings of the 2018 ACM SIGSAC Conference on Computer and Communications Security*, pp. 364–379, 2018.
12. Sagduyu, Y.E., Shi, Y., Erpek, T., IoT network security from the perspective of adversarial deep learning, in: *2019 16th Annual IEEE International Conference on Sensing, Communication, and Networking (SECON)*, pp. 1–9, 2019.
13. Ullah, F., Naeem, H., Jabbar, S., Khalid, S., Latif, M.A., Al-Turjman, F., Mostarda, L., Cybersecurity threats detection in internet of things using deep learning approach. *IEEE Access*, 7, 124379–124389, 2019.
14. Shafiq, M., Tian, Z., Sun, Y., Du, X., Guizani, M., Selection of effective machine learning algorithm and Bot-IoT attacks traffic identification for internet of things in smart city. *Future Gener. Comput. Syst.*, 107, 433–442, 2020.

15. Qiu, H., Zheng, Q., Zhang, T., Qiu, M., Memmi, G., Lu, J., Towards secure and efficient deep learning inference in dependable IoT systems. *IEEE Internet Things J.*, 2020.

16. Parra, G.D.L.T., Rad, P., Choo, K.K.R., Beebe, N., Detecting Internet of Things attacks using distributed deep learning. *J. Netw. Comput. Appl.*, 102662, 2020.

17. Rezvy, S., Luo, Y., Petridis, M., Lasebae, A., Zebin, T., An efficient deep learning model for intrusion classification and prediction in 5G and IoT networks, in: *2019 53rd Annual Conference on Information Sciences and Systems (CISS)*, pp. 1–6, 2019.

18. Ibitoye, O., Shafiq, O., Matrawy, A., Analyzing adversarial attacks against deep learning for intrusion detection in IoT networks, in: *2019 IEEE Global Communications Conference (GLOBECOM)*, pp. 1–6, 2019.

19. Deshmukh, R. and Hwang, I., Incremental-Learning-Based Unsupervised Anomaly Detection Algorithm for Terminal Airspace Operations. *J. Aerosp. Inf. Syst.*, 16, 9, 362–384, 2019.

20. Constantinides, C., Shiaeles, S., Ghita, B., Kolokotronis, N., A novel online incremental learning intrusion prevention system, in: *IEEE 10th IFIP International Conference on New Technologies, Mobility and Security (NTMS)*, pp. 1–6, 2019.

21. Fan, X., Li, C., Dong, X., A real-time network security visualization system based on incremental learning (ChinaVis 2018). *J. Vis.*, 22, 1, 215–229, 2019.

22. Reis, L.H.A., Murillo Piedrahita, A., Rueda, S., Fernandes, N.C., Medeiros, D.S., de Amorim, M.D., Mattos, D.M., Unsupervised and incremental learning orchestration for cyber-physical security. *Trans. Emerg. Telecommun. Technol.*, e4011, 2020.

23. Li, J., Xue, D., Wu, W., Wang, J., Incremental Learning for Malware Classification in Small Datasets. *Secur. Commun. Netw.*, 2020.

24. Zhao, W., Li, L., Alam, S., Wang, Y., An Incremental Clustering Method for Anomaly Detection in Flight Data. *Transp. Res. Part C: Emerg. Tech.*, 132, 103406, 2021. arXiv preprint arXiv:2005.09874.

25. Almusaylim, Z.A. and Zaman, N., A review on smart home present state and challenges: linked to context-awareness internet of things (IoT). *Wirel. Netw.*, 25, 6, 3193–204, 2019 Aug.

26. Jha, S., Kumar, R., Chatterjee, J.M., Khari, M., Collaborative handshaking approaches between internet of computing and internet of things towards a smart world: a review from 2009–2017. *Telecommun. Syst.*, 70, 4, 617–34, 2019 Apr.

2

Integration of Big Data Analytics Into Cyber-Physical Systems

Nandhini R.S.* and Ramanathan L.

Computer Science and Engineering, Vellore Institute of Technology, Vellore, India

Abstract

The evolving Cyber-Physical Systems technology advances the big data analytics and processing. The chapter discusses the topics of Big Data which are required for Cyber-Physical Systems across all data streams including the heterogeneous data resource integration. The challenges such as integration of data generated from multiple sources into cyber-physical systems, big data for conventional databases and offline processing, scalability are further considered. The control and management of big data is aided by the architecture of cyber-physical system with cyber layer, physical layer and communication layer is designed which not only integrates but also helps cyber-physical system in decision making. The case study that aids big data processing and analytics in cyber-physical system is stated.

Keywords: Cyber-Physical systems, big data analytics and processing, Internet of Things, data mining

2.1 Introduction

The rapid growth in things or devices in particular sensors and actuators made the development to control the smart physical things, smart objects and digital technologies such as machines in smart manufacturing and structures in smart cities, etc. possible. The communication technologies and physical devices are merged to generate systems that are effective, productive, safe called intelligent systems, where the integrations and interactions are combined to create a global cyber-physical system.

Corresponding author: rameshsneka.nandhini@vit.ac.in

Uzzal Sharma, Parma Nand, Jyotir Moy Chatterjee, Vishal Jain, Noor Zaman Jhanjhi and R. Sujatha (eds.)
Cyber-Physical Systems: Foundations and Techniques, (19–42) © 2022 Scrivener Publishing LLC

A cyber-physical system is the association of cyber and physical components that have been specifically engineered to monitor, coordinate and control based on computational algorithms. It is a 3C technology—communication, computation, and control. Cyber-physical systems capture the data from the wireless sensor devices and monitor them, the control of the physical devices is based on the physical data using actuators, thus interacting both with the physical and cyber world in the real environment. These systems are interconnected with each other on a universal scale using different network and communication resources. The physical control is efficient when the data collected from the sensors are processed for information with data mining techniques. The interaction among the users from context perspective, the physical device's surroundings and the process in the cyber-physical systems are observed when the features of cyber-physical system are considered. However, the integration rules, interoperation among the devices, control of cyber-physical system are the functions that are globally distributed and networked in real-time [1]. This system is used extensively in many applications such as industries, transport and vehicular industry, medical and health management, smart grids, military applications, weather forecasting and many more.

An enormous measure of data is generated from various digital technologies like wireless detectors and sensors, mobile phones, storage devices connected to the internet where a continuous data stream is produced. Cyber-physical system has a computational capability that needs to be scaled to provide efficiency as the increasing sensors, digital technologies and devices that are networked create a huge volume of data. To develop a system that is more efficient, intelligent, reliable, trustworthy and self-adaptable integration of big data into a cyber-physical system is mandatory. Computing and computational resources are comparatively lower than the huge data generated from various resources. The big data analytics techniques aim to examine, process and handle the big data characteristics of data to identify the patterns, obtain the information that is needed and relationships in the data sets also the innovative forms of data can be obtained for decision making and process control. The insights about how to model, capture, specify, transfer, organize and manage the data efficiently can be discovered [2]. Conventional data analytics processes the data sets the whole size or type, whereas big data analytics collect, process the data and manage them with low latency and typical data such as unorganized data, data gathered from the sensors including the ones that have spatiotemporal characteristics and the data produced in real-time considered as the stream of data flow can be composed with faster results during real-time processing. Machine learning (ML), artificial neural networks (ANN), statistics, dynamic Bayesian networks (DBA), deep learning, and natural language processing are some of the advanced big data techniques. The merging the big data analytics with the cyber-physical system is inevitable as it is the key to productive, efficient and adaptable cyber-physical system to sustain.

The following are the contents discussed in the chapter. Section 2.2 contains the architecture of cyber-physical system from a big data model for cyber-physical system. Section 2.3 explains the issues and challenges when big data is integrated with cyber-physical system, integration of CPS and BDA and its control and management. The storage and its communication of big data for cyber-physical system are stated in Section 2.4. Data processing techniques and models of big data such as cloud and multi-cloud processing, clustering in big data and cyber-physical system and big data analytics models are stated in Section 2.5. Applications of big data-enabled CPS are stated in Section 2.6 particularly manufacturing, smart grids and smart cities, healthcare and smart transportation. The data security and privacy from the CPS applications and loop holes that cause cyber threats in big data analytics are further discussed.

2.2   Big Data Model for Cyber-Physical System

The big data characteristics can be understood by 5V architecture—volume, variety, veracity, velocity and value [3]. Big data analytics (BDA) is applied in many distinct domains such as e-commerce, enterprise to predict the patterns of customers' interest, and weather forecasting, where changes in the weather can be analyzed and pattern prediction is done based on past data, etc. The data characteristics are varied and the implementation of aggregated data cost is considered due to which smart data was proposed. The concept of smart data is to make sure to eliminate the noise so that important and relevant data can be obtained, which can further be used for application purpose in cyber-physical system to monitor and control so that accurate decision can be made which impacts the physical device in the real-time environment [4]. The present BDA models that are used focus on mining the data, functions that process the data along with data storage and visualization instead of exploring the ways that big data acquire smart data from raw data which makes the integration vulnerable and lowering the analytic capabilities of the system. The BDA architecture should improve the effectiveness and intelligence of the cyber-physical system. The communication layer is included in the system architecture for smart data purpose, data source layer is included in the BDA model which integrates smart methods for data mining and visualizing layer that aids in the integration of collection, pre-processing, storage, mining and visualization of data functions in CPS [5].

2.2.1   Cyber-Physical System Architecture

The BDA enabled CPS design comprises of three layers namely—a physical layer, a cyber layer and a communication layer.

Physical layer—Sensors that are locally distributed across the CPS application fields generate data that are accumulated in the layer for further process. This data contains noise and are uncertain which can be termed as raw data and needs to be processed.

Communication layer—This layer pre-processes the raw data into smart data and converts the decisions from the cyber layer to executable commands. Cyber layer—Controlling and monitoring decisions are made by analysing the data that reflects in the infrastructure of the physical layer.

State sensing, intelligent analysis in real-time, accurate execution and self-optimization are some of the main functions of the architecture from a data processing perspective.

2.2.2   Big Data Analytics Model

The BDA is the other section of the architecture—a vast amount of raw data is processed so that decisions are made faster and better. The learning process in the BDA model is inspired by the human brain, techniques (support vector machine, fuzzy clustering, convolutional neural networks, auto-encoders, deep learning models) that are integrated with data processing techniques [6]. The big data analytics model contains four layers—the data source layer, smart data warehouse layer, smart data mining layer and smart visualization layer.

Data source layer—Many technologies are used to gather data in this layer. Raw data is collected from distributed wireless sensors that include industrial applications, social media, the internet, etc. from the physical CPS devices.

Smart data warehouse layer—This layer manages and maintains historical data that aids decision making and provides an environment to analyse information [7]. The raw data is processed into information with the aid of a data cleaning module that removes the inaccurate record, a data integration module that integrates data with different formats, a data reduction module that reduces data to a more simplified form, data transformation module converts raw data to same formats and data discretization module that converts attributes to discrete intervals.

Smart data mining layer—This layer consists of five modules—extraction model, training model, analytic model, data mining model, and prediction model. Different BDA techniques are used in each model for better results.

Smart data visualization model—This layer can be designed according to users' preferences. The analytic results are displayed to gain perception into the modelled data through visualization techniques.

2.3   Big Data and Cyber-Physical System Integration

Big data analytics is necessary for cyber-physical system as it produces a massive amount of data dynamically, which needs to be explored and examined to obtain useful information and predict patterns. It is undoubtedly proven that the integration of BDA into CPS is inevitable. The big data-enabled CPS must process all the complex data to ensure that the correct operation is carried out so that the system can make the decision and control the dynamic continuous changing behavior of the physical devices. To implement the big data-enabled CPS many concepts are to be adapted and introduced such as data structures, big data features and characteristics and spatial and temporal constraints. However, this integration does not fit the offline processing data solutions which are conventional as the system deals with the real world where the decisions made are critical and takes place in the real-time. The consequences of big data in real-time need to be resolved by a suitable non-classic, vertically integrated solution that handles real-time stream processing for control purposes and batch processing for learning purposes.

2.3.1   Big Data Analytics and Cyber-Physical System

Integrating the cyber-physical system with big data analytics, the CPS focuses on the streaming data produced by the sensors and the data analytics part, where the computation and communication systems collect the data. The features of big data need to be considered in the integration process where the Volume estimates the total amount of data volume, Velocity determines the pace with which the data is created and aggregated, Variety tells the richness in the data representation, and Value estimates the information from the raw data to make decisions. Apart from this, spatial data is also taken into account as it plays important part in the big data-enabled cyber-physical systems.

2.3.1.1 Integration of CPS With BDA

To enable the integration of two systems, an Architecture Analysis and Design Language (AADL) [8], Modelica modeling language—Modelicaml [9] and clock theory [10] integration ensures that the requirements of big data are met and are implemented on the platforms of big data and its properties are considered [11]. A vector-logical big data processing approach, that lets cyber-physical systems control the operations and a computing automation model that impacts performance and hardware intricacy is proposed in the aid of the integration [12].

2.3.1.2 Control and Management of Cyber-Physical System With Big Data Analytics

The so-called system controls the interconnected devices and systems between the physical environment and the computational capabilities in a real-time dynamic environment and manages them. Self-awareness, self-configuration and self-repairing are some of the abilities that cyber-physical system has to adapt for the system to sustain.

The big data environment handles the data as a service to deal with, where this service will be able to manage big data characteristics such as volume, velocity and variety while gathering the generated data from the sensors and the machine controls, and organize them based on the multi-dimensional feature spaces and apply in the industry 4.0 to function [13]. Some of the challenges here faced are big data acquisition and storage, widespread data relevance, data stream elaboration, analysing the data and machine similarity identification, the human–machine interfaces (HMI) based on certain applications and feedback-control mechanisms.

Managing and control of cyber-physical system always depend on the modes created by the humans, but hard to verify and maintain as they are incomplete which leads us to data-driven approaches where the huge amount of data collected by the CPS are modeled such that they learn automatically the models. Cognitive reference architecture is best preferred in this context [14]. This analysis of cyber-physical systems includes different interfaces that interconnect with each other. The big data platform is an interface that all the relevant raw data from the machines and sensors are gathered and prepared for analysis and interpretation. The next interface is learning algorithms that brief about the anomaly detection used for monitoring conditions and predictive maintenance from the data. The information provided from the learning algorithm interface is combined with specific domain knowledge to identify faults and semantic context is added to the results in this conceptual layer. The results from the conceptual layer are converted in a human-understandable manner and implemented to achieve better standardization, efficiency and repeatability in task-specific HMI. Another conceptual layer is placed where the use of knowledge is done to recognize actions that are needed to be taken under the users' decisions which are needed to be communicated to the next interface. The final interface is the adaption layer where the computation of commands takes place in real-time, which communicates changes to the control system that reflects in the physical device.

Modeling the cyber-physical with big data should consider the chaotic features caused by the control of cyber-physical system as it deals with the vast amount of data and its control so that it may lead to unpredicted results. The cyber-physical system responds to all the minor changes and disturbances which cause the system to be sensitive. A fuzzy feedback linearization model followed by a time prediction algorithm is initiated to tackle the chaotic control problems in CPS and also including the synchronization control problem [15].

2.3.2   Issues and Challenges for Big Data-Enabled Cyber-Physical System

The big data-driven CPS will consider the special characteristics and attributes, restrictions, demands and constraints along with the basic big data properties—volume, velocity, variety, volatility, value, veracity and validity that are met during the development of certain system domain integrated with big data. The functional components of big data in CPS are system infrastructure and data analytics which should be considered during the integration. Real-time communication between the physical and cyber devices, where capturing the data, monitoring the database and its functionalities and the distributed computing is part of the system infrastructure component. Data analytics deals with product actualization and resource efficiency and organization along with predictive and descriptive analysis. Some other important issues that deal with both the components are adaptability, flexibility, security and reliability.

In cyber-physical system, a vast amount of data from networking sensors, machines, and several other embedded devices are collected from the physical environment. These data-producing devices such as sensors are not restricted to a certain time or space and also several category and forms such as temperature, speed, geographical data, environmental data, astronomical data, health and logistics data from different sectors and also from digital equipment, transportation and public facilities and smart homes. This leads us to spatiotemporal data requirements, where the system mostly functions in a real-time environment which makes us consider the spatial and temporal data. Geographical data, time-series data, data from remote locations and from moving object trajectories—where data contains movement history of objects are considered as spatiotemporal data.

The time and space correlations are to be considered as important cyber-physical system data features, where the dimensions of such data are observed during analysis and processing. The heterogeneous data are most common in cyber-physical system and the data representation and model makes the data more insightful. Real-time support, sensing and communication services availability, maintenance, infrastructure for the system, evolvability, modularity challenges are persistent when the integration takes place. This integration also questions the infrastructure of the cyber-physical system where the communication and computational capabilities needed to be inspected. Security is another important challenge as its standards vary from applications when they interact with different devices. The control decisions, the trustworthiness of data and authentication of devices and their management where there is a necessity to interpret the protocols and approach towards the system in specific applications as security demands [16].

2.4 Storage and Communication of Big Data for Cyber-Physical System

The management of data and communication in the real environment is key for a successful system to function and sustain constantly with efficiency. Managing the storage operation for cyber-physical system with big data solutions should be regarded alongside caching and routing as there is a huge amount of traffic from the social media applications, people health data, traffic and weather monitoring applications and other smart home appliances which led to the researchers find solutions in storage and communications of big data CPS. Enhancing the performance of system needs to concentrate on the improvement of data collection, data processing techniques from a storage perspective.

2.4.1   Big Data Storage for Cyber-Physical System

Storing the persistent and continual data from numerous resources demands that the approaches be efficient and effective from a scalability, cost and flexibility perspective. Combining the cloud/edge computing facilities with big data analytics can give significant results for data storage objectives. Innovative measures should be applied such as proactive content caching in the networks and its characteristics that predict the user behaviour is the motivation for big data-enabled architectures where data and statistical analysis and visualizations methods are taken into account at base stations. To satisfy the users the data is controlled and used for content popularity estimation and content caching in which cyber-physical system has a high interest [17].

Pre-cache technologies are used with big data for higher performances during the transfer of data from sensors to servers, given that cyber-physical system generates a vast amount of data, where network traffics are caused. Two differential algorithms namely Data Filter Algorithm (DFA) and Data Assembler on Server Algorithm (DASA) are used to reduce the traffic in the networks during the data transfer [18]. This can be implied as an optimal trade-off solution that resolves the network traffic problem effectively and also the data accuracy problem where the data captured by the sensors are changed slightly due to the accuracy of the sensors. The data accuracy is dealt with by choosing the relevant parameters and the algorithm functions before sending the data to the servers by using filters and places them in the sensors and a measure is assigned to each.

Performing the caching on the wireless sensor networks, device-to-device networks in wireless environment and its caching and other data generation devices like base stations rather than on the clouds offers a positive impact on data management. Coded multi transmission is used at the base stations for caching in a realistic environment which allows sharp attributes and quality of the throughput in the asymptotic regime of the sensors which is based on a simple protocol model that uses geometric link conflict constraints and captures elementary aspects of the interference and spatial spectrum reuse [19]. The integration of big data with real-time CPS finds these caching and storage techniques very useful where reliability and predictability are preferred first and different strategies to enhance the CPS performance can be used to speed up the data collection, processing and distribution and the correct use of caching techniques makes the system more manageable.

2.4.2   Big Data Communication for Cyber-Physical System

Cyber-physical system makes decisions considering the data generated from the sensors newly created by the digital technologies which provide information and is used for processing. The innovations in big data technologies provide new insights into the effect of strategic communication, the communication process needs to be analyzed and controlled along with the management of information in real-time evaluation. Modern ways of thinking and decision making are one of the prominent promises that big data computing offers. The data is always made available to the users' advantage so that optimal decisions can be made by determining the latest information which gives more accurate results. Big data delivery technology can be a key technology that does computing better. The big data transmission requirements are to be considered and met among the big data characteristics, which is challenging to process the data where the limited transmission capabilities are to be observed.

The big data environment should be made familiar for cyber-physical systems by proposing new architectures, network infrastructure and other services that have become vital. The data delivery performance should be improved for betterment in the device-to-device (D2D) communications. Without support from the network infrastructure or central control units, the data is exchanged among the nodes. There are certain limitations in the data delivery capacity in D2D communications when the quality and mobility of the nodes are considered. As the cognitive radio technology is integrated with D2D communications, the cognitive radio technology gives the device-to-device the ability to improve the data delivery capacity and makes D2D an alternative that acts as supporting system for the applications of big data [20]. The routing algorithms for D2D cognitive radio networks should be appropriately chosen along with its communication. Integrating the wireless sensor network with mobile cloud computing creates significant advantages where WSN have distributed sensors spatially that monitor the physical conditions such as temperature, sound, pressure, motion, light etc. that changed the way that interaction takes place with the physical world, whereas mobile cloud computing appears to be the new computing model with efficiency, powerful and unique computing basics such as processors, storage, applications and services offered in networks which can be accessed easily on demand. Lower operating cost, high scalability, easy accessibility and maintenance expense are some of the advantages of MCC. Integrating WSN and MCC, where WSN collects the information from the deployed sensors and process them to the cloud and powerful cloud computing is utilized to store and process them to users on demand so that they have the information available to them through simple devices [21]. The sensory data processing framework decreases the storage information of the sensors and reducing the traffic load during the data transmissions is done through WSNs where the transmissions are done in a fast, reliable and secure way. The analytical approach for big data technologies for communication in a real-time environment involves the fusion of data models such as relational, semantic and data and metadata-based in big data along with the provision of distributed computing [22].

These technologies help to find a solution for handling the data speed and data processing in the storage perspective along with easy communication and transmission of the data for systems.

2.5   Big Data Processing in Cyber-Physical System

Big data management can be made better if the processing speed is at a good pace. Computing and clustering help the parallel processing, execution, queries and scheduling tasks in the real-time cloud environment. Big data analytics lets the cyber-physical system discover the patterns, correlations and useful information from the data collected in the physical environment through relevant techniques.

2.5.1   Data Processing

It is impossible to process the huge dynamic data using conventional methods and in a centralized manner. The data needs to be distributed to speed up the processing methods. Parallel processing techniques are applied over traditional processing techniques to handle the data along with its characteristics, scalability issues, availability of resources and programming inefficiency and also the limitations of the database that could not keep with the latest techniques of processing. The following are some of the processing methods and techniques that can be used to overcome the limitations in processing of data—cloud and multi-cloud data processing, clustering in big data.

2.5.1.1   Data Processing in the Cloud and Multi-Cloud Computing

Parallel processing methods have an advantage over conventional processing as they have dedicated servers to process the data. Processing the data in large amounts remains a challenging task in many aspects as efficient data processing has become mandatory due to which the computing and networking infrastructures need to be reconsidered. The method of data processing in big data methods differs in cloud servers, and public cloud proves to be more efficient in terms of resources provisioning, tasks task scheduling and impact of networking on performance in big data. This offers the option to hire the resources such as computing and storage to users in a pay-as-you-go manner [23].

A distributed algorithm is used to adapt the allocated resources and also to support the query rate. This is a resource algorithm in the dynamic environment that carries out computations in the presence of queries. The communication bandwidth and the computation capacity limit the query rate when the network computation performance is limited. The communication of big data with the network resources is understood with the help of a communication network graph, computation nodes to balance the computation loads and network nodes to schedule the processed data transmission [24]. Cloud adapted a new similarity check based compression technique that uses a weighted fast compression distance method instead of traditional data compression techniques due to velocity and volume of big data and lack of efficiency and scalability in the data processing. The adapted data compression techniques are established on similarity calculations within the data chunks that are partitioned along the restoration functions and predictions also improving the efficiency and affordable data loss [25].

The flow of data processing including the data collection, generation and computation, analysis is assigned to individual computing entities breaking the workflow in many big data, IoT and CPS applications. Data and intensive computing workflow are deployed in multi-cloud computing, where data transfer within the cloud affects the workflow standards. In the multi-cloud environments, mathematical models examine the intra and inter cloud execution procedure of the workflow and optimize the network performance of the workflow [26]. The distributed virtual machines run on both single and multi-level platform. An asynchronous deployment protocol is used for the multi-cloud framework that accelerates the deployment process. The global big data analytics for IoT, other models of cloud such as private, hybrid and multi-cloud uses this framework that uses a domain-specific language (DML) [27]. The large-scale multi-cloud environment also has multiple data centers for the big data processing platform. The computing requirement for multi-cloud services is given by the data-driven and feedback enhanced trust (DFET) design over the multiple data centres. The indicator that monitors data is the basis for the computing pattern that integrates the service indicators into computing so that it is applied to service-oriented cloud applications. Hierarchical feedback is associated with this computing model, which considers the relationship among users, monitors and service providers and enhances robustness and reliability [28].

2.5.1.2   Clustering in Big Data

Clustering is a method of unsupervised learning and is used in statistical data analysis. The data clustering partitions a set of objects into groups that are of the same features. It categorizes the data and recognizes the hidden patterns. There is a need for data clustering in big data applications, where the vast amount of data needs to be analyzed. Clustering helps in the distribution of data for storage purposes and task execution. Hierarchical clustering and centroid-based clustering are operated in big data applications frequently. Multiple clustering analysis is a clustering technique that is used in automation systems to explore the patterns in big data which considers the requirements of different clustering. A tensor-based multiple clustering (TMC) and a multiple services and analytic framework cluster the dissimilar data objects in cyber-physical systems, measuring the importance of attributes combination [29]. The most popularly used k-means clustering algorithm increases the number of iterations for convergence as the numbers of iterations increases the numbers of clusters increases which prove that tractions it is not advisable for the applications of big data. The enhanced versions of traditional clustering algorithm should be used, such as supervising the cluster about the initial centroid, data points, etc.

Since big data uses distributed computing, that can be achieved using MapReduce, with the help of the Hadoop platform. For initial computations, the enhanced k-means algorithm averages the data points and selects the initial centroids of clustering rather than the random selection which makes it more efficient than the traditional k-means algorithm and also attain cluster formation accuracy [30]. A clustering based on the summary statistic (coss) is an algorithm that is established on the grounds of summary statistics. The threshold for micro clusters different from one another that is a threshold setting mechanism which adapts is used. All the clusters are combined for a fitting and appropriate clustering algorithm. This results in efficiency and refined clustering [31]. These are a few data clustering algorithms that can be used in big data applications.

2.5.1.3   Clustering in Cyber-Physical System

The CPS when combined with big data has numerous applications such as traffic control system, signaling systems in railways, intelligent transportation, military application, etc. The sensor nodes in the large-scale sensor-based system are intelligently organized and designed to have a long network lifetime. An inter cluster communication relay algorithm where the set of clusters is based on the structured sensor network so that the energy efficiency and its distance is based on the distance that connects the cluster head work and base station also called data collections centers [32].

A density-based data stream clustering algorithm called FlockStream algorithm is used for monitoring the data streams, a big data-enabled cyber-physical system. The flocking behavior is used as the base for agents in this algorithm [33]. The data is processed efficiently in the cloud and multi-cloud environments as CPS application in big data deals with real-time data with a large volume.

2.5.2   Big Data Analytics

Big data analytical approach is used to fulfil the requirements of cloud computing services so that they can be efficiently processed and analysed to enhance their performance. The following are the concepts that are useful for the integration.

Data mining: The process of obtaining the information from raw data can be referred to as data mining. The data mining process reduces the data complexity by capturing the important data. Data mining follows some processing steps before useful information can be obtained from raw data such as selection, pre-processing and data transmission.

Automated decision making and control are key characteristics of the system. Cyber-physical system objects are expected to interact with other objects, perform computations, make decisions and let the decisions reflect in the real world. Huge data are collected from the physical environment into information, data mining techniques are availed. Dimensionality reduction is one such important technique for CPS applications that can alter the features of data.

Principal Component Analysis (PCA) is a dimensionality reduction technique that is used to reduce the dimensions of very huge data sets. The data collected from sensors may contain certain errors as different methods are used for the collection process and some heterogeneous dynamic patterns. These data may also contain noise and are multi-dimensional. Neural networks, when combined with the basic clustering method through Principal Component Analysis (PCA) deals with the complexity issues in the data [34]. The raw data that has unknown patterns and correlations needs to be transformed to useful information through knowledge discovery in databases. Predictive analysis assign scores to data based on the data attributes to analyze data behavior.

Real-time analytics: Real-time analytics lets big data-enabled CPS deal with the challenges in the data gathered from the real-time CPS, which are unstructured and need to be converted to use structured data before analyzing. The data from the social networks, medical devices, traffic monitoring, household appliances, etc. fall under this category.

Spatial–temporal analysis: The data collected have challenges in data storage, scalability and efficiency. The data is collected from the spatio-temporal distributed cyber-physical system sensor nodes, determines the information on the locations. Artificial intelligence algorithms such as Particle Swarm Optimization (PSO) are used to assess and detect the location and update them [35].

2.6 Applications of Big Data for Cyber-Physical System

Big data-enabled cyber-physical system applications impact our daily lives in different fields like automatic cars, smart manufacturing, smart grids, intelligent manufacturing, transportation, medical and healthcare, smart cities and disaster event applications, military applications, etc. A huge volume of data is produced through big data-enabled CPS applications and needs to be processed to utilize in the applications' performance.

Manufacturing, smart grids and smart cities, and healthcare are some of the emerging applications of big data-enabled CPS.

2.6.1 Manufacturing

Digital manufacturing integrates the methods of manufacturing with computer-based technology and computation and communication to create a product. Analytics and visualization collaborate to form computer-based technologies in digital manufacturing. Digital manufacturing is combined with control and automation to define cyber-physical system based manufacturing. The fourth industrial revolution, Industry 4.0 has a great impact on manufacturing. Flexibility, reducing the time, altering according to the customer needs, and services are the advantages offered by Industry 4.0 [36].

Decentralized factory environments are created using interconnected cyber-physical systems along with a combination of tracking technology and component-based assembly line. Agile techniques are included in the entire development phase. A Cyber-Physical Human System (CPHS) offers the possibility of product modification during manufacturing [37]. RFIDs, sensors, microprocessors or embedded system are physical entities in CPSs that collect data from the environment and process the data by connecting and communicating with other systems to proceed for further process. Logistics, human robot interaction and surveillance as a service are some of the applications of CPS used in manufacturing [38]. The optimization can be achieved by the productivity of manufacturing using predictive productive systems [39].

2.6.2   Smart Grids and Smart Cities

Smart grids—Advances in sensing and signal processing make a sustainable energy environment more popular. Home sensors and appliances generate huge volume of data and communicate with the embedded power sensors. Sensing technologies are used in smart grids, however, applied to many large scale challenges such as data processing, analysis and management of the information are to be considered. Smart grids assure improved efficiency and reliability. A big data architecture that consists of data resources, transmission, storage and analysis elements are used in smart grids [40]. In smart grids cyber-physical environment, the communication with the smart grid is done through the control center. This modern cyber-physical system has a hierarchical architecture that has a cyber and a physical plane. All the smart devices are located in the physical plane but the control center is in the cyber plane [41].

Smart cities—Smart cities include traffic management, automatic operation of lights in the cities on roads, electricity management in the city, water management, green city maintenance, garbage collection and automatic disposal, identifying threats causing the situation to the citizens, etc. Smart cities are possible by deploying sensors in the environment and are emergent these days. Analyzing the traffic patterns so that smart users can reach their destinations faster is also a part of smart cities. Smart transportation can be achieved through a graph-oriented mechanism. The overall traffic information can be obtained along with the location and speed of each vehicle. Road sensors are deployed for this purpose, where the obtained information is processed using big data tools [42].

IoT is associated with smart things and hence with smart cities. An architecture that is based on the architecture of IoT that helps in the applications of smart cities. The architecture contains the following layers—technologies, middleware, management and service layer [43].

2.6.3 Healthcare

Cyber-physical system plays a prominent role in medical and healthcare systems. Many wireless sensor networks, dedicated medical sensors such as blood pressure, EEG, oxygen saturation heart rate, magnetic field, temperature, etc. are developed along with the computation techniques for healthcare applications of CPS. More people are now depending upon smart health devices to track their daily activities, where smartwatches are the ones, most commonly used in wearables to track the heart rate, count the number of steps and track other physical activities like running, jogging, swimming, sports, etc. It also monitors the sleep patterns and water intake amount. Various biomedical sensors are designed for designated purposes to monitor the patient's condition and their daily progress.

A Medical Cyber-Physical System (MCPS) is the heterogeneous data from different kinds of medical sensors and other medical devices in a seamless manner are analyzed, shared and appropriate and accurate decisions are made [44]. The cyber-physical system is integrated with Wireless Body Area Network (WBAN), where the wearable devices are used by patients. Local action and data collections are offered by such wearable devices. These can be applied to elderly people who require constant care, mild cognitive impairment and disabilities [45].

2.6.4 Smart Transportation

For transportation to be smart or intelligent, the internet should be associated with it. The objects or the vehicles across different locations should be interconnected with one another for data communication, information and other requirement purposes and need to be connected to the cloud. Incorporating the CPS technology mechanisms—communication, computation and control and by combining the cyber world with the real world, smart transportation can be achieved successfully. These smart transportations rely on technological advancements such as the increase in sensors and the embedded systems.

Vehicular Cyber-Physical System (VCPS) uses a reinforcement approach to deal with smart transportation. It considers the entire challenge of transportation associated with the internet as a game and Nash Equilibrium (NE) balances the problem making it faster and better where past behavior and mistakes from other players are considered as input to tackle the present situation. The information about the past is accessed from the cloud [46]. The social media information such as local traffic information, drivers' condition, other parameters of the vehicles and the surrounding infrastructure information are uploaded into the cloud technology. The big data analysis processes the data in the cloud and the relevant information are passed to drivers through an interface like predicting the destination, driving skills of the driver, etc. which benefits both the customer and the driver [47]. Artificial Intelligence (AI) in real-time applications, control and computing let the embedded Cyber-Physical Vehicle Systems (CPVSs) sustain and overcome the challenges. Optimization in CPVS is done only at design and run time, considering the cyber and physical system co-optimization and the response to both. The pattern across the time, feedback, control of the cyber physical vehicle system is observed to make intelligent transportation better [48].

Smart transportation helps in the progress of autonomous vehicles, communication between vehicles in real-time, robotic transportation, aerospace applications and other challenges in smart transportation.

2.7   Security and Privacy

The physical device gathers the raw data and sends it to the cyber part where the processing takes place. During the transmission, the data is exposed to security threats. It is crucial to protect the system from internal and external attacks, as the data is stored in the cloud networks in real-time. The data storage, access to it and its processing and analysis, all need security as they are exposed to cyber threats and attacks.

Privacy invasion and malicious attacks are possible in the cloud where the continuous stream of data from the CPS applications is stored. The cloud operators and the third party providing the cloud services may have access to the data. The security for cloud services must be revised, made stronger and frequent inspection must be done so that important data from business, industries or government department so that the cloud's credibility does not decrease. The protection of cloud data's security and privacy is of utmost importance. The file that is needed to be stored in the cloud is broken into several files and stored at different locations in the distributed servers of the cloud, where the cloud operators would not have access to the entire file which improves the security of the data stored and the information is contained privately [49]. Big data is very complex to deal with, as it is distributed, has many characteristics, the models of big data also process the data into information and predicts the situation and outcome using the past and the present data. The entire data is processed by the big data and kept in the cloud, where the cryptography techniques can be considered to overcome security and privacy issues. Data can be encrypted on sending to the cloud and decrypted when retrieved when used [50].

A secure big data analytics model provides a strong trust in the cybersecurity and privacy of the data. Certain measures are supposed to be overlooked to provide the security such on [51].

- New strategies of security and privacy can be developed for business, financial industries and government agencies.
- A centralized data management infrastructure should be adapted and frequent security checks on the analytics model should be carried out.
- Network monitoring, suspicious alerts must be implemented and security should be ensured to priority databases such as government and military databases all the time without fail.
- Monitor the real-time stream data and anomaly detection in the network traffic must be guaranteed.

Different strategies must be applied to the cloud that ensures advanced security to the data stored to provide robustness, reliability and privacy to cyber-physical systems application where a stream of dynamic and sensitive data is generated.

2.8   Conclusion

The big data-enabled CPS technology benefits both the big data processing and analysis and the technological advancements in the system. Cyber-physical system is all about the integration of the physical system with a cyber system where communication, computation and control aid in the integration. To make faster and better control decisions the BDA enable CPS architecture is availed where it adapts the characteristics of the system by including the communication layer. The integration of big data analytics with cyber-physical system focuses on basic characteristics of big data and some specialized features of the cyber-physical system and the issues and challenges of integrating big data and CPS are discussed along with the control and management. The storage and communication when the cyber-physical system combined with big data and the data processing in the cloud and multi-cloud technologies, clustering methods in big data and CPS, and big data analytics such as data mining, real-time analytics, spatial–temporal analytics overcome the computational challenges. The CPS big data collection, storage, transmission is considered. The applications of big data-driven CPS such as manufacturing, smart grids, smart cities, healthcare and smart intelligence are discussed from the cyber-physical system perspective. The data generated from the various cyber-physical system through sensors, digital networks, physical devices for particular applications such as military, government, smart girds, manufacturing, aerospace, etc. are of high importance where security and privacy must be provided to those data. The issues and challenges of security and privacy to the cloud containing the sensitive data must be strongly protected along with the big data analytical techniques that process the data and store it in the cloud.

References

1. Broy, M., Engineering cyber-physical systems: Challenges and foundations. *CSD&M*, pp. 1–13, 2013.
2. Chen, M., Mao, S., Liu, Y., Big data: A survey. *Mobile Netw Appl.*, *19*, 2, 171–209, 2014.
3. Chan, J.O., An architecture for big data analytics. *CIIMA*, *13*, 2, 1, 2013.
4. García-Gil, D., Luengo, J., García, S., Herrera, F., Enabling smart data: noise filtering in big data classification. *Inf. Sci.*, *479*, 135–152, 2019.
5. Luo, S., Liu, H., Qi, E., Big data analytics–enabled cyber-physical system: model and applications. *Ind. Manage. Data. Syst.*, 119, 5, 1072–1088, 2019.
6. Hawkins, J., George, D., Niemasik, J., Sequence memory for prediction, inference and behaviour. *Philos. Trans. R. Soc B.*, *364*, 1521, 1203–1209, 2009.
7. Golfarelli, M. and Rizzi, S., A survey on temporal data warehousing. *IJDWM.*, 5, 1, 1–17, 2009.
8. Zhang, L., Designing big data driven cyber physical systems based on AADL. *IEEE SMCS.*, 3072–3077, 2014, October.
9. Schamai, W., *Modelica modeling language (ModelicaML): A UML profile for Modelica*, Linköping University Electronic Press, Linköping, 2009.
10. Jifeng, H., A clock-based framework for construction of hybrid systems. *ICTAC*, Springer, Berlin, Heidelberg, pp. 22–41, 2013, September.
11. Zhang, L., A framework to model big data driven complex cyber physical control systems, in: *ICAC*, pp. 283–288, IEEE, Cranfield, UK, 2014, September.
12. Hahanov, V., Gharibi, W., Litvinova, E., Chumachenko, S., Big data driven cyber analytic system. *IEEE BigData Congress*, 615–622, 2015, June.
13. Marini, A. and Bianchini, D., Big Data As A Service For Monitoring Cyber-Physical Production Systems. *ECMS*, pp. 579–586, 2016, May.
14. Niggemann, O., Biswas, G., Kinnebrew, J.S., Khorasgani, H., Volgmann, S., Bunte, A., Data-Driven Monitoring of Cyber-Physical Systems Leveraging on

Big Data and the Internet-of-Things for Diagnosis and Control. *Proceedings of the 26th International Workshop on Principles of Diagnosis*, 185–192, 2015, August. DX@ Safeprocess.

15. Liu, L., Zhao, S., Yu, Z., Dai, H., A big data inspired chaotic solution for fuzzy feedback linearization model in cyber-physical systems. *Ad. Hoc. Netw.*, 35, 97–104, 2015.

16. Ray, I. and Ray, I., *Proc. NSF Workshop Cyber-Phys. Syst.*, 1–5, 2009, July.AU: Please provide article title and volume number.

17. Zeydan, E., Bastug, E., Bennis, M., Kader, M.A., Karatepe, I.A., Er, A.S., Debbah, M., Big data caching for networking: Moving from cloud to edge. *IEEE Commun. Mag.*, 54, 9, 36–42, 2016.

18. Zhao, H., Gai, K., Li, J., He, X., Novel differential schema for high performance big data telehealth systems using pre-cache. *IEEE HPCC. CSS. ICESS*, 2015, August1412-1417.

19. Ji, M., Caire, G., Molisch, A.F., Wireless device-to-device caching networks: Basic principles and system performance. *IEEE. J. Sel. Areas Commun.*, 34, 1, 176–189, 2015.

20. Huang, J., Wang, S., Cheng, X., Bi, J., Big data routing in D2D communications with cognitive radio capability. *IEEE Wirel. Commun.*, 23, 4, 45–51, 2016.

21. Zhu, C., Wang, H., Liu, X., Shu, L., Yang, L.T., Leung, V.C., A novel sensory data processing framework to integrate sensor networks with mobile cloud. *ISJ.*, 10, 3, 1125–1136, 2014.

22. Jabbar, S., Malik, K.R., Ahmad, M., Aldabbas, O., Asif, M., Khalid, S., Ahmed, S.H., A methodology of real-time data fusion for localized big data analytics. *IEEE Access*, 6, 24510–24520, 2018.

23. Wang, D. and Liu, J., Optimizing big data processing performance in the public cloud: opportunities and approaches. *IEEE Netw.*, 29, 5, 31–35, 2015.

24. Destounis, A., Paschos, G.S., Koutsopoulos, I., Streaming big data meets backpressure in distributed network computation. *IEEE INFOCOM*, pp. 1–9, 2016, April.

25. Yang, C. and Chen, J., A scalable data chunk similarity based compression approach for efficient big sensing data processing on cloud. *IEEE Trans. Knowl. Data Eng.*, 29, 6, 1144–1157, 2016.

26. Wu, C.Q. and Cao, H., Optimizing the performance of big data workflows in multi-cloud environments under budget constraint. *IEEE SCC*, pp. 138–145, 2016, June.

27. Pham, L.M., Tchana, A., Donsez, D., Zurczak, V., Gibello, P.Y., De Palma, N., An adaptable framework to deploy complex applications onto multi-cloud platforms. *IEEE RIVF ICC – RIVF*, pp. 169–174, 2015, January.

28. Li, X., Ma, H., Yao, W., Gui, X., Data-driven and feedback-enhanced trust computing pattern for large-scale multi-cloud collaborative services. *IEEE Trans. Serv. Comput.*, 11, 4, 671–684, 2015.

29. Zhao, Y., Yang, L.T., Zhang, R., A tensor-based multiple clustering approach with its applications in automation systems. *IEEE Trans. Ind. Informat.*, 14, 1, 283–291.

30. Shettar, R. and Purohit, B.V., A MapReduce framework to implement enhanced K-means algorithm. *IEEE ICATCCT.*, 361–363, 2015, October.

31. Fu, J., Liu, Y., Zhang, Z., Xiong, F., Big data clustering based on summary statistics. *IEEE CCITSA.*, 87–91, 2015, December.

32. Cao, J. and Li, H., Energy-efficient structuralized clustering for sensor-based cyber physical systems. 234–239, 2009, July.

33. Spezzano, G. and Vinci, A., Pattern detection in cyber-physical systems. *Proc. Comput. Sci.*, 52, 1016–1021, 2015.

34. Chen, T.C., Sanga, S., Chou, T.Y., Cristini, V., Edgerton, M.E., Neural network with K-means clustering via PCA for gene expression profile analysis. *IEEE WRI. CSIE.*, 3, 670–673, 2009, March.

35. Ding, G., Tan, Z., Wu, J., Zeng, J., Zhang, L., Indoor fingerprinting localization and tracking system using particle swarm optimization and Kalman filter. *IEICE.*, 98, 3, 502–514, 2015.

36. Wang, L. and Wang, G., Big data in cyber-physical systems, digital manufacturing and industry 4.0. *IJEM.*, 6, 4, 1–8, 2016.

37. Scheuermann, C., Verclas, S., Bruegge, B., Agile factory-an example of an industry 4.0 manufacturing process. *IEEE CPSNA*, 2015, August 43-47.

38. Thoben, K.D., Wiesner, S., Wuest, T., Industrie 4.0" and smart manufacturing-a review of research issues and application examples. *Int. J. Autom. Technol.*, 11, 1, 4–16, 2017.

39. Lee, J., Jin, C., Bagheri, B., Cyber physical systems for predictive production systems. *J. Prod. Eng.*, 11, 2, 155–165, 2017.

40. Wang, K., Wang, Y., Hu, X., Sun, Y., Deng, D.J., Vinel, A., Zhang, Y., Wireless big data computing in smart grid. *IEEE Wirel. Commun.*, 24, 2, 58–64, 2017.

41. Kumar, N., Zeadally, S., Misra, S.C., Mobile cloud networking for efficient energy management in smart grid cyber-physical systems. *IEEE Wirel. Commun.*, 23, 5, 100–108, 2016.

42. Rathore, M.M., Ahmad, A., Paul, A., Jeon, G., Efficient graph-oriented smart transportation using internet of things generated big data. *IEEE SITIS*, 2015512-519.

43. Moreno, M.V., Terroso-Sáenz, F., González-Vidal, A., Valdés-Vela, M., Skarmeta, A.F., Zamora, M.A., Chang, V., Applicability of big data techniques to smart cities deployments. *IEEE Tran. Ind. Informat.*, 13, 2, 800–809, 2016.

44. Alhumud, M.A., Hossain, M.A., Masud, M., Perspective of health data interoperability on cloud-based medical cyber-physical systems. *IEEE ICMEW*, pp. 1–6, 2016, July.

45. De Venuto, D. and Annese, V.F., Sangiovanni-Vincentelli, A. L. (2016, May). The ultimate IoT application: A cyber-physical system for ambient assisted living. *IEEE ISCAS*, pp. 2042–2045.

46. Kumar, N., Bali, R.S., Iqbal, R., Chilamkurti, N., Rho, S., Optimized clustering for data dissemination using stochastic coalition game in vehicular cyber-physical systems. *J. Supercomput.*, 71, 9, 3258–3287, 2015.
47. Nawa, K., Chandrasiri, N.P., Yanagihara, T., Oguchi, K., Cyber physical system for vehicle application. *Trans. Inst. Meas. Control.*, 36, 7, 898–905, 2014.
48. Bradley, J.M. and Atkins, E.M., Optimization and control of cyber-physical vehicle systems. *Sensors*, 15, 9, 23020–23049, 2015.
49. Gai, K., Qiu, M., Zhao, H., Security-aware efficient mass distributed storage approach for cloud systems in big data. *IEEE BigDataSecurity HPSC. IDS*, pp. 140–145, 2016, April.
50. Sekar, K. and Padmavathamma, M., Comparative study of encryption algorithm over big data in cloud systems. *IEEE INDIACom*, pp. 1571–1574, 2016, March.
51. Mahmood, T. and Afzal, U., Security analytics: Big data analytics for cybersecurity: A review of trends, techniques and tools. *IEEE NCIA*, pp. 129–134, 2013, December.

3

Machine Learning: A Key Towards Smart Cyber-Physical Systems

Rashmi Kapoor[1]*, Chandragiri Radhacharan[2] and Sung-ho Hur[3]

[1]Department of EEE, VNR VJIET, Hyderabad, India
[2]Department of EEE, JNTUH University College of Engineering Jagtial, Nachupally (Kondagattu), India
[3]School of Electronics Engineering, College of IT Engineering, Kyungpook National University, Daegu, South Korea

Abstract

Machine learning is one of the important components of cyber physical systems. Either development or implementation about cloud computing or edge computing, machine learning, deep learning and AI techniques are key to develop a smart cyber physical system. Machine learning has applications in almost all streams of engineering. It is considered as a subset of Artificial Intelligence (AI) but can be seen as an extension of AI that has broadened the application areas of AI.

AI was initiated to make computers mimic human behaviour, considering human to be most intelligent creature on the earth. Although, later when discussions concluded that human behaviour cannot always be considered as intelligent, modified to "mimicking ideal human behaviour". Modern AI techniques are extracting intelligence not only from human but also from many other creatures like Ant, Bee, Monkey, birds, fishes and many more.

Machine learning added a new feature to AI by trying to make our computer system learn from the data they are receiving. By using Machine Learning techniques, the computers are now not only processing the data, but also extracting the information from that data to give us better results in every next iteration.

Two major thrust research areas in Electrical engineering are Smart Grid and Electric Vehicles. Both these areas are applied to make the power systems and power electronic converters smarter with help of smart inter-disciplinary techniques like machine learning, deep learning, different AI optimization tools etc.

*Corresponding author: rashmi_k@vnrvjiet.in

Uzzal Sharma, Parma Nand, Jyotir Moy Chatterjee, Vishal Jain, Noor Zaman Jhanjhi and R. Sujatha (eds.) *Cyber-Physical Systems: Foundations and Techniques*, (43–62) © 2022 Scrivener Publishing LLC

So, it is the need of the day for the researchers from different streams to equip themselves with these modern tools.

Machine learning can be applied to various classification applications in electrical engineering like detecting power system faults, transformer faults, machine health monitoring etc. It can also be applied for regression applications like solar radiation prediction, selective harmonic elimination for multi-level inverters, electrical load forecasting etc.

In this chapter basics of machine learning, different machine learning algorithms, stages in machine learning based implementations are discussed. At last Electrical engineering related applications of this mezzanine technology are discussed. Two, end to end applications one in power system and another in power electronics are also covered. Implementation on MATLAB as well as Python platforms are demonstrated through simple examples.

Various Hardware's that supports machine learning in a cyber-physical system are also discussed and Raspberry-Pi, as a tool for development of machine learning based cyber physical systems is also demonstrated through example.

Keywords: Machine learning, power systems, power electronic converters, MATLAB, python, artificial neural network, artificial intelligence, smart grid

3.1 Introduction

When a computer network, embedded system and physical process are deeply inter-connected to make complete system more efficient, user friendly and/or reliable, such a system is cyber physical system. Smart grid and autonomous vehicles are two main examples of cyber physical systems related to electrical engineering. One of the key components in such systems is artificial intelligence, which adds an extra feature to the system by adding some intelligence to it. The present chapter deals with the basics of Machine learning techniques. Embedding these techniques in a cyber-physical system [20] can make the system intelligent and user friendly.

Artificial Intelligence Techniques [14] are developed to add intelligence to our systems. These techniques extract intelligence from many natural phenomena. Artificial neural networks are evolved by mimicking the structure of human brain, the body part which is responsible for human intelligence. Fuzzy logic is developed by human's reasoning and decision-making ability. Genetic Algorithm from human evolution system. Ant colony, Particle swam, Bee colony and many other algorithms [1] are developed by mimicking the intelligence in different creatures. The thrust of human to make intelligent machines has led to the development of different algorithms extracting intelligence from different creatures and their behaviour.

One of the main features of intelligence is the "ability to learn". If this ability to learn can be embedded in our machines that are our computers, it forms a machine learning system. This can be possible only through computer programs that are actual interface between the machine and the human. So, the aim in machine learning is to develop computer programs, that not only process the data to generate output, but also gain information from that data simultaneously, to improve its performance in every next run. For example, if my personal inverter has a computer program, that can learn from data, it may do load scheduling for my home so that battery can last for long duration. Another example can be a microwave, if it also has a machine learning based module, it can learn to predict the cooking time required for a particular item based on the quantity of the food item kept. Personalised house cleaner can be another daily life example, where a computer program can be made to learn from the data. Then, the question may arise about difference between a machine learning algorithm and any other computer program. If your computer program only follows the instruction given, it is not a machine learning program but if along with following instructions it is also learning from experiences (in the form of data), then, it is an intelligent program or can be considered as machine learning, since our machine that is computer is learning with experience like a human. The learning process [13, 15] can be supervised learning [19], unsupervised learning, or reinforcement learning. In case of supervised learning labelled data is available to the machine to learn. In unsupervised learning unlabelled data, it means only input is available to machine to extract some information from it. Whereas in reinforcement learning, unlabelled data with an agent is available for machine to extract fruitful information from the data.

Different applications of Machine learning are divided in some basic streams, like classification, regression, clustering, association, etc. [2]. Classification applications are the cases when the input is kept in one of the two or more predefined classes. The examples of classification applications can be classifying a medical data into healthy and not healthy patient groups or classifying power system voltage and current signals in healthy and faulty power distribution or transmission system. These are the case with binary or two class classification. Similarly, if current and voltages from an electrical distribution system are kept in one of the multiple classes like healthy system, system with LG, LLG, or any other type of fault it became a multi class classification example.

In case of classification applications, the target (or expected outcomes) will be zero and one, if it is a binary classification, or zero, one and two if it is a three-class classification. Thus, the expected outcomes will always be discrete numbers in case of classification applications. Whereas applications like predicting stock market or predicting solar irradiance or electrical loads all will have continuous expected outcome in some range, such applications are regression applications. Although both classification and regression applications come under supervised learning, the type of target data or dependent variable splits them as two different types of applications.

Association and clustering are other applications areas of machine learning that comes under unsupervised learning technique.

3.2   Different Machine Learning Algorithms

Logistic regression is the basic algorithm for classification applications [3], which is based on artificial neural network. Artificial neural network is inspired from human brain or neuron structure. The structure of basic artificial neuron is shown in Figure 3.1(a). Here x1 and x2 represent input to the network, w1 is the weight for connection from input 1 to neuron whereas w2 is weight for connection from input 2 to neuron. So now weighted inputs that are x1 * w1 and x2 * w2, will reach the artificial neuron, where it will first cross through a summation block. Then, this summation output represented by Z in the figure will be acted upon by a function called activation function, to generate the output of the artificial neuron. For logistic regression [18], this function is usually a sigmoidal activation, shown in Figure 3.1(b). This algorithm is suited for binary or two class classification problems. If output of the neuron is close to zero (<0.5), input belongs to one class, if it close to 1 (>0.5), input belongs to other class. Thus z = 0 becomes the partitioning line equation between the two classes. The equation of this partitioning line depends on value of weights w1 and w2. Finding the correct value of w1 and w2 (may be w3, w4... depending upon number of inputs) is the training process. By using large data set of input and output, the optimal values of weights are determined, which gives correct partitioning line between the two classes, so that any new data point can be placed in one of the two classes. The line partitioning will be useful only if, the data to be classified are linearly separable, for linearly non separable data polynomial classification is required by using multi-layer networks. If logistic regression algorithm is required to be used for multiclass classification [6], then OVR (one vs rest) technique can be used. But mostly for multiclass classification problems the sigmoidal activation is replaced by soft-max function and cross entropy loss function is used for training the network.

K nearest neighbor and decision tree [5, 6] are the two non-parametric methods that can be used for classification as well as regression applications.

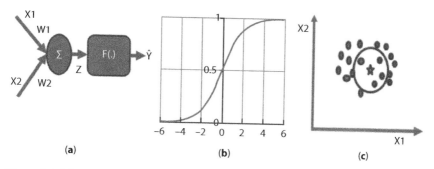

Figure 3.1 (a) Structure of basic artificial neuron, (b) sigmoidal activation function and (c) K nearest neighbor classifier.

For classification applications, K nearest neighbor determines its 'k' nearest neighbors (k = 5, case shown in Figure 3.1(c)), to the unknown data point from the training set and by voting among those 'k' neighbors the class of unknown data point is estimated. Various distance formulas are used to find nearest neighbors like Euclidean distance, hamming distance, Manhattan distance, etc. choosing the correct value of 'k' is very important for performance of this algorithm.

Decision tree method is a hierarchical model-based method [2, 3, 5], where we traverse from root node to terminal or leaf node through various branches and nodes. The splitting of branches from nodes is done through feature at that node. The leaf node determines the class of unknown input in case of classification applications, whereas output value, in case of regression applications.

Linear regression is the basic regression algorithm [5, 6] in machine learning, which is again an artificial neural network approach, but instead of sigmoidal activation function as in logistic regression, now the activation function would be linear activation function. Since activation function is linear, the output is not limited between 0 and 1, it can be any value, based on learning parameters.Support vector machine [6, 10] (SVM) improves the performance of logistic and linear regression by considering the support vectors. These support vectors help in finding optimal plane or hyper plane for classification applications. They also provide optimal fitting for data points in case of regression applications. The support vectors are the vectors from classification boundary to nearby data points. The example of choosing the optimal classification line is shown in Figure 3.2(a), where center line is the optimal line as its distance from the neighboring training points (support vectors) is largest.

Naïve Bayes algorithm is based on Bayes theorem [2], where probability of the occurrence of an event is calculated if another event has already

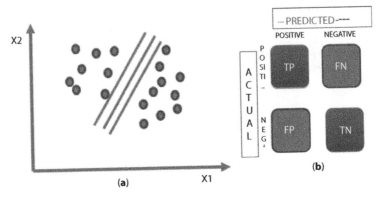

Figure 3.2 (a) SVM Classifier and (b) structure of confusion matrix.

happened. This algorithm assumes that all the input features or variables are independent to each other and each has equal contribution towards the output. Ensemble machine learning [4] algorithms are advanced machine learning algorithms to boost the performance the algorithms by combining the different basic techniques.

3.2.1 Performance Measures for Machine Learning Algorithms

Performance of any machine learning algorithm is determined by validating its performing on test data. The numerical measure of this performance can be done by different parameters [19, 20]. These parameters will be helpful in comparing different algorithms for a particular application. For classification problems, confusion matrix is one of the important parameters to determine the performance of any algorithm. Confusion matrix is the matrix, that determines how much confused the trained model is, to classify any test point in correct class. The rows of this matrix are actual values, while the columns are predicted output values, for test samples. Figure 3.2(b) shows the confusion matrix for a binary classification problem. The element at first row and first column represented as 'TP', i.e., True positive, these are the number of test samples that belongs to positive class and being predicted by the model to be in positive class. So, they are true positive samples. 'FN' represent False negative, that are the number of test samples that belongs to positive class but being predicted by the model to be in negative class, so, the negative class prediction by the model is false for these number of samples that is why it is 'false negative'. Similarly in second row there are 'false positive' and 'true negative' number of test samples. False negative, are the number of incorrect negative class predictions by the model whereas 'True positive' are the number of samples that are correctly predicted by the model to be in negative class. There are many parameters that can be determined from this confusion matrix for comparing different classification algorithms. Some of these parameters are:

Accuracy: Accuracy is defined as ratio of number of correct classifications by the trained model over total number of test samples given to the model.
Precision: It is defined as ratio of number of correct positive class prediction over total positive class predictions made by the model.
Recall/sensitivity: Sensitivity of the model is the number of correct positive class prediction over actual number of positive class samples.
Specificity: Specificity of the model is number of correct negative class prediction over actual number of negative class samples.
F1 score: This parameter summarises Recall and precision by taking harmonic mean of these two parameters.

Trade-off between different parameters needs to be taken base on application requirement, precision may be more important performance criterion for some applications than sensitivity and vice versa.
For regression applications, mean square error, mean absolute error and R2 error or coefficient of determination, are generally used for comparing different algorithms. Mean square error is the mostly used performance measure for regression applications.

3.2.2 Steps to Implement ML Algorithms

The effectiveness of any ML algorithm depends on quantity and quality of data [5, 22]. The first step to implement any ML algorithm is the collection of data. The data can be collected by running the system under different possible conditions and tabulating the input and target variables. Sometimes running actual system under different conditions is not practically feasible, in that case a dummy system model can be developed for collection of data set. Sometimes data collection can be done through a simulated system. But it is essential to validate the simulated data before using it as training data for any implementation. Data can also be downloaded from various online platforms like Kaggle or different government and non-government organizations websites. The next step is to visualize and analyse this raw data, so that any missing or incorrect sample can be corrected or omitted from the data set. Various types of plots are available in MATLAB, Python and R programming platforms available for machine learning implementation that helps in visualization of the data like bar plot, scattered plot, box plot, etc. Different techniques are available to handle missing data if any in the data set. The missing data samples if detected can be ignored or can be predicted from other samples using a machine learning technique. Once the complete data set is available, based on visualization and analysis, features are selected for the model. These featured are independent variables that decide the output of the model. Less number of features may cause under or overfitting of the model, whereas large number of features makes the model complicated and bulky. Once the features are selected, data set is required to be normalized. This step converts the independent variables into zero mean and unit variance, so that all the features get equal dominance towards output determination. Now the data set is ready to be applied to any machine learning algorithm for training. The complete data set is divided in two parts, training set and testing set. The training set is used for training the machine learning model whereas the testing set or validation set is used to validate the performance of the trained model by using various performance measures. Once the best model is achieved, it can be used for inference for unknown data by developing an API or by deploying it on suitable hardware.

3.2.3 Various Platforms Available for Implementation

MATLAB, Python and R programming [12] are the three most popular platforms for implementation of any machine learning based application. All these three provide user friendly instruction set/GUIs for the user. Latest version of MATLAB provides GUI to implement both classification and regression applications that are very good for basic level implementation of any machine learning based application. MATLAB also provides a huge instruction set for programming any machine learning algorithm. Python and 'R' are another user-friendly platform that has good number of inbuilt functions for programming any machine learning algorithm very easily.

3.2.4 Applications of Machine Learning in Electrical Engineering

Machine learning can be applied to various electrical engineering applications. Many electrical engineers are working towards development of smart grid, which consists of smart generation, transmission, distribution, and utilization. Machine learning can be an important tool in the development of smart grid. Machine learning based controllers for generators can be developed. Machine learning can also play an important role in increasing the reliability of the electrical grid by developing machine learning based fault detection and isolation systems for different components of the grid like transformer, alternators, and transmission lines. Maintenance of the generating station where human intervention is risky or time consuming can also be done through machine learning. The machine learning based smart loads are already in market like smart air conditioners, air purifiers, washing machines, etc. Artificial intelligence techniques are also playing a role in integrating renewable energy sources with the conventional grid. The forecasting of electrical loads and solar irradiations can be another example where machine learning can be used.

Machine learning also has wide applications in electric vehicle development. Battery health monitoring systems, smart driver assistant system can be developed for electric vehicles using machine learning techniques. Machine learning can also be applied for fault detection and control of various power electronics equipment in the vehicle. For example, dc to dc converters controller and health monitoring system can be developed by using machine learning techniques.

There are various other areas in electrical engineering where machine learning can make the complete system less complicated and more reliable. For example, in electrical drives, safety systems can be developed using machine learning, electrical motor control and health monitoring can also be done using machine learning techniques.

3.3   ML Use-Case in MATLAB

In this section, one example implementation of machine learning algorithms is discussed to classify electrical distribution system line faults. Point of common coupling voltages and neutral current are the independent variables or the input features. The trained machine learning model will be able to classify the system as healthy system or system with LG fault or system with LL faults, etc. The platform demonstrated in this segment is MATLAB. It is a classification application for the machine learning, so different classification algorithms of machine learning can be compared. As discussed, the first step will be to collect dataset for training and testing of different algorithms. Since it is difficult to get huge fault data for any electrical distribution system, either a laboratory dummy model or a simulated distribution system is required to generate different fault condition dataset. In this case, a Simulink model is used to generate PCC voltage and neutral current for different fault cases and healthy power system at different loading conditions. This Simulink scope data will be voltages and current

Table 3.1 Sample data set for power system fault classification.

IN1	IN2	IN3	IN4	IN5	IN6	IN7	Target
9.00E–05	0.002468	0.001717	200654.5	200656.7	200666.6	1.02E–13	0
0.012805	1.341397	1.539374	0.013685	213347.2	199668.7	224021.9	1
0.960094	0.002615	0.904782	199445.7	0.002778	213384.6	223686.6	1
0.056628	0.079739	0.026991	213557.8	199485.2	0.028794	224088.5	1
0.067671	0.082547	0.031251	42504.31	42496.08	185594.7	579.1227	2
1.939036	3.01543	2.393509	185609.1	42495.55	42523.11	570.2783	2
1.691694	1.860545	2.426165	42622.63	185792.5	42623.51	563.3078	2

values with corresponding time value. Since it is time-based data, it cannot be directly used as input feature or independent variable for any machine learning model. This time-based data can be converted to time-based features like average value, RMS value or max value etc. This time-based data can also be converted to frequency-based features by using fast Fourier transform or wavelet transform. In the present work fast Fourier transform is used to convert the time-based data to frequency domain and then band power in different frequency ranges based on power spectrum has been chosen to extract features from voltages and current. Seven features are being extracted for each case to complete the data set.

Table 3.1 shows the sample data set extracted for three class classification are: healthy system (target = 0), system with LG fault (target = 1) and system with LL fault (target = 2). Now, features are ready but their distribution is not appropriate, so normalization of data set is required so that it can be in zero mean and unit variance form. The Matlab code for the same is shown in Table 3.2, where each sample is subtracted by mean of its column and divided by standard deviation for the same column.

Table 3.2 Code for data normalization in Matlab.

```
for f=1:7
    P14(:,f)=(P(:,f)-mean(P(:,f)))/std(P(:,f))
end
```

This normalized data set can now be used to train any machine learning classification model.

Two cases of implementation can be seen here in MATLAB, first by using GUI app in MATLAB for machine learning that is classification learner application and other by writing an m-file for this implementation.

Let us first see the implementation in classification learner app [16]. This app can be found under APPS tab of MATLAB. After opening the app, clicking on import data will open a new window having three steps as shown in Figure 3.3. The first step is to select the data set from MATLAB workspace. Once data is selected, columns need to be specified as predictor or response in the second step. The predictor means input variables and response means the target value. For this case of classifying the faults, the first seven columns are input features, while the last column is the target output or predictor. In the third step, validation method is selected. Three options available in this step are cross validation, hold out and no validation. In cross validation, data is divided in different parts or folds (the number of folds needs to be specified by the user). One part is kept aside as testing set and remaining parts are used as training set. The performance of the model is evaluated on test set. The complete process is repeated by considering each portion of the data set as test set. This method of validation is particularly suitable for the case when data set is not sufficiently large, as in this case model will be tested on each type of input instead of being tested only on small portion of data. If the data set is sufficiently large the "hold out" validation can be selected in

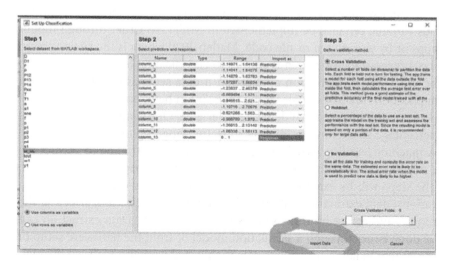

Figure 3.3 Classification learner app in Matlab.

step 3. In this type of validation, a percentage of data is kept aside as testing data for validation of the trained model. The user may also choose 'no validation' option in step 3.

After completing import of data, visualization of data can be done through scattered plot option available in app, and later training can be done by selecting different algorithms and comparing the performance using confusion matrix and ROC curve. The comparison window of various algorithms is also available in the app. The best model can be exported to Matlab workspace for further testing of the model. Once the model is exported simple 'predict' command is used to get inferences from the trained machine learning model. The code for the trained machine learning model can also be generated from the classification learner app. This can be easy way to start and understand the machine learning implementation without writing code.

These machine learning models can also be developed by writing an m-file code in MATLAB. Right from importing and handling the data to visualizing the data, MATLAB provides simple inbuilt functions like import, gscatter. MATLAB also provides inbuilt functions for each basic machine learning algorithm, for example, classificationKNN, ClassificationTree, NaiveBayes, svmtrain and svmclassify are some MATLAB functions [17] for K nearest neighbor, decision tree, Naïve Bayes and SVM algorithm, respectively. Matlab also has inbuilt function 'confusionmat' for determining confusion matrix, similarly ROC curve and accuracy curves can also be plotted through simple instructions. A simple program for classification using programming in MATLAB is shown in Table 3.4.

Similarly, any regression application where target response is continuous variable can also be implemented in MATLAB either through inbuilt apps or by writing am m-file code. Matlab 2020 which is the latest version has a regression app which is similar to classification learner app that can be used for any regression application if data set is available. Regression applications are based on learning the relation between different independent variables to predict a dependent variable. One simple example can be percentage shortening prediction in stator wingding of induction motor. A machine learning based regression model can be trained to predict the percentage shortening in stator winding with the help of stator current. The steps will be exactly same as what discussed for classification applications; data extraction, data visualization, feature selection, selecting the model, and at last training and testing of algorithm. Data extraction can be done either through a simulation model or from the hardware setup of the system in laboratory. Once data is collected it will be analysed through various visualization tools available, for choosing independent variable or features for the model. The features can be frequency-based features like power spectrum density by performing FFT or wave let transforms. The features can also be sequence component based, that can be obtained by converting three phase stator current to sequence components. Since turn shortening in stator winding causes unbalance in stator winding, so negative or/and zero sequence components can be used for feature extraction. Once features are selected machine learning algorithms can be applied to get a trained model, either through app or by writing a code. A sample regression implementation through Matlab m-file is shown in Table 3.3.

Table 3.3 A sample regression implementation through Matlab m-file.

```
load data_regression.mat  % loading the data file
data1=data_regression(:,2:3) % removing the unwanted columns from data
    here first column was serial no. so omitted
[train_data,test_data ] = holdout(data1,70 );% spilitting the data set as train
    and test, here 70% for training and 30% for testing
In_train=train_data(:,1:end-1); % defining column 1 last-1 as independent
    variables or input features
Tr_train=train_data(:,end);% and last column as response or dependent
    variable
In_test=test_data(:,1:end-1); % for both train and test data set
Tr_test=test_data(:,end);
N=length(In_train)
M=length(In_test)
Model1 = fitlm(In_train,Tr_train);% fitlm is inbuilt function for linear
    regression model training
W=Model1.Coefficients{:,1}% to check the trained model parameters
%% Mean Square Error
predicted_output=predict(Model1,In_test); % applied test inputs to trained
    model for      %prediction
mse2=sqrt(mean((predicted_output-Tr_test).^2)) % performance evaluation
    through mean %square error
figure
hold on
scatter(In_test,Tr_test) % scattered plot for test data set
fplot(W(1)+W(2)*x) %  plotting the fitted line of the model
xlabel({'Input'});
ylabel({'output'});
title({'Regression Using Inbuilt MATLAB Function'});
xlim([-3 3])
hold off
```

Table 3.4 A sample Classification implementation through Matlab m-file.

```
LR_Model=mnrfit(In_train,Tr_train) % function for multinomial logistic
   regression
% for two class classification 'fitmodel' or 'fitconstrainedmodel' functions can
   be used.
% testing the trained LR model with new samples that are not used for training
Predicted_op = Model.predict(In_test);
% to validate the performance the confusion matrix is determined
C_matrix = confusionmat(op_test),Predicted_op);
knn = ClassificationKNN.fit(In_train,Tr_train,'Distance','seuclidean');
% testing the trained KNN model with new samples that are not used for
   training
KNN_predicted = knn.predict(In_test);
% to validate the performance the confusion matrix is determined
KNN_confusion_Mat = confusionmat(Op_test, KNN_predicted);
Op_Nb = NaiveBayes.fit(In_train,Op_train,'Distribution',dist);
% testing the trained Naïve Bayes model with new samples that are not used
   for training
NB_predicted = Nb.predict(In_test);
% to validate the performance the confusion matrix is determined
NB_confusion_Mat = confusionmat(Op_test, NB_predicted);
Svm_Model= svmtrain(In_train,Op_train,'kernel_
   function','rbf','kktviolationlevel',0.1,'options',opts);
% testing the trained SVM model with new samples that are not used for
   training
Op_svm = svmclassify(Svm_Model, In_test);
C_svm = confusionmat(Op_test,Op_svm);
```

In the similar way, for any classification application, after loading the classification dataset a code can be written in Matlab. Table 3.4 shows the implementation of different algorithms in an m-file.

3.4   ML Use-Case in Python

Python is a high-level programming language which has a large standard library that facilitated user to complete any complicated task also with small set of instructions or functions. Spyder (scientific python development

Table 3.5 Calling the libraries in python.

```
import numpy as np
import pandas as pd
import matplotlib.pyplot as plt
```

environment) is an open-source IDE (integrated development environment) to develop and run any python program. The Jupyter notebook is a web-based application where python code along with interactive text based easily sharable notebook can be developed. Pycharm and thonny are other popular IDEs for python. Scikit learn (sklearn) [7, 8, 11] is a machine learning library in python that provides inbuilt functions for various basic machine learning algorithms. Numpy (numerical python) is also a library in python that helps in handling n dimensional arrays. Pandas library in python [8, 9] are used to handle large tabular data sets with labels in a machine learning based program.

To show the implementation of a machine learning classification application, sample data set is generated for power system fault classification as a demonstration. The data is saved as comma separated values (.csv) file, which is loaded in Jupyter notebook. To demonstrate the pandas library data handling, the data set is saved as .csv file and each input column is labeled as I1 to I7 and target column as T.

Before loading the data important libraries need to be called like numpy and pandas for data handling, matplotlib for different plotting functions related to data visualization, error curve plotting, etc. Table 3.5 shows calling of some important python libraries.

Now data set can be loaded using csv_read function available in Pandas. To see some of the initial or ending values of the data "data.head()" or "data.tail()" functions can be used. Pandas library also provides "data.shape" function to find the dimensions of the data set. The complete code for logistic regression and K nearest neighbor algorithm is shown in Table 3.6.

Similarly regression algorithms can also be implemented in python. A sample code is shown in Table 3.7.

Table 3.6 Logistic regression and K nearest neighbor algorithm in python.

```
data = pd.read_csv('.csv file with path')    # reading .csv file using pandas library
data.head()                                  #displaying first five
data.tail()                                  # and last five values from data set
data.shape                                   #displaying size of data set
input_param = data.iloc[:,[0,1,2,3,4,5,6]].values  #saving first seven columns of data as input
    variable
output_param = data['T'].values              # last column as target variable
from sklearn.preprocessing import StandardScaler    # calling library StandardScalar
sc = StandardScaler()    # it will convert the independent variable to zero mean and unit    # #
    variance
sc.fit(input_param)  # input data input_param will be normalized.
input_param = sc.transform(input_param)
from sklearn.model_selection import train_test_split#importing function train_test_slpit to
    #splitdata set as train set and test set.
Train_in, Test_in , Train_op, Test_op = train_test_split(input_param, output_param, test_size =
    0.25, random_state = 1)
from sklearn.linear_model import LogisticRegression    #calling logistic regression from #sikit
    learnlibrary
from sklearn.metrics import accuracy_score    # calling the functions for performance
    #validation
from sklearn.metrics import precision_score          #evaluation of the algorithm: accuracy,
from sklearn.metrics import recall_score             # precision, recall
model = LogisticRegression()                         # defining the model
model.fit(Train_in, Train_op)                        #training the model with data set
pred_train = model.predict(Test_in)                  # evaluating the model
print(pd.crosstab(Test_in, pred_train,               # finding confusion matrix
rownames=['Actual'], colnames=['Predicted']))
print('\nTrain accuracy:',accuracy_score(Train_op, pred_train))
print('\nTrain precision:', precision_score(Train_op, pred_train, average='macro'))
print('\nTrain recall:', recall_score(Train_op, pred_train,average='macro'))
from sklearn.metrics import classification_report
print(classification_report(Train_op, model.predict(Train_in)))
from sklearn.neighbors import KNeighborsClassifier       #implementation of k nearest
    #neighbor
from sklearn.model_selection import KFold, cross_val_score
model_knn = KNeighborsClassifier()
model_knn.fit(Train_in, Train_op)
pred_train = model_knn.predict(Train_in)
print('\nTrain accuracy:',accuracy_score(Train_op, pred_train))
print('\nTrain precision:', precision_score(Train_op, pred_train,average='macro'))
print('\nTrain recall:', recall_score(Train_op, pred_train,average='macro'))
from sklearn.metrics import classification_report
print(classification_report(Train_op, model_knn.predict(Train_in)))
from sklearn.model_selection import cross_val_score
cvs= cross_val_score(model_knn, Train_in, Train_op, cv=5, scoring = "accuracy")
print("Scores:", cvs)
print('Cross validated mean accuracy:', cvs.mean())
```

Table 3.7 Regression algorithm in python.

```
import numpy as np
import pandas as pd
import matplotlib.pyplot as plt
data=pd.read_csv('C:/Users/Rashmi_PC/Documents/rashmi_docs/MATLAB/
    data_regression1.csv')
data.head()
X_data1 = data['delta'].values
y_data1= data['percentage shortning'].values
from sklearn.linear_model import LinearRegression  # LinearRegression
    function from  #
# sklearn
plt.scatter(x=X_data1,y=y_data1)   # library, scattered plot of input data
X = np.array(X_data1).reshape(-1, 1)
y = np.array(y_data1).reshape(-1, 1)
Train_in, Test_in, Train_op, Test_op = train_test_split(X, y, test_size = 0.25)
regr = LinearRegression()
regr.fit(Train_in, Train_op)
print(regr.score(Test_in, Test_op))
out_pred = regr.predict(Test_in)
plt.scatter(Test_in, Test_op, color ='b')
plt.plot(Test_in, out_pred, color ='k')
plt.show()
```

3.4.1   ML Model Deployment

The process of utilizing trained machine learning model in a cyber-physical system requires deploying the trained machine learning model on suitable hardware that can be embedded in a cyber-physical system. Microcontrollers makes it easier, to include any machine learning algorithm in cyber physical system, thus making it an edge intelligence system.

To load the trained model on a microcontroller it is required to convert the model in embedded C code that can be loaded in a microcontroller. Although it's not an easy task for everyone to write a machine learning code in embedded C as it does not provide user friendly libraries, to develop a machine learning model. Other easy way is to write a python code for machine learning and deploy that code on raspberry pi, where python libraries can be loaded, and inference can be drawn from the trained model. Raspberry pi, because of hardware limitation, will not be suitable for complex applications. Nvidia provides small portable GPUs like Jetson Nano for fast inferences from large deep learning models. These high-end systems are especially useful for complicated real-time inferences like computer vision applications, or handling time series data using deep neural networks (RNN or LSTM).

3.5   Conclusion

The chapter has given complete basics on machine learning algorithms. The readers can utilize this knowledge to develop their own cyber physical systems for different application areas. Various application areas for electrical engineers to be explored, especially in the field of smart grid and electric vehicles are also discussed. The implementation of basic machine learning algorithms is demonstrated through MATLAB application as well as coding platform and through Python coding.

References

1. Neapolitan, R.E. and Jiang, X., Artificial Intelligence, With an Introduction to Machine Learning, 2nd Edition, United States, CRC Press, 2018.
2. Alpaydın, E., *Introduction to Machine Learning*, Second Edition, The MIT Press Cambridge, Massachusetts, London, England, 2010.
3. Murphy, K.P., *Machine Learning: A Probabilistic Perspective*, The MIT Press Cambridge, Massachusetts, London, England, 2012.
4. Zhang, C. and Ma, Y. (Eds.), Computational Intelligence and Complexity, in: *Ensemble Machine Learning Methods and Applications*, Springer, 2012.
5. Mitchell, T.M., *Machine Learning*, McGraw-Hill Education, New York, 1997.
6. Mohri, M., Rostamizadeh, A., Talwalkar, A., *Foundations of Machine Learning*, Second edition, The MIT Press Cambridge, Massachusetts, London, England, 2018.
7. Géron, A., *Hands-On Machine Learning with Scikit-Learn and Tensor Flow*, 2nd Edition, O'Reilly Media, Inc, September 2019.
8. Sarkar, D., Bali, R., Sharma, T., *Practical machine learning with Python*, Springer, 2018.
9. Muller, A.C. and Guido, S., *Introduction to Machine learning with Python*, O'Reilly Media, October 2016.
10. Burkov A. *The Hundred-Page Machine Learning Book*, 1st ed. Quebec City: Andriy Burkov, 2019.
11. Brownlee, J., *Machine Learning Mastery With Python :Understand Your Data, Create Accurate Models and Work Projects End-To-End*, Machine Learning Mastery, 2021.

12. Lantz, B., *Machine Learning with R*, Second Edition, Packt Publishing, July 2015.
13. Simeone, O., *A Brief Introduction to Machine Learning for Engineers*, 17th, pp. 1–231, now Publishers Inc. Hanover, MA United States May, 2018.
14. Russell, S.J. and Norvig, P., *Artificial Intelligence: A Modern Approach*, Prentice Hall, Eaglewood Cliffs, New Jersey, 2020.
15. E. Alpaydin, *Introduction to Machine Learning*, 3rd ed. Cambridge, MA: MIT Press, 2014.
16. *Math Works*™, https://www.mathworks.com/help/stats/machine-learning-in-matlab.html.
17. Paluszek, M. and Thomas, S., *MATLAB Machine Learning*, Springer, January 2017.
18. Rogers, S. and Girolami, M., *A First Course in Machine Learning*. CRC Press, London, 2015.
19. Chatterjee, J.M., Kumar, A., Rathore, P.S., Jain, V. (Eds.), *Internet of Things and Machine Learning in Agriculture: Technological Impacts and Challenges*, vol. 8, Walter de Gruyter GmbH & Co KG, 2021.
20. Vasaki, P., Jhanjhi, N.Z., Humayun., M., Fostering Public-Private Partnership: Between Governments and Technologists in Developing National Cybersecurity Framework, in: *Employing Recent Technologies for Improved Digital Governance*, pp. 237–255, IGI Global, 2020.

Precise Risk Assessment and Management

Ambika N.

*Department of Computer Science and Applications, St. Francis College
Bangalore, India*

Abstract

Cyber network is a huge system consisting of lot of terminals, hand-held devices with varying sizes and capacities communicating with each other. The size of the system has made it impossible or takes a lot of time to trace the terminals. Hence the hackers can introduce different kinds of attacks into the network without being traced for a very long time. As some of the confidential data is transmitted over the network, it becomes essential to safeguard the data and the terminals attached to the network.

The previous work suggested uses multi-criteria decision analysis. It evaluates the danger in a digital framework. It potentially selects an ideal therapeutic technique. The creators ascertain the general danger score utilizing the measures compared to the TVC segments. The standards separate into sub-criteria, etc. Its score is the weighted amount of the sub-criteria scores. On the most reduced level, scores for the rules can be allowed by topic specialists or gotten from quantifiable information. Utilizing a similar MCDA approach, countermeasures can be scored and organized. Scores allocate depending on how it compels the countermeasure is at the moderation of every part of the danger. Notwithstanding adequacy, countermeasure scores incorporate other models regarded significant by the partners and network protection supervisors, for example, cost and time. The incorporation of countermeasure prioritizes bringing the system past danger evaluation and toward hazard the board. The suggestion uses a better methodology to assess the risk of the framework. The client's sources are jolted down to prioritize what has to be given preference. Based on the sources different risk issues are evaluated. It measures the risk based on the priority, usage of a particular technology and the risks associated with them. The contribution evaluates the same based on a particular scenario.

Email: Ambika.nagaraj76@gmail.com

Uzzal Sharma, Parma Nand, Jyotir Moy Chatterjee, Vishal Jain, Noor Zaman Jhanjhi and R. Sujatha (eds.)
Cyber-Physical Systems: Foundations and Techniques, (63–84) © 2022 Scrivener Publishing LLC

Keywords: Cyber security, multi-criteria decision analysis, risk issues, priority-based analysis, area-based analysis

4.1   Introduction

The Internet is an enormous network encompassing different kinds of terminals, devices, and gateways. The number of users is sizable in number. Hence, keeping track of each user doing is quite complicated. The clients can have the intent to inject different kinds of attacks. The expenses on the criminals are very less. They just need a computer, internet connection and a program that fructify their intentions. It also provides them the facility to reach beyond geographical location. On the other end, the identity of the guilty is difficult to be traced. Based on the report conducted by Symantec 69% of the population became victims of different types of cyber attacks [1–3]. The survey tells that more than one million attacks fructify a day. Hence it becomes essential to detect them and provide countermeasure to the same.

The previous work [4] uses multi-criteria decision analysis. It evaluates the danger in a digital framework. It potentially selects an ideal therapeutic technique. The creators ascertain the general danger score utilizing the measures compared to the TVC segments. The standards separate into sub-criteria, etc. Its score is the weighted amount of the sub-criteria scores. On the most reduced level, scores for the rules can be allowed by topic specialists or gotten from quantifiable information. Utilizing a similar MCDA approach, countermeasures can be scored and organized. Scores allocate depending on how it compels the countermeasure is at the moderation of every part of the danger. Notwithstanding adequacy, countermeasure scores incorporate other models regarded significant by the partners and network protection supervisors, for example, cost and time. The incorporation of countermeasure prioritizes bringing the system past danger evaluation and toward hazard the board. The suggestion uses a better methodology to assess the risk of the framework. The client's sources are jolted down to prioritize what has to be given preference. Based on the sources different risk issues are evaluated. It measures the risk based on the priority, usage of a particular technology and the risks associated with them. The contribution evaluates the same based on a particular scenario.

The introduction starts in Section 4.1. The need for security is detailed in Section 4.2. Section 4.3 details different kinds of attacks existing over the Internet. Literary study is elaborated in Section 4.4. The proposed study is represented in Section 4.5. The contribution is concluded in Section 4.6.

4.2 Need for Security

The WannaCry ransomware exploits a natural weakness of Microsoft Windows, effectively investigated by the U.S. Public safety Bureau for concealed reconnaissance purposes. Other than influencing singular PCs, the WannaCry essentially upsets the regular activity of a few huge business and administrative organizations counting FedEx, Deutsche Bahn, Megafon, Telefónica, the Russian Central Bank, Russian Railways, and Russia's Interior Service. In the United Kingdom, the cyber attack disabled the data innovation frameworks of medical clinics across the National Wellness Service. The final product of task drops, medical clinics put on redirection status, and wellbeing data reports, for example, diligent evidence being made inaccessible in both England and Scotland. Primer proof focuses on North Korea's multitude of programmers as the primary guilty party of what has been advised by the network protection organization F-Secure is the greatest ransomware flare-up ever. The recurrence of cyber attacks has been dramatically expanding, with a few comparative occasions. It details in the United States in the previous few years, the most eminent one on February 2016, when the Hollywood Presbyterian Examination location in Los Angeles wound up salaried $17,000 emancipation in bitcoins to recapture control of its data innovation organization.

4.2.1 Confidentiality

The property [5] data isn't made accessible or unveiled to unapproved people, elements, or cycles. Secrecy secures information away and in transmission. Privacy undermines at any point data can be seen or perused by unapproved substances or uncovered out of the 'need to know' gathering or local area. This trade-off could be either physical or electronic. The electronic secrecy bargains incorporate end-clients or elements getting to data, information, or assets does not imply for them. It guarantees that data is uncovered to approved clients as it were. The classification includes the ideas of information protection, encryption, and figure or cryptography.

The OCTAVE system [6] decides hazard levels and for arranging against digital assaults. Its design intends to limit association openness to dangers and to anticipate the likely results of assaults and address the ones that succeed. The structure is part into three complete stages—building resource-based danger profiles, distinguishing foundation weaknesses, and creating security systems and plans. There are two renditions of OCTAVE, with OCTAVE-S, giving an improved adaptation pointed at more modest associations with level progressive designs. OCTAVE Allegro is exhaustive form focused on huge organizations with diverse designs.

4.2.2 Integrity

It is the capacity [7, 8] to guarantee that data doesn't change. It implies that information can't alter without approval. Trustworthiness guarantees that the information has not been modified away or potentially in transmission. Honesty penetrates at whatever point data changes without express approval by the data proprietor. This trade-off could bring about the commission or oversight of either approved client or unapproved substance. Honesty bargain could be either unplanned or deliberate and through malevolent purpose. Pernicious uprightness bargain could be that a material purposefully adds, erases, or changes data set records. It can happen either through an approved gathering or by an unapproved party when the client approaches that they shouldn't have. Inadvertent trustworthiness bargain is the point at which a framework alters or erases records that it shouldn't. It can happen when an infection contaminates a framework or when a client accomplishes something that he didn't mean to do. It frequently checks that you need a document erased before it does as such. Respectability alludes to the reliability of data assets.

4.2.3 Availability

It guarantees [9] that data resources are available at whatever point is required. It is a significant property since any disturbance of administration may unfavourably influence the business activities of SMEs. Accessibility [10] guarantees that an approved client or element or unit can get to a framework asset when a legitimate solicitation is made. Assuming this asset is a strategic resource, accessibility necessitates that reinforcement or excess arrangements ensure its accessibility. Its trade-off could happen because of inadvertent activities or mishaps or by pernicious or purposeful demonstrations, for example, a Denial-of-Service assault or botnets. Accessibility bargains could likewise arrange as specialized, human, or marvels, such as flood, quake, or blackout.

4.2.4 Accountability

The rule [11, 12] that an individual is endowed to protect and control hardware, keying material, and data and is responsible to an appropriate expert for the misfortune or abuse of that gear or data. The aspect expresses that each individual who works with an information model has explicit responsibility regarding information assertion. The errands for which a person is able are primary for the unspecific information surety arrangement and can be quickly quantitative by a single person who has administrative responsibility regarding information verification. One framework organizes a description that all representatives should try not to innovate external programming on an arrangement having information structure. The person responsible for information safety performs infrequent verification on the planning. People should know about the anticipated from them and guide persistent improvement.

4.2.5 Auditing

The motivation behind a network safety review [13] is to approve the strategies by the online protection group. There are control components set up to authorize them. An examination is formal than an evaluation. The free outsider of the association performs a review. The outsider has a certificate. An association can have an inner review group. The group should go about as a free organization. The network safety review discovers the presence of controls. The evaluators seldom test the viability of those controls. It doesn't imply that it is taking care of its responsibility to alleviate the digital danger. A network protection review program has a period and a spot. Most reviews won't uncover the genuine viability of the security controls you have set up.

4.3 Different Kinds of Attacks

4.3.1 Malware

It alludes to a gathering of attacks stacking on a model. It bargains the structure to the reward of a foe. Some model category of attack integrates corruptness [14], worms [15], Trojan [16], spyware [17], and bot executable [18]. Malware pollutes model in a categorization of framework proliferation from tainted devices, betraying clients to open debased evidences, or pleasing customers to see malware dissemination website. In more concrete instances of malware contamination, malware may pile itself onto a USB drive enclosed into a corrupt appliance and subsequently taint every framework into which that device embeds. Malware may engender from appliance and kind of mechanism that contain implanted model and procedure rationale. So, malware can be embedded anytime in the framework existence cycle. Victims of malware can trial anything from the end client frameworks, servers, network gadgets, and cycle dominance frameworks like Supervisory Command and Information Attainment.

The assaults occur at an only mark of boundary among instrumentation, types of gear, planning parts, or network tier victimization ofactive design and execution weaknesses at each layer. It ensures each asset, the edge protection methodology use dominantly to put a divider outside all inner assets to shield everything internal from any unenviable disruption from external. The border safeguard device uses a security system and hostile to ill health planning initiate inside disruption expectancy/discovery model. Any assemblage coming from external is captured and inspected to assurance there is no malware entering into within possession. Unspecific acceptance of this boundary precaution framework has occurred because it is far uncomplicated and little costly to get one borderline than to get a large measure of uses or countless interior organizations. The entrance control instruments utilize related to the edge protection system.

It composes as research often to characteristic safety weaknesses or now and again to display differentiated susceptibility. Today, the malware uses chiefly to take delicate private, monetary, or commercial enterprise information to support others. As per the report, Trojans represent part of the dangers. In 2009, Trojans were reported to have made up 60% of all malware. In 2011 it was 73%. The current pace exhibit that almost three out of each four fresh malware deformation made in 2011 were Trojans and shows that it is the arm of judgment for digital hoodlums to lead network disruption and info fetching.

Spam [19] adverts were used to send unimportant, unseen, and impulsive communication to millions of participant role. Spam has ended up being particular in the marketplace since junk e-mail is sent secretly without any reimbursement needed. Because of such devalued obstruction to the passage, electronic mail is different, and the measure of impulsive mail has formed hugely.

Phishing [20] is a methodology of undertaking to gain delicate info, for example, username, secret phrase, or Visa credentials by fetching on the happening of a reliable substance. Most phishing pranks depend on misleading a customer into seeing a noxious website affirmation to be from genuine firm and agency. The uninformed customer enters secluded information is then therefore utilized by noxious crooks. The strategies use specialized trickery supposed to make a relation in an email appear to have a place with an authentic unification, as a noteworthy financial institution. Incorrectly spelled URLs or the utilization of sub-spaces are basic deed used by phishers.

Drive-by Downloads [21] concern the accidental transfer of malware from the Cyberspace and are used by the aggressors to dispersed malware quickly. Drive-by transfer happen in a mixture of fortune. It initiates when a customer travel to a website while viewing an electronic mail content, or when customer click on a deceptive season up framework. However, the most well-known drive-by downloads happen by a broad border when seeing website.

4.3.2 Man-in-the-Middle Assault

Man-in-the-middle assault [22] occurs when the attacker tamper between the deuce agreement closes. Each content conveyed from origin A to communicator B comes at the assailant earlier arriving at its aim. The chances contain unapproved admittance to touchy data or conceivable outcomes to adjust the data/message.

4.3.3 Brute Force Assault

This [23] involves rehashed endeavors to access ensured data till the precise credential is established, and information will reach. The creator proposes [24] another technique known as the beast power assault approach to produce AEs against AI-based frameworks in online protection. The procedure is easy to carry out and maintains a strategic distance from the drawn-out preparation of GAN-based assault techniques. The tactics are slope-free techniques. It controls the highlights of info vectors in a determinate manner. It makes the strategy more reasonable for the ill-disposed assaults in network protection. It produces AEs dependent on the certainty scores of the objective classifiers heuristically. It is a discovery assault technique for which the designs and boundaries of the objective classifiers are pointless for assaults. The certainty scores of the objective models are the lone expected information to deliver AEs.

4.3.4 Distributed Denial of Service

This [25] is an attack that deals the availability of message. The assailant floods the injured party with orders, in this style acquiring unserviceable. The creator proposes [26] an insightful security framework against DDoS assaults in correspondence networks. It has two parts. A screen for recognition of DDoS assaults and a discriminator for the locate clients in the framework with noxious plans. A tale versatile continuous alteration-component model that trail the progressions in Mahalanobis spacing between examined highlight variables in the checked framework represents conceivable DDoS assaults. A grouping framework that trial over the comparability scores of personal conduct standards among the clients isolates the vindictive from the guiltless. It empowers the screen to adjust to the typical traffic system and diurnal or occasional varieties while simultaneously staying delicate to unusual changes. It is a solo way to deal with distinguishes traffic peculiarities. The framework makes noticed informing traffic type and power and doesn't need any extra data, for example, trace backs. A strange change in the rush hour gridlock system proclaims on the off chance that the Mahalanobis spacing arrangement of the province variables in progressive period windows surpasses a limit work. It sets to a steady as an element of system boundaries or then again can be adaptive set.

4.4   Literature Survey

This section details the previous contributions made by various authors across different horizons. The work [4] uses multi-criteria decision analysis. It evaluates the danger in a digital framework. It potentially selects an ideal therapeutic technique. The creators ascertain the general danger score utilizing the measures compared to the TVC segments. The standards separate into sub-criteria, etc. Its score is the weighted amount of the sub-criteria scores. On the most reduced level, scores for the rules can be allowed by topic specialists or gotten from quantifiable information. Utilizing a similar MCDA approach, countermeasures can be scored and organized. Scores allocate depending on how it compels the countermeasure is at the moderation of every part of the danger. Notwithstanding adequacy, countermeasure scores incorporate other models regarded significant by the partners and network protection supervisors, for example, cost and time. The incorporation of countermeasure prioritizes bringing the system past danger evaluation and toward hazard the board. The proposal uses a better methodology to assess the risk of the framework.

The methodology [27] contains two circles. The external circle features that STPA-SafeSec is an iterative methodology that should be reapplied in the framework to deal with this advancing existence. In its center, STPA is about imperatives and the control circles of the framework. Each control circle is dissected independently during the investigation. The imperatives refine for the framework all in all dependent on the disasters. At that point, these requirements get refined and planned to the control layer. Risks and ensuing misfortunes occur when control activities disregard at least one of the recently characterized requirements supposed unsafe control moves. The examination gives the way to infer the causal elements that lead to unsafe control activities. These causal variables reach out by STPA-SafeSec to incorporate safety contemplation. The theoretical activity tier acquires planned to an execution explicit part tier. This segment layer gives the way to refine the limitations and determine more explicit causative variables. It can additionally control inside and out security investigation. The outcomes are a bunch of changes that apply to the framework engineering. It guarantees misfortune-free activities are at long last determined. It depends on the situations that portray risky control activities.

The principle objective of CySeMoL [28] is to permit clients to make models of their designs and make computations on the probability of various digital assaults being fruitful. The model remembers the hypothesis for how credits in the article model rely upon one another security skill from the client of CySeMoL. Clients should model their framework engineering and indicate their properties to make computations conceivable. The classes in CySeMoL incorporate different IT parts like Operating System and Firewall, cycles, for example, Security Awareness Program, and Persons that are clients. Every element has qualities that can be either assaults steps made against the substance or countermeasures related to it. These ascribe are connected differently. The passwords of secret-word records have a probability of this assault being fruitful. It relies upon an individual possessing the secret word account is in a security mindfulness program. Each trait in CySeMoL can have the worth true or False and addresses either the probability of an assault being fruitful or the probability of a countermeasure being utilitarian.

The creators [29] utilize the MulVAL assault diagram tool stash. It can reach out to other assault charts comparing with semantics. The MulVAL thinking framework can consolidate CVSS measurements from NVD information sources and yield the AC metric. Attack Action Node model has the presence of an assailant effectively misusing the system. A separate AAN assault hub opposes sharing a solitary device. The new instrument acquaints with the model the incorrect perception. A circular segment from the original state to the perception state addresses the way that the perception. It uses restrictive probabilities. It does not qualify with and or hubs. When an aggressor is available and sending the record worker an NFS shell abuse parcel, this activity identifies an organization-based IDS. Tripwire screen could report a dubious record adjustment. Every hub in a Bayesian organization relates with a CPT which is the likelihood dispersion of the hub's potential states adapted on the guardians' states. They use the specific qualities relating to possibility. They utilize the center estimations of the reaches comparing to other probability are some examples.

The work [30] breaks down the digital protection of the PSSE in the SCADA framework. They describe the aggressor by characterizing a bunch of goals. The approach incorporates subtle trickiness assaults, both for straight and non-linear assessors. Assaults influencing the assembly of the PSSE are identified with information accessibility, as they view as DoS attacks. They evaluate compromises between model precision and conceivable assault sway for various BDD plans. The PSSE issues find the solution using a measuring structure. It is a non-linear component focusing on the frame of the energy system used. It has a variable having zero-mean Gaussian measurements in the covariance system. It results in estimation value considered to minimize in different scenarios. These measures satisfy the first level conditions used to find optimization. It symbolizes Jacobian resultant. The answer obtained is symbolization resulting from Newton's methodology. It is the result of using the iterative method to find an accurate value. The hessian resultant obtained is due to merging collapse. The second-order computation is expensive. The same applies to the PSSE methodology. The resultant leads to the Gauss–Newton resultant.

The CBC-MAC calculation [31] depends on the Triple Information Encryption Standard. It characterizes in subset-037 v.3.1.0 of the ERTMS particular. The credential material trades through credential administration framework secured by various solution substances. The system uses Tetrad unique keys, which orders in trio tiers. Session keys, KSMACs, are created from the verification key material, KMAC, for every meeting. This system depicts in detail in subset-037. It Exchanges two arbitrary numbers in content between two elements. It performs the 3DES-CBC-MAC calculation multiple times, utilizing these two arbitrary numbers as seed material and three squares of 64 bits taken from KMAC as keys.

The creators [32] have investigated the cost, effect, and hazard of ACT in the SHARPE programming bundle. ROA and ROI calculation completes by characterizing capacities in SHARPE. The measurements, for example, assault cost and ROA mirrors have security venture cost, hazard, effect, and ROI address the protector's perspective. Cost and effect of assault were utilized as measures by Schneier for investigation of AT. In the ACT, the cost can be of two sorts; cost of assault and security speculation cost. When at least one occasion rehashes in the ACT, Rauzy's calculation builds the double choice chart (BDD) relating to the ACT. The effect of the ACT min-cut shows the significant effect as assault sway for the ACT. Security venture cost registers by adding the expense of executing countermeasures in the ACT. Hazard calculation performs by the result of the likelihood of assault and effect. ROA is an action that evaluates the advantage acquired from a specific assault.

The digital actual security investigation approach [33] remembers experimentation for sensible testbeds. Methods and skills distinguish framework-level weaknesses. Results if the weak are misused, and secure ways to deal with kill the weak. Framework-level outcomes are hard to decide whether different defects abuses at the same time. Experiment on usable frameworks or test-beds is in deciding framework-level effects. Experiment on functional frameworks in nearly all the happening is beyond the realm of imagination on account of the danger to the operational framework and its central goal. Building a trial framework indistinguishable from the operational framework is cost restrictive. Programming models of the gadgets and framework are ordinarily not accessible or, if accessible, need highlights identified with network protection investigation. A compelling approach to make a digital actual security experimentation stage is through a half-breed testbed. The strategy empowers construction framework of both the SCADA framework and the framework. The framework of the SCADA incorporates its availability to the different commercial enterprise and the Cyberspace. The actual framework is chosen from divergent resolve for the framework under examination. In a half and half examination, the SCADA framework occasions and the framework occasions are participated in lockstep to make sensitive activity.

Undertaking design [34] is a way to deal with the executives of data structures. It includes control frameworks. It depends on models of the frameworks and their current circumstances. They portray how security speculations join with building models to reason arranged design models. Assault trees are graphical documentation advanced from deficiency trees, where the fundamental objective of an attacker. The numerical derivation motor that impact graphs give permits demonstrating complex choice issues. Coupled to this numerical motor is likewise graphical documentation where the factors address as a chart. The models permit thinking about the outcomes of different situations and accordingly support dynamic. A theoretical model involves four parts entities, entity connections, properties, and trait connections. The initial three of these segments can be perceived from standard demonstrating dialects, for example, the class outlines of the UML. Elements are a focal segment in demonstrating dialects. It is an in-class graph used to address ideas of pertinence for the model.

The theoretical model [35] starts by proof assortment. A security appraisal commonly includes information assortment regarding interviews, documentation examines, log surveys, determining different measurements, infiltration tests, and then some. One part of this data assortment recognizes the elements that researchers and their relationship to one another. Another piece of the information assortment concerns the nature of different ascribes and investigating how these characteristics impact security. Putting together a theoretical model concerning an all-encompassing impact chart that communicates the guard diagram has direct advantages. It guarantees that the model utilized for appraisal, and therefore the information gathered for it, contains the information expected for creating and surveying security using guard charts. The model covers the parts that are of significance to the evaluation. The appraisal will zero in on things of importance to its outcome. Besides, it is from a launched conceptual model direct and upheld by devices to infer and ascribes characteristic links and restrictive likelihood tables. Utilizing a theoretical model, the modeler will demonstrate the substances, their connections, and the condition w.r.t properties to survey the security. It starts up in the solid model. The relationship among them determines the organization of qualities. This organization will compare to an all-inclusive impact outline communicating a safeguard diagram. It ascribes to be incorporated can be gotten from the elements.

VAPT system [36] directs in deuce significant parts. The primary incomplete designed with the Investigation and Insight of active Weakness. The subsequent half patterns are with the Victimization of the important agreement of Weakness. It assesses their Intensity and Impacts over the Prey model. Weakness evaluation is an aloof method through infiltration testing is an operative method where safety proficients animate conflict and trial the target locate and its repercussion power against attacks. VAPT analyzer targets identifying essential data about the test target and examining the objective to discover the weaknesses. Weakness appraisal is a technique that follows the precise and proactive way to deal with find weakness. It is polished to find known and obscure issues in the framework.

The I4.0 creation plant Smart Factory OWL [37] portrays and breaks down the design of cloud-based administrations and their information. A creation framework for preparing mass material is considered a utilization case. It improves the item quality, accomplishes higher framework accessibility, and builds efficiency. In this way, information-based assistance for plant checking and enhancement dissects as a cloud arrangement. The sensors [38] procure information. The application is a reason for a hazard investigation. It determines the utilization case of "Condition Based Maintenance", including availability and related information streams. This application is a plant administrator employing cloud administration. The rationale either peruses crude information or effectively totalled information from the sensor or plays out an ensuing information examination. It plays out condition-based support. It gives support rationale requires a ton of skill, specifically about the application. A merchant of programming arrangements may give this aptitude as a Cloud administration. The assistance facilitates by a Cloud specialist co-op and associated employing multi-point associations.

The work [39] follows an objective situated methodology for security danger displaying and examination by utilizing visual model components. The fundamental UAV model characterizes as a blend of six isolated frameworks: Data obtaining module, Elevation, and Direction Quotation Scheme, Transportation Organization, Dominance Component, Information Work Compartment, and the Measurement Compartment. The correspondence framework has not appeared as it incorporates every one of the component and control signs and information signals that goes through it. The UAV was planned by distinguishing significant segments of the framework and the UAV. The related and conceivable assault characterize alongside the potential dangers in the danger model of the framework.

4.5 Proposed Work

The work [4] uses multi-criteria decision analysis. It evaluates the danger in a digital framework. It potentially selects an ideal therapeutic technique. The creators ascertain the general danger score utilizing the measures compared to the TVC segments. The standards separate into sub-criteria, etc. Its score is the weighted amount of the sub-criteria scores. On the most reduced level, scores for the rules can be allowed by topic specialists or gotten from quantifiable information. Utilizing a similar MCDA approach, countermeasures can be scored and organized. Scores allocate depending on how it compels the countermeasure is at the moderation of every part of the danger. Notwithstanding adequacy, countermeasure scores incorporate other models regarded significant by the partners and network protection supervisors, for example, cost and time. The incorporation of countermeasure prioritizes bringing the system past danger evaluation and toward hazard the board. The proposal uses a better methodology to assess the risk of the framework.

4.5.1 Objective

- To evaluate appropriate risk and provide adequate countermeasure for the same that the customer is keen for.

- Prioritize the risk in the network. Sources of risk can be evaluated and appropriate measure can be adopted. The client can rank based on the facilities or the sources they are utilizing.

4.5.2 Notations Used in the Contribution

Table 4.1 represents the notations used in the contribution.

Table 4.1 Notations used in the contribution.

Notations	Description
R	Total risk factor
S_i	Source risk
P_i	Priority assigned
ω_i	Weight of ith risk
R_i	ith risk

4.5.3 Methodology

Based on different kinds of vulnerabilities and threats, the area based risk-score is computed. Figure 4.1 represents the different kinds of breaching incidents. Figure 4.2 provides the amount of malware infections year-wise.

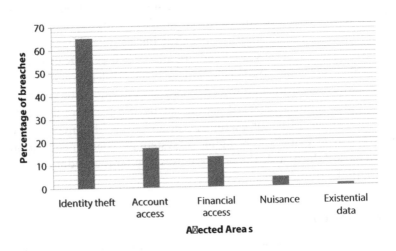

Figure 4.1 Cyber threats area-wise.

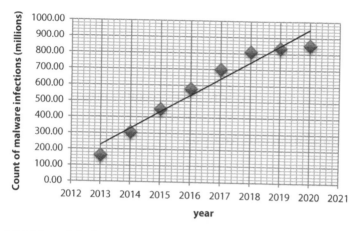

Figure 4.2 Malware infections year-wise.

The previous work [4] uses multi-criteria decision analysis. It evaluates the total work and the danger is in a digital framework. It potentially selects an ideal therapeutic technique. The creators ascertain the general danger score utilizing the measures compared to the TVC segments. The standards separate into sub-criteria, etc. Its score is the weighted amount of the sub-criteria scores. On the most reduced level, scores for the rules can be allowed by topic specialists or gotten from quantifiable information. Utilizing a similar MCDA approach, countermeasures can be scored and organized. Scores allocate depending on how it compels the countermeasure is at the moderation of every part of the danger. Notwithstanding adequacy, countermeasure scores incorporate other models regarded significant by the partners and network protection supervisors, for example, cost and time. The incorporation of countermeasure prioritizes bringing the system past danger evaluation and toward hazard the board.

The suggestions use a better methodology to assess the risk of the framework. The client's sources are jolted down to prioritize what has to be given preference. Based on the sources different risk issues are evaluated. Let S_i be the source from which a risk issue R_i is analyzed. It weighs ω_i. Based on its usage (w.r.t client) its priority is set. Let its priority by P_i. The total risk R is calculated. Eq. (4.1) is used to calculate the risk factor based on source used by the clients. The sources used very often are given higher priority.

$$S_i = P_i \sum_{i=0}^{n} \omega_i R_i \qquad (4.1)$$

Total risk is calculated using Eq. (4.2)

$$R = \sum_{i=0}^{n} S_i \tag{4.2}$$

Based on the client's necessity, the risk counter measure is suggested.

4.5.4   Simulation and Analysis

The work [4] uses multi-criteria decision analysis. It evaluates the danger in a digital framework. It potentially selects an ideal therapeutic technique. The creators ascertain the general danger score utilizing the measures compared to the TVC segments. The standards separate into sub-criteria, etc. Its score is the weighted amount of the sub-criteria scores. On the most reduced level, scores for the rules can be allowed by topic specialists or gotten from quantifiable information. Utilizing a similar MCDA approach, countermeasures can be scored and organized. Scores allocate depending on how it compels the countermeasure is at the moderation of every part of the danger. Notwithstanding adequacy, countermeasure scores incorporate other models regarded significant by the partners and network protection supervisors, for example, cost and time. The incorporation of countermeasure prioritizes bringing the system past danger evaluation and toward hazard the board. The proposal uses a better methodology to assess the risk of the framework. Table 4.2 represents sources and its priorities. Table 4.3 represents the parameters used in the simulation.

Table 4.2 Representation of sources and its priorities.

Sources	Number of employees	Access frequency per employee	Priority
Financial access (specific to account department employees)	3	Once a day (for a client)	10
Data access (provided to employees under manager-level and above)	5	three times a day	5
Email (used by all the employees regularly)	40	six times a day	2

Table 4.3 Simulation parameters.

Parameters	Description
Number of terminals used	40 (five of them are given special access to data + 3 are given access to do online transactions)
Maximum limit to send email	24,000 bytes
Maximum limit to download or upload data	20,000 bytes
Amount of data transmitted during online money transaction	800 bytes
Maximum time limit to transit online money	4 min
Total simulation time	30 min

The following assumptions are made in the simulation:

- The client uses more of email, followed by data access, and later financial access.
- The priority is given based on their usage.

Figure 4.3 jolts down the parameters used in simulating the work.

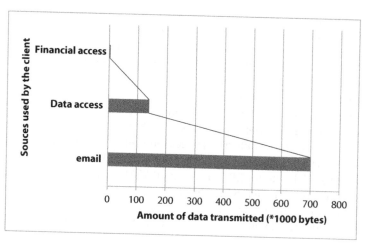

Figure 4.3 Simulated results.

4.6   Conclusion

Cyber security is an essential component in the system. The system or a part of the system may be under different kinds of threats. It becomes essential to detect them and find the countermeasure for the same. The previous contribution uses multi-criteria decision analysis. It evaluates the danger in a digital framework. It potentially selects an ideal therapeutic technique. The creators ascertain the general danger score utilizing the measures compared to the TVC segments. The standards separate into sub-criteria, etc. Its score is the weighted amount of the sub-criteria scores. On the most reduced level, scores for the rules can be allowed by topic specialists or gotten from quantifiable information. Utilizing a similar MCDA approach, countermeasures can be scored and organized. Scores allocate depending on how it compels the countermeasure is at the moderation of every part of the danger. Notwithstanding adequacy, countermeasure scores incorporate other models regarded significant by the partners and network protection supervisors, for example, cost and time. The incorporation of countermeasure prioritizes bringing the system past danger evaluation and toward hazard the board. The suggested proposal is aimed to satisfy client according to his needs. It measures the risk based on the priority, usage of a particular technology and the risks associated with them. The contribution evaluates the same based on a particular scenario.

References

1. Ambika, N., Chaubey, N.K., Prajapati, B.B., Improved Methodology to Detect Advanced Persistent Threat Attacks, in: *Quantum Cryptography and the Future of Cyber Security*, pp. 184–202, IGI Global, US, 2020.
2. Ambika, N. and Al-Turjman, F., An Improved Solution to Tackle Cyber Attacks, in: *Advanced Controllers for Smart Cities: An Industry 4.0 Perspective*, pp. 15–23, Springer, Switzerland, 2021.
3. Ten, C.W., Hong, J., Liu, C.C., Anomaly detection for cybersecurity of the substations. *IEEE Trans. Smart Grid.*, 2, 4, 865–873, 2011.
4. Ganin, A.A. *et al.*, Multicriteria decision framework for cybersecurity risk assessment and management. *Risk Anal.*, 40, 1, 183–199, 2020.
5. Gamage, T.T., Roth, T.P., McMillin, B.M.M., Confidentiality preserving security properties for cyber-physical systems. *IEEE 35th Annual Computer Software and Applications Conference*, IEEE, Germany, pp. 28–37, 2011.
6. Aminzade, M., Confidentiality, integrity and availability–finding a balanced IT framework. *Int. J. Netw. Secur.*, 2018, 5, 9–11, 2018.

7. Reed, J.H., Gonzalez, C.R.A., Gatlinburg, T.N., Enhancing smart grid cyber security using power fingerprinting: Integrity assessment and intrusion detection. *Future of Instrumentation International Workshop (FIIW)*, IEEE., USA, pp. 1–3, 2012.

8. Mo, Y. and Sinopoli, B., On the performance degradation of cyber-physical systems under stealthy integrity attacks. *IEEE Trans. Automat. Contr.*, 61, 9, 2618–2624, 2015.

9. Parvin, S. *et al.*, Multi-cyber framework for availability enhancement of cyber physical systems. *Comput. J.*, 95, 927–948, 2013.

10. Walker-Roberts, S., Hammoudeh, M., Dehghantanha, A., A systematic review of the availability and efficacy of countermeasures to internal threats in healthcare critical infrastructure. *IEEE Access*, 6, 25167–25177, 2018.

11. Liu, J., Xiao, Y., Gao, J., Achieving accountability in smart grid. *IEEE Syst. J.*, 8, 2, 493–508, 2013.

12. Kacianka, S. and Pretschner, A., Understanding and formalizing accountability for cyber-physical systems. *IEEE International Conference on Systems, Man, and Cybernetics (SMC)*, IEEE, Miyazaki, Japan, pp. 3165–3170, 2018.

13. Greitzer, F.L. and Frincke, D.A., Combining traditional cyber security audit data with psychosocial data: towards predictive modeling for insider threat mitigation, in: *Insider threats in cyber security*, pp. 85–113, s.l. : Springer, Boston, MA, 2010.

14. Bou-Harb, E., Debbabi, M., Assi, C., A novel cyber security capability: Inferring Internet-scale infections by correlating malware and probing activities. *Comput. Netw.*, 94, 327–343, 2016.

15. Chaudhary, P., Gupta, S., Gupta, B.B., Auditing defense against XSS worms in online social network-based web applications, in: *Handbook of research on modern cryptographic solutions for computer and cyber security*, pp. 216–245, IGI Global., US, 2016.

16. Vincent, H. *et al.*, Trojan detection and side-channel analyses for cyber-security in cyber-physical manufacturing systems. *43rd North American Manufacturing Research Conference*, vol. 1, elsevier, North Carolina, United States, 201577-85.

17. Boiko, A., Shendryk, V., Boiko, O., Information systems for supply chain management: uncertainties, risks and cyber security, in: *ICTE in Transportation and Logistics 2018*, vol. 149, s.l. : elsevier, Elsevier journal Procedia Computer Science, 201965-70. http://www.wikicfp.com/cfp/servlet/event.showcfp?eventid=72728&copyownerid=13988

18. Chatterjee, M., Namin, A.S., Datta, P., Evidence fusion for malicious bot detection in IoT. *IEEE International Conference on Big Data*, IEEE., Seattle WA, USA, pp. 4545–4548, 2018.

19. Abdulhamid, S., II *et al.*, Comparative Analysis of Classification Algorithms for Email Spam Detection. *Int. J. Comput. Netw.*, 10, 1, 60–67, 2018.

20. Dodge, Jr, R. C., Carver, C., Ferguson, A.J., Phishing for user security awareness. *Comput. Secur.*, 26, 1, 73–80, 2007.

21. Egele, M. *et al.*, Defending browsers against drive-by downloads: Mitigating heap-spraying code injection attacks. *International Conference on Detection of Intrusions and Malware, and Vulnerability Assessment*, s.l. : Springer, Berlin, Heidelberg, pp. 88–106, 2009.

22. Yang, Y. *et al.*, Man-in-the-middle attack test-bed investigating cyber-security vulnerabilities in smart grid SCADA systems. *International Conference on Sustainable Power Generation and Supply (SUPERGEN 2012)*, IET, Hangzhou, China, pp. 138–146, 2012.

23. Hafiz, M.M. and Ali, F.H.M., Profiling and mitigating brute force attack in home wireless LAN. *International Conference on Computational Science and Technology (ICCST)*, IEEE, Kota Kinabalu, Malaysia, pp. 1–6, 2014.

24. Zhang, S., Xie, X., Xu, Y., A Brute-Force Black-Box Method to Attack Machine Learning-Based Systems in Cybersecurity. *IEEE Access*, 8, 128250–128263, 2020.

25. Spyridopoulos, T. *et al.*, A game theoretic defence framework against DoS/DDoS cyber attacks. *Comput. Secur.*, 38, 39–50, 2013.

26. Semerci, M., Cemgil, A.T., Sankur, B., An intelligent cyber security system against DDoS attacks in SIP networks. *Comput. Netw.*, 136, 137–154, 2018.

27. Friedberg, I. *et al.*, STPA-SafeSec: Safety and security analysis for cyber-physical systems. *J. Inf. Secur. Appl.*, 34, 183–196, 2017.

28. Holm, H. *et al.*, CySeMoL: A tool for cyber security analysis of enterprises. *22nd International Conference and Exhibition on Electricity Distribution (CIRED 2013)*, IET, Stockholm, pp. 1–4, 2013.

29. Xie, P. *et al.*, Using Bayesian networks for cyber security analysis. *IEEE/IFIP International Conference on Dependable Systems & Networks (DSN)*, IEEE, Chicago, IL, USA, pp. 211–220, 2010.

30. Teixeira, A. *et al.*, Cyber security analysis of state estimators in electric power systems. *49th IEEE conference on decision and control (CDC)*, IEEE, Atlanta, GA, USA, pp. 5991–5998, 2010.

31. Lopez, I. and Aguado, M., Cyber security analysis of the European train control system. *IEEE Commun. Mag.*, 53, 10, 110–116, 2015.

32. Roy, A., Kim, D.S., Trivedi, K.S., Cyber security analysis using attack counter-measure trees. *Sixth Annual Workshop on Cyber Security and Information Intelligence Research*, ACM, Oak Ridge Tennessee, USA, pp. 1–4, 2010.

33. Urias, V., Van Leeuwen, B., Richardson, B., Supervisory Command and Data Acquisition (SCADA) system cyber security analysis using a live, virtual, and constructive (LVC) testbed. *IEEE Military Communications Conference*, IEEE, Orlando, FL, USA, pp. 1–8, 2012.

34. Ekstedt, M. and Sommestad, T., Enterprise architecture models for cyber security analysis. *IEEE/PES Power Systems Conference and Exposition*, IEEE., Seattle, WA, USA, pp. 1–6, 2009.

35. Sommestad, T., Ekstedt, M., Johnson, P., Cyber security risks assessment with bayesian defense graphs and architectural models. *42nd Hawaii International Conference on System Sciences*, IEEE., Waikoloa, HI, USA, pp. 1–10, 2009.

36. Shinde, P.S. and Ardhapurkar, S.B., Cyber security analysis using vulnerability assessment and penetration testing. *World Conference on Futuristic Trends in Research and Innovation for Social Welfare (Startup Conclave)*, IEEE, Coimbatore, India, pp. 1–5, 2016.

37. Flatt, H. *et al.*, Analysis of the Cyber-Security of industry 4.0 technologies based on RAMI 4.0 and identification of requirements. *IEEE 21st International Conference on Emerging Technologies and Factory Automation (ETFA)*, IEEE, Berlin, Germany, pp. 1–4, 2016.

38. Dewal, P. *et al.*, Security attacks in wireless sensor networks: a survey. In Cyber Security. *J. Cybersecur*, 729, 47–58, 2018.

39. Javaid, A.Y. *et al.*, Cyber security threat analysis and modeling of an unmanned aerial vehicle system. *IEEE Conference on Technologies for Homeland Security (HST)*, IEEE, Waltham, MA, USA, pp. 585–590, 2012.

5

A Detailed Review on Security Issues in Layered Architectures and Distributed Denial Service of Attacks Over IoT Environment

Rajarajan Ganesarathinam[1]*, Muthukumaran Singaravelu[2] and K.N. Padma Pooja[3]

[1]*School of Computer Science and Engineering, Vellore Institute of Technology, Vellore, India*
[2]*Department of Computer Science and Engineering, Anna University, Chennai, India*
[3]*Department of Computer Science and Engineering, Thiagarajar College of Engineering, Madurai, India*

Abstract

The promising nature of the Internet, its related technologies, and the applications has brought a significant impact on human beings' day-to-day activities in the past three decades. As a part of its evolution, the current trend is the Internet of Technology (IoT), which brings automation to the next level via connecting the devices through the Internet, and its benefits are tremendous. Meanwhile, the threats and attacks are also evolving and become an unstoppable menace to IoT users and applications. In this chapter, we are presenting the various security loopholes and concerns in the existing layered architectures of IoT. Out of many attacks and threats over IoT, we have specifically chosen Distributed Denial of Service (DDoS) attacks because of its severity in the IoT environment and dealt extensively with the different categories of DDoS impact as well as a review of existing countermeasures against DDoS in IoT. Further, this chapter addresses critical challenges and future research directions concerning IoT security that gives insights to the new researchers in this domain.

Corresponding author: rajarajan.g@vit.ac.in

Uzzal Sharma, Parma Nand, Jyotir Moy Chatterjee, Vishal Jain, Noor Zaman Jhanjhi and R. Sujatha (eds.)
Cyber-Physical Systems: Foundations and Techniques, (85–122) © 2022 Scrivener Publishing LLC

Keywords: IoT security, internet attacks, distributed denial of service, layered architecture, cyber systems

5.1   Introduction

Undoubtedly, the Internet has become an indispensable entity in all walks of human life. Due to its tremendous growth, it becomes a basic need for millions of people to meet their demands. The Internet is used by approximately half of the world's population [1, 2]. Taking advantage of the Internet's numerous benefits, another area known as the Internet of Things uses the Internet to link objects and machines to communicate with one another [3]. The aim of this cutting-edge technology is to improve automation by linking objects through the Internet. As a result, sectors like government, healthcare, logistics, agriculture, business, education, etc., are experiencing the impact of IoT in socio-economic aspects and encouraging the researchers to explore further in this technology to raise this digital world into another level [4–7]. Thus, IoT is a digital ecosystem that caters applications to multiple domains, as shown in Figure 5.1, by interoperability among the physical devices. Because of its better outcomes and

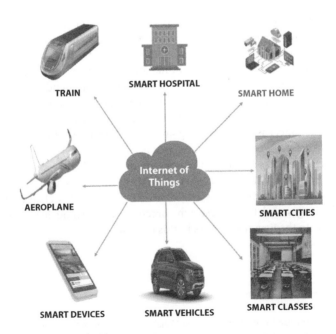

Figure 5.1 Applications of IoT.

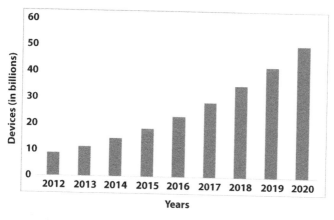

Figure 5.2 Growth of IoT devices in billions.

comforts in human life, the numbers of IoT devices are increasing year by year. Figure 5.2 shows the trend of IoT devices population. Gartner Inc. [8] forecasted that more than 125 billion Internet-linked gadgets would be in practice, and by average, each person owns 15 connected devices in 2030. To achieve the interconnectivity among the IoT devices as well as to form a well-established infrastructure for IoT ecosystem, multiple heterogeneous platforms, elements, architectures [9] are needed, that will be discussed in next subsequent section.

On the other hand, by recognizing the buzz of IoT in market shares, many firms and organizations have been driven to develop more IoT devices as quickly as possible to sustain their positions, with the motive of functionality, not on security. As a result, IoT security has been severely affected [10, 11]. In the security perspective, the rush in the IoT revolution so far with less focus on the security of IoT devices, leads to the foundation of potential disaster [12]. Not only benefits, but there are also multiple challenges like energy efficiency, interoperability of heterogeneous platforms, poor management, device identification, privacy and trust encompassing IoT architecture [13]. The most important of these concerns are security and privacy. Unless it is focused on proper motive and care, IoT becomes the Internet of dangerous threats and attacks. The infusion of more and more non-secure devices from the market and its interconnectivity poison the IoT digital ecosystem [14–16]. Thus, the abundance of IoT devices has the possibility of being prey to a variety of malwares [17], which solicit attackers to inflict havoc in Figure 5.3. Further details about the extensive nature of DDoS will be covered in the subsequent sections.

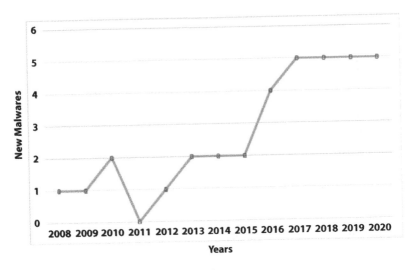

Figure 5.3 DDoS capable IoT malware growth.

Out of many attacks in which IoT is subjected to, Distributed Denial of Service (DDoS) is the complicated and dangerous attack over IoT. The significant reason for considering this attack is due to its severity, complex nature of perpetration, difficulty in the prevention and mainly its gruesome impact. DDoS is the magnified form of Denial of Service (DoS) attacks, which involves a group of remotely distributed bots [17, 18] that interrupt and deny services for users by flooding the target machine or communication links with massive amount of traffic in a network. This attack gained so much of popularity in the year 2016, because of DDoSing the IoT network with the help of a malware called "Mirai" [19, 20] which infects hundreds of IoT devices with the volume of 1.2 Tbps. This remains the most massive DDoS attack over IoT till now and becomes an eye-opener of security concerns in IoT platforms. By using Mirai malware, attackers exploited the IoT using massive DDoS attacks through simple procedures [21, 22]. The progressive nature of DDoS capable malwares over IoT is shown.

The objectives of this chapter are manifold:

- Highlight the different models of IoT layered architecture and its security concerns.
- Give a picture of DDoS attacks and its taxonomy.
- Address the pros and cons of existing solution mechanisms for DDoS attacks and security loopholes in the IoT environment

- Provide insights about critical challenges and future research in this arena.

The rest of the chapter is organized as follows: Section 5.2 briefs about IoT components, different layers of IoT architecture and its security loopholes. Section 5.3 overviews about DDoS attacks, its working mechanisms, classification and its impact over IoT in a detailed manner. The extensive literature survey about solution mechanisms specific to DDoS attacks in IoT are discussed in Section 5.4. Section 5.5 suggests the research challenges and further directions towards DDoS-free IoT. Section 5.6 concludes this review chapter.

5.2 IoT Components, Layered Architectures, Security Threats

As highlighted in the introductory section, IoT is the heterogeneous composition of different technologies, platforms and devices embedded with softwares.

5.2.1 IoT Components

Generically, there are six components involved in IoT infrastructure, as shown in Figure 5.4. The details of the components are as follows:

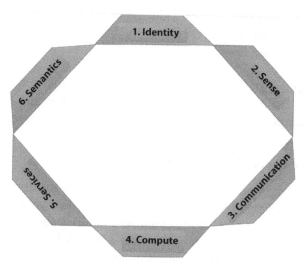

Figure 5.4 IoT components.

(a) Identification: It facilitates the process of identifying every device in the IoT network through naming and addressing. Naming means assigning a special name to each object while addressing refers assigning a unique address to every device. For example, Electron Product Codes (EPC), ubiquitous codes, IPv6 are the popular conventions commonly used [23].

(b) Sensing: it is the process of collecting the information through various objects like actuators, smart sensors, wearable sensing objects, RFID tags, etc., and transferring it to the cloud storage.

(c) Communication: Communication focuses mainly on sending and receiving of files and other related information among the devices through various technologies like Bluetooth [24], RFID [25], LTE [26] and NFC [27].

(d) Computation: It means processing the collected information obtained through sensors, and the type of computation varies with respect to the application. Many hardware and software platforms like Arduino, Raspberry Pi, Intel Galileo, Tiny OS [28], LiteOS [29], Android, etc., are supporting this computation phase

(e) Services: There are the following four services provided by IoT applications [30, 31].

    (i)   Identity-related service
    (ii) Information aggregation service
    (iii) Collaboration Service
    (iv) Ubiquitous Service.

(f) Semantics: It is a significant component of IoT to carry out its responsibilities. It collects the related information and commands individual decisions to devices on demand.

5.2.2   IoT Layered Architectures

According to our findings, there is no single, uniform IoT architecture that has been agreed upon by all researchers around the world. To meet the demands of the moment, the research community suggested a variety of architectures. Thus, the point of the architecture of the IoT ecosystem is evolutionary; not a predefined one. This subsection analyzes the pros and cons of the existing layered architecture of IoT.

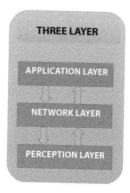

Figure 5.5 3-Layer architecture.

5.2.2.1 3-Layer Architecture

This is the very fundamental architecture to meet out the basic idea of IoT. As shown in Figure 5.5, it has three layers, namely Perception, Network (transport) and Application layers [32–34]. The perception layer, also called as sensor layer, is responsible for identifying devices in the IoT population and collects the information from those objects. The type of sensors deployed in the IoT environment depends on the application. The next layer is the network layer or transport layer acts as a bridge between the application and perception layer. The primary responsibility of the transport layer is to collaborate smart objects, networking elements and networks with each other. The medium of communication may be either wired or wireless. The application layer, the final layer, is in charge of delivering services to applications such as smart homes, animal tracking, smart cities, healthcare, and so on.

5.2.2.2 4-Layer Architecture

The above stated 3-layer architecture is to fulfil only the basic need of IoT, and there is no point of addressing security goals like authentication, authorization, trust and confidentiality [35]. Hence, researchers proposed a 4-layer architecture [36] to implement the missing features of the 3-layer architecture. The following Figure 5.6 shows that it has an extra one layer called the support layer. The responsibility of the remaining three layers like perception, network, and application is similar to the 3-layer architecture with extra care of device protection and encryption mechanism.

The support layer comes in between perception and network layer. The primary responsibility of this new layer in this architecture is to provide

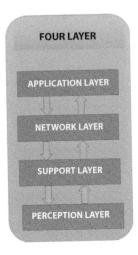

Figure 5.6 4-Layer architecture.

authentication and protection. That is, it allows the only authenticated source of information to network layer through applying valid mechanisms like pre-shared secret keys, passwords, etc. Also, it encrypts the authenticated information so that confidentiality can be ensured.

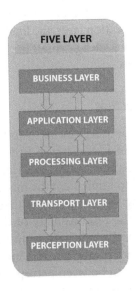

Figure 5.7 5-Layer architecture.

5.2.2.3   5-Layer Architecture

Researchers proposed another level of architecture called 5-layer architecture [37–39] as an enhancement to the 4-layer scenario. Apart from perception, network and application layer, it has an extra two layers, namely processing and business layer, as shown in Figure 5.7. The processing layer acts as a middleware that collects the information from the network layer and eliminates unnecessary extra information. That is, it performs the role of extracting the needful information from the volume of information collected by sensors. Hence, it overcomes the problem of big data processing and reduces the overhead involved. Another new layer called business layer that acts as a manager of the entire system. The primary responsibility includes privacy, managing and controlling the applications, modeling the secure and robust data storage.

5.2.3   Associated Threats in the Layers

By analyzing the loopholes in the infrastructure of IoT, attackers are posing threats with multiple variations, and as a result, the impact is acute. Table 5.1 shows the possible attacks over different layers.

5.2.3.1   Node Capture

This is a serious assault on the IoT's perception layer. An attacker compromises a main node, such as a gateway router, and gains complete control over it. As a result, all information stored in memory can be leaked, and it is a big menace [40].

5.2.3.2   Playback Attack

It is also known as a replay attack because it involves an attacker intruding on the correspondence between the sender and the receiver and capturing the genuine information from the sender's end. Thus, an attacker sends the same authenticated data to the receiver (victim) by spoofing his identity and authenticity as the normal sender, so that victim believes that message is from valid source [41].

5.2.3.3   Fake Node Augmentation

Here, an attacker gains control over IoT devices by adding a malicious node into the system and inputs fake data. The underlying motive behind this attack is to block the transmission of real information. Likewise, if many fake nodes are added, it paves the way for a massive collapse of IoT infrastructure.

5.2.3.4   Timing Attack

By analyzing how long it takes to respond to a query, processing time, and cryptographic algorithms, an attacker may identify vulnerabilities in the system and extract critical information. This type of attack is commonly possible in devices with less computing capabilities [42].

5.2.3.5   Bootstrap Attack

Before two devices start to communicate confidential information, some assurance is needed to ensure that devices should be trusted. As a consequence, a mechanism for configuring nodes during initial network setup, also known as bootstrapping, is needed [43]. An attacker exploits this mechanism during the bootstrapping phase to gain access to the device.

5.2.3.6   Jamming Attack

The attackers use jammers, which operate on the same frequency spectrum as other communication devices and interfere with legal signal transmission [44, 45].

5.2.3.7   Kill Command Attack

This attack occurs only in RFID devices. During the manufacturing of RFID tags, they have a password with write-protected access. Because of the memory and processing limitations, an attacker can use brute force to break the password, resulting in the tags being disabled [46].

5.2.3.8   Denial-of-Service (DoS) Attack

This DoS attack is the most famous attack in which an attacker compromises the system and denies the services to legitimate devices or users. The most dangerous form of DoS attack is Distributive DoS attack [47] is explained in the next section.

5.2.3.9   Storage Attack

The collected information from sensors is stored in the cloud environment or storage devices. The attackers exploit the cloud storage and modify the correct details is called storage attack.

5.2.3.10 Exploit Attack

This attack is the substandard form DoS attack in which the attacker probes the devices, system configuration, protocols, and extracts the vulnerabilities in the system. Therefore, the attackers gain control and breach the security limit [48].

5.2.3.11 Man-In-The-Middle (MITM) Attack

It is similar to Replay attack such that an intruder gains the control between communications of two nodes as well as fabricate the legitimate information with vulnerable source codes like worms, virus, trojans, etc. The attacker hides his presence and lets the participating devices to believe that information is from authenticated sources [49].

5.2.3.12 XSS Attack

It is a form of attack scenario that allows attackers to embed a malicious client-side script into a popular website. Thus, attackers could change the contents of the application and use the application in an illegal manner [50].

5.2.3.13 Malicious Insider Attack

This type of attack is rare but possible. It happens from the compromised user of IoT environment to do illegal activities. That is, authorized user being an attacker malfunctions the complete IoT ecosystem from inside [51, 52].

5.2.3.14 Malwares

The main motive behind the injection of malware into IoT is to steal the confidentiality of information [53]. That is, applying worms, viruses, spywares, trojans, adwares, etc., to interact with the system.

5.2.3.15 Zero-Day Attack

This refers to a security flaw in an application that the vendor is unfamiliar with. As a result, the intruder uses it to gain power without the user's permission or understanding [54, 55].

Table 5.1 Attacks in every layer of IoT architecture.

Attacks	Layer involved	Impact
Node Capture [18]	Perception	Memory leak
Playback attack [19]	Perception	Repudiation
Fake node Augmentation	Perception	Blocking real node data transmission
Timing attack [20]	Perception	Indefinite delay in data transfer
Bootstrapping attack [21]	Perception	Illegal intrusion and exploitation
Jamming attack [22, 23]	Perception	Blocking of wireless channels
Kill command attack [24]	Perception	Disabling RFID tags
Denial of Service attack [25]	Network	Resource Exhaustion, device crash
Storage attack	Network	Modification of original information
Exploit Attack [26]	Network	Improper functionality of protocol
MITM attack [27]	Network	Repudiation
Cross site scripting attack [28]	Application	Illegal modification of contents in application
HTTP flooding attack	Application	Severe congestion, Resource exhaustion
Regular expression attack	Application	Exhaustion of resources
Hash collision attack	Application	More collision in hash tables
Reprogramming attack	Application	Illegal code modification in application
Malicious insider attack [29, 30]	Support	Authorized user with illegal activities
Malwares [31]	Processing	Loss of confidentiality
Zero day attack [32, 33]	Business	Unpredictable

All types of attacks are harmful, and measures should be taken to prevent or avoid these attacks. Out of many attacks which we discussed, the most significant, dangerous, impactful attack over IoT environment is Distributed Denial of Service Attacks (DDoS). The next section deals with the DDoS attack over IoT in a significant manner.

5.3   Taxonomy of DDoS Attacks and Its Working Mechanism in IoT

The Internet Telecommunication Union (ITU-T) defines DDoS as "prevention of authorized access to resources or delay of time-critical operations". This is a massive coordinated attack on the availability of victims' or active network services, which is covertly launched through many compromised nodes [56].

DDoS attacks are not specific to IoT; Even before the advent of IoT, DDoS menace exists in Internetworks from the year 2000 onward. However, the arrival of IoT makes the DDoS attack more complex and powerful than ever. Most of the attacks, including DDoS, understand the following security issues on the Internet and perpetuate a variety of threats over it.

(a) Internet is interdependent: It makes no difference how protected the victim is; its vulnerability to DDoS attacks is determined by the protection of the rest of the Internet.

(b) Limited resources: The Internet entities like hosts, network, services, etc., have limited resources that can be saturated by attackers.

(c) No accountability: An IP packet contains field like source IP and Destination IP. The entities like routers, gateways simply process the source IP, destination IP entries without validation. Thus, attacker perpetrates spoofing related threats.(d). Distributed control: On the Internet, of course, there is no way to deploy a global or centralized security mechanism. Every network has its policies defined by its administrators. Thus, it becomes a possibility of attackers to gain control over some network. The research work in [57] proposed Automated Trust Negotiation (ATN) to deal with complex components of the Internet, but still, solutions against evolving new threats are unaddressed.

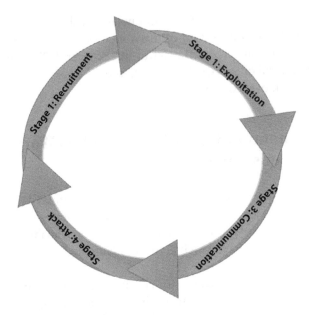

Figure 5.8 Phases of DDoS attack.

As shown in Figure 5.8, the DDoS attacks should go through the following phases to perpetuate its strategy over victim [58, 59].

(i) Recruitment Phase: The attacker scans for vulnerable devices in the IoT network. If found, it can be compromised and used for further stages of attacks. Earlier, this work was done manually; thereafter, automated tools are evolved to scan the entire network for vulnerability in just one click.

(ii) Exploitation Phase: The recruited machines with vulnerabilities are injected with malicious code or software like worms, viruses and Trojans to turn it into a botnet. The botnetwork is the network of compromised nodes in IoT.

(iii) Communication Phase: The attacker mostly using command-and-control infrastructure to communicate among botnets. In this phase, all the attack-related information like nature, longevity, type of attack, etc., can be communicated to botnets.

(iv) Attack Phase: Finally, the attacker commands the botnets to target the victim based on the communicated information between attacker (master) and botnets (slaves).

In modern-day DDoS attacks, most of the attackers spoofing their identity to complicate the traceback mechanism.

5.3.1 Taxonomy of DDoS Attacks

There are lots of classifications of DDoS attacks have been proposed in the literature over the past few years. This section presents our improved classification of DDoS attacks, which was generated by combining the taxonomies proposed by [59–66]. We classified the DDoS attacks based on the 12 parameters: Architecture, Vulnerability, Protocol, Automation, Impact over the victim, Rate of attack, Persistence of agent set, Victim type, Validity of Source address, Scanning, Propagation and Attack traffic distribution.

5.3.1.1 Architectural Model

As highlighted in this section, most of the DDoS attack is perpetrated using the mechanism called command-and-control Infrastructure [18]. Based on this, there are four different types of architecture namely Agent Handler model, Internet Relay Chat model, Reflector Model and Peer-to-Peer model used by attackers to carry out DDoS over victim.

The Agent-Handler mechanism (Figure 5.9(a)) contains three entities: Client, Master (Handler) and slaves (Agents). The client is a device that the attacker will use to communicate with agents. The agents (bots) are the true perpetrators of DDoS attacks, acting on the client's and handler's instructions. [62].

The Agent–Handler model is improved by the Reflector model (Figure 5.9(b)). Like the Agent–Handler model, it has client, handler, agent but it has an extra component called a reflector. The reflectors are uninfected machines induced by handlers to perpetrate attack over victim; instead of agents. That is, agents, spoof the IP address of the victim and intentionally send the request to the reflector with spoofed source IP address of the victim. As a result, reflectors flood the response to the victim, which leads to a crash of the target. This type of DDoS is also called as "Distributive Reflective Denial of Service" (DRDoS) [67, 68].

The Internet Relay Chat (IRC) based model is very similar to Agent-Handler except that IRC protocol is connecting client and bots (Figure 5.9(c)) and it has advantages in attackers' point of view like high invisibility, low traceability and high survivability [69].

The Peer-to-Peer (P2P) based model differs from C&C infrastructure (Figure 5.9(d)) such that attacker issues commands to botnets relying on

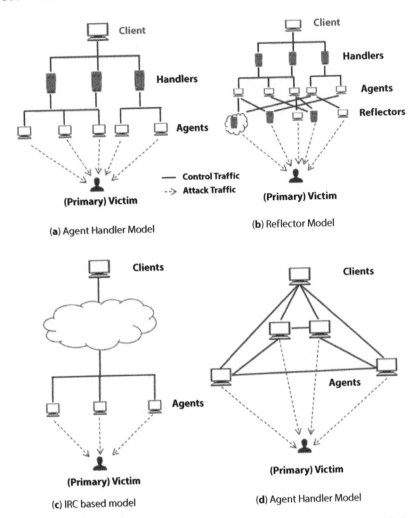

Figure 5.9 (a) Agent-Handler Model; (b) Reflector Model; (c) IRC based model; (d) Peer-to-Peer model.

P2P network, not on C&C based network. As a result, the attacker has some benefits like robustness, fault-tolerance compared to C&C model.

5.3.1.2   Exploited Vulnerability

Based on the vulnerability in the network, DDoS attacks are classified into two different categories [18, 61, 63, 66]:

- Resource Depletion
- Bandwidth Depletion.

When a resource is depleted, malformed packets or mechanisms that exploit an application are used to deny service. That is, either by exploiting the vulnerabilities in the protocol like TCP-SYN, PUSH and ACK or tampered IP packets are used to harm the network resources.

In bandwidth depletion attacks, the focus is clogging the network bandwidth, CPU processing time, memory with the huge number of legitimate traffic either through flooding or amplification mechanism [18, 59, 60, 66, 69–71].

5.3.1.3   Protocol Level

Based on the attacks on protocols of different layers of the TCP/IP model, DDoS can be classified into two categories:

- Network-level
- Application-level.

In the network level, protocols in the network or transport layer like TCP, UDP, ICMP, etc., are exploited to conduct the attack and block the services. On the other hand, application layer protocols like DNS, HTTP, SMTP, etc., are used for flooding and amplification attack [71–73].

5.3.1.4   Degree of Automation

Based on how the attack is initiated, it can be classified into three categories [18, 58, 59]:

- Manual
- Semi-automatic
- Automatic.

Nowadays, most of the attacks are fully automated so that impact is severe and traceability is difficult.

5.3.1.5   Scanning Techniques

DDoS attacks can be classified into four groups based on how the attacker searches the network for vulnerabilities and recruits bots for attacks [18, 58].

- Random Scanning
- Hitlist Scanning
- Permutation Scanning
- Local subnet Scanning.

In random scanning, no specific technique is used by the attacker to scan the devices in the network for vulnerability. The attacker randomly scans the IP address space and finds vulnerable hosts. The process of scanning the list of hosts based on the known facts about the devices and its vulnerabilities is called Hitlist scanning. In permutation scanning, identities of objects are found out by pseudo-random permutation of IP address space.

5.3.1.6 Propagation Mechanism

Based on how the attack code is injected into devices, DDoS can be categorized into three classes [18, 58]:

- Central Source Propagation
- Back-Chaining Propagation
- Autonomous Propagation.

In the central source propagation, the handler or malicious package is stored in a central server. After recruiting vulnerable hosts, the attacker injects the malicious code from the centralized source. However, there is a possibility of a point of failure of centralized infrastructure. The attack code is downloaded from the host and used to hack the device in the Back-chaining technique. On the other hand, most of the modern-day DDoS attackers make use of the autonomous propagation such that malicious codes are directly injected into the host at the time of infection itself. This is completely automated and no need for any third-party intervention.

5.3.1.7 Impact Over the Victim

Based on the impact of DDoS attacks over the victim [58, 59], it can be categorized as:

- Disruptive
- Degrading.

DDoS attacks that interrupt the victim's services to legitimate users for an extended period of time are known as disruptive DDoS attacks. Anyhow recovering from this disruptive attack depends on the sustenance of victim infrastructure as well as the nature of DDoS attack. The Degrading category means the motive of the attack is not to disrupt all the service altogether, but stopping the most critical service in IoT for a significant period.

5.3.1.8   Rate of Attack

Depending on the attack rate over the victim, the DDoS attack can be classified into the following:

- Constant Rate
- Variable Rate.

Constant rate DDoS attacks are described as attackers continuously flooding packets towards the victim at peak rates. Variable-rate DDoS attacks occur when the rate varies over time. Though the constant rate has a large impact, the variable rate is better at hiding the existence of a DDoS attack.

5.3.1.9   Persistence of Agents

The attackers use the same set of recruited agents during the attack period or sometimes randomly vary the agents' availability in order to complicate the traceability. As a result, DDoS can be classified as either a constant agent set or a variable agent set, depending on how the agent sets are deployed.

5.3.1.10   Validity of Source Address

Depending on the source IP address of agents, DDoS can be classified as spoofed source DDoS and Valid source DDoS. In spoofed source IP, the attacker hides his presence under the mask of any random host IP, and it further complicates the traceability features. It is an infrequent occasion in the modern-day scenario that attackers are using actual valid source IP address.

5.3.1.11   Type of Victim

Based on the target victim to be attacked, DDoS can be classified as Host, Application, Network and Infrastructure based DDoS attacks.

5.3.1.12   Attack Traffic Distribution

The traffic rate can be either similar or dissimilar during the attack period. Based on the traffic of packets distribution, DDoS can be classified into following [65, 74]:

- Isotropic
- Non-Isotropic.

In the case of Isotropic DDoS, the traffic distribution is uniform throughout the attack duration. But in Non-Isotropic DDoS, it varies at specific devices.

5.3.2   Working Mechanism of DDoS Attack

The overall scenario of modern-day DDoS attacks is represented in Figure 5.10. In general, the working mechanism of DDoS attack can be divided into three phases: Attacking phase, Handling phase and Target phase.

The two crucial components in the attacking phase are bots and botmaster. A bot is a malware package that includes rootkits, scanners, SQL templates, image scripts, and other components and serves as a command and control server. Based on the nature of attack and functionality, botmaster selects a specific set of the botnet [75, 76]. With the help of agents, the attacker (botmaster) understands the various loopholes in terms of security and its related features and left those security holes to remain open for further phases. The attacker will find more and more vulnerable IoT objects by consistently searching the web with bots.

The handling phase has three essential components, namely C&C server, loader and report server. A database (MySQL) of infected devices and

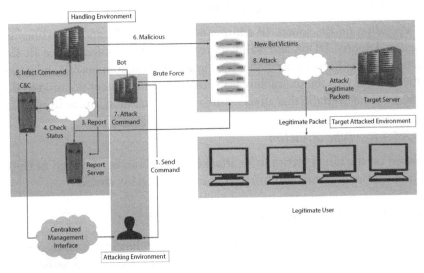

Figure 5.10 Working mechanism of DDoS attacks.

related information is held on the C&C server. Most of the DDoS attackers communicate with C&C server and agents through IRC mode, whereas recent studies show HTTP botnets are also popular [77, 78]. That is, HTTP protocol is used for communication between the attacker and C&C server. Later, the control panel of the C&C server is installed in the infected machine so that attacker can exploit whatever in those IoT devices without the knowledge of the owner of the device. Since the victim host interacts with the C&C server at this stage, agents can easily carry out attacks.

The target process consists of two components: newly infected devices and the target server. Following the injection of malicious code into hosts, all of the victim's actions and original files are added to key generators, which are then executed alongside the victim's other applications. When a user fills out a request, the username and password are communicated automatically to the C&C server. After confirming the botnets' active status, the attacker directs the agents to attack the victim. The command includes significant parameters like nature of the attack, duration, time-to-live (TTL) and port number, etc.

5.4   Existing Solution Mechanisms Against DDoS Over IoT

An extensive literature study has been conducted with respect to solution mechanisms against DDoS in IoT, and the findings have been categorized into detection and prevention strategies. That is, some work is focusing only on how to detect variable rate DDoS attacks low-rate DDoS and its related variants. Meanwhile, some researchers proposed prevention mechanism against DDoS. Hybrid strategies include both detection and prevention mechanisms. This section elaborates the literature details on existing countermeasures against DDoS in IoT and compares the pros and cons of the work.

5.4.1   Detection Techniques

In [79], the honeynet solution is proposed against the effortless detection of DDoS attacks. Honeypots are the decoy systems which lure the attacker to probe the system [80]. This work combined the honeypots and proposed a system called "Honeycloud". These honeypots fingerprint the attacker's activities whenever suspicious known attack or blacklisted IP contacted the IoT devices. Based on this, further processing can be done to avoid

DDoS impact. It is effective only if the attacker is unaware of the presence of honeypots. Otherwise, this technique itself is a serious threat to existing IoT devices.

Many researchers proposed mechanisms to improve processing time and scalability to counter the malicious attacks. In either case, attackers' state-of-the-art strategies nullify the proposed mechanisms and increase response time due to long latency. In the continuation of such effort, [81] used Fog computing techniques to withstand DDoS attacks. The authors proposed a model called "FOCUS—Fog Computing based Security System" which provides two-level protection system. That is, a VPN is used to secure the communication medium at the first level, followed by the challenge–response authentication approach to detect illegitimate traffic from a DDoS attack at the second level. The advantage of this mechanism is less response time compared to other techniques and less bandwidth consumption. However, accurate network traffic classifier is essential for the second level (challenge–response mechanism) to detect a DDoS attack with zero false-positive rates.

[82] proposed an innovative Intrusion Detection System based on Artificial Neural Network. This ANN-IDS can be used as an offline framework to capture and analyze traffic between multiple IoT devices, as well as to detect DDoS attacks in the IoT network. The experimental demonstration showed that this mechanism is 99% accurate in classifying legitimate and malicious traffic. However, it is not effective against real-time responses.

In [83], the detection mechanism for both high-rate and low-rate DDoS attack is proposed. In general, high-rate DDoS causes a sudden surge in prompt traffic and low-rate DDoS happens at aperiodic intervals so that it is complicated to detect. The authors proposed a two-layer approach to detect these two variants of DDoS attacks. The metrics are passed through the Detection with Average Filters unit in the first stage to filter out the high-rate DDoS traffic (DAF). The remaining metrics are passed through Detection with Discrete Fourier Transform (DDFT) to detect low-rate DDoS traffic at the second stage. The main drawback of this approach is high overhead and ineffective when high-rate and low-rate malicious traffic are close enough.

Adeilson et al. [84] proposed a real-time DDoS detection system for the Internet of Things (IoT) based on the rapidly increasing technology of "Complex Event Processing" (CEP). This CEP architecture consists of three main layers: Event filter, Event processor and Action Engine. The event filter tests and tracks network traffic when the IoT system experiences traffic flooding. The packet analyzer and attack detection tools modules in the Event processor evaluate the type of DDoS attack and record its existence and properties. The action engine—the final layer—deals with suspicious attack traffic and blocks links to relevant resources. This technique is advantageous in detecting the attack traffic with high accuracy, but the false positive rate is computed as around 8%, which is unacceptable in a real-time scenario.

The research work presented in [85] is about detecting the botnets based on Power Spectral Density (PSD). The authors presented a model called PsyBOG—a signal processing technique that finds the main frequencies by using botnets' periodic DNS queries. By observing the simultaneous behavioral pattern as well as the periodic behavioral pattern of DNS traffic, the botnet traffic, legitimate traffic and infrequent traffic can be separated. The simulation-based experiment results showed that this approach is viable for large-scale IoT systems as scalability is not affected by voluminous traffic.

In [86], the use of machine learning techniques to detect malicious traffic is proposed. This work presented a model called T-IDS: Advanced Traffic-based Intrusion Detection System, which uses a network traffic feature collection, feature selection techniques, and a randomized data partitioned learning model to detect intrusions (RDPLM). Voronoi-based data partitioning and clustering is preferred for data reduction after the dataset has been collected and preprocessed. Finally, based on the input dataset's heterogeneity, a meta-learning prototype with multiple randomized trees is developed. This makes it easier to detect malicious traffic, but the downside is that when dealing with large sets of data, the running time and computing capability of this model grows exponentially.

In [87], the behavioral study of DNS registration is used to detect the botnets. This approach focuses on early detection by analyzing the bots during DNS registrations as well as communication with C&C servers. By using the domain name generating algorithms and other tracking services, the suspicious bots should be blacklisted. Since this methodology is entirely focused on botnet datasets, such datasets must be provided with care.

The detection of mobile botnet is a bit complicated than static botnetworks. [88] proposed signature-based mobile botnet detection. This approach has three modules, namely the multi-agent system, signature-based detection and decision-action module. The multi-agent system manages traffic and gathers information from various Android devices. The detection module gathers data from the central server and uses pattern-matching algorithms to identify known botnets. Finally, decision-module decides the eviction of botnets from IoT. The main drawback in this approach is it is ineffective against new variants of botnets. It is limited to discover only known botnets, not new attacks.

The DDoS attacks over the android platform are significantly increased from the last 3 years. The authors of [89] suggested a structure analysis testing framework-based methodology. This approach comprises of five modules with the objective of detecting DDoS attacks on android platforms only. The first module collects the normal as well as botnet applications installed among all IoT devices to perform structured analysis. The second module uses the Android Asset Packaging Tool (AAPT) to remove the android manifest file and decompress the.apk file. The rest of the modules, segregate botnets from the legitimate applications by applying machine learning algorithms. The experimental results showed that it is very effective in case of DDoS over android platforms than previous strategies.

Natarajan et al. [90] presented a detection technique of stegabots based on analysis of image entropy. It is useful because the change in entropies shows a massive difference in the botnet binaries before and after the image. However, scalability is a problem with this method. Anitha et al. [91] extended this image entropy-based detection to check whether a user is a bot or not. This work focuses mainly on detecting stegabot in social media networks.

The real-time DDoS detection protocol is proposed by [92] for connection-oriented service in the network. The authors proposed a novel system called sliding-mode observer, which is installed in gateway routers and firewalls that diagnose attack traffic based on real-time queue length. NS-2 based simulation experiments show that this approach is practical.

5.4.2   Prevention Mechanisms

Senie et al. [93] suggested ingress–egress filtering as a packet filtering technique. That is, filtering out the incoming and outgoing malicious packets with the spoofed IP address. This mechanism gained popularity at the early stages, but it was failed when DDoS attackers using legitimate IP addresses. Lee et al. [94] presented a score based packet filtering technique to drop malicious packets. That is, based on the traffic features of both incoming and outgoing packets, a score count is assigned to it. If the difference between the measured and threshold scores is greater than the threshold, the packet is considered an attack and is discarded. In real-time DDoS, this feature predicted the malicious packets and dropped them with the success rate of 80%.

A weight-fair throttling mechanism is proposed in [95] to avoid DDoS attacks on the web server at the upstream router. The leaky bucket algorithm at the upstream router regulates the packet flow towards the web server. If the voluminous traffic more than the capacity of the server reaches the edge router, this mechanism throttle the flow and prevent the crash of the web server. Secure Overlay Service (SOS) is also once considered as a prevention mechanism against DDoS, but its scope is narrow, and it is ineffective against new routing protocol having in-built security loopholes. The working mechanism of SOS is presented in [96].

Nowadays, DDoS attackers are exploiting the features of Software Defined Networking (SDN) and making it as a source platform for conducting DDoS attacks over IoT environment [97] introduced the S-Flow technique, which combines the potential of SDN with traffic flow and defines a metric called DCN to quantify packet flow distribution and intensity. As an extension of this work, [98] presented floodlight-based guard system in which anti-spoofing module of source IP and S-Flow technology is combined to make sFlow-RT is efficient against IP spoofing based DDoS attacks in SDN.

The work presented in [99] is exclusively for Service Oriented Architecture of IoT to deal against DDoS attacks. The authors proposed a model called Learning Automata to thwart DDoS in SOA based IoT platforms. The significant feature in this approach is that it builds on the top of cross-layer technology and so it is instrumental in capturing attack packets with less overhead. The more in-depth analysis of this working mechanism is found in [99].

To minimize the effect of DDoS attacks, [100] proposes a constructive auto-responsive honeypot architecture. The main goal of this system is to keep the network stable by making resources inaccessible to DDoS attackers. The NS-2 based simulation results proved that this technique had reduced the false-negative rate. But the main drawback is more overhead in the network. The classifier System DDoS is introduced in [101] as a way to detect and prevent DDoS attacks by sorting incoming packets and making an inference using classifiers. The authors proposed four different classifiers to segregate and blacklist malicious traffic with the assumption that IP spoofing is not involved. Therefore, it is working only for legitimate IP packets, not for spoofed IP addresses. The experimental results were tested using k-fold validation, which showed that it is 97% accurate with a kappa coefficient of 0.89 under single attack and 94% accurate with a kappa coefficient of 0.9 under multiple attacks.

The collaborative efforts by IBM and Akamai lead to the development of multi-faceted prevention mechanism against DDoS attack called "Kona Site Defender". This is robust in handling DDoS attacks in such a way that request traffic load is redirected to various geographically distributed

Table 5.2 Summary of existing countermeasures against DDoS attacks.

Existing countermeasures	Mode	Operation scenario	Advantages	Disadvantages
Honeynet cloud [79]	Detection	Eavesdropping of attackers' activities	• Attackers mode of operations can be known • Effective fingerprinting of attacker's signature	• High overhead • False positive rate is high
FOCUS [81]	Detection	VPN and Challenge response authentication method	• Less overhead • Quick detection of attacks • Less processing time and bandwidth	• Accurate network classifier is needed; otherwise false positive rate would be high
ANN-IDS [82]	Detection	Artificial Neural Network based traffic analysis	• 99% accurate	• Unreliable against real-time attack packets
Variable Rate DDoS detection [83]	Detection	Detection Average Filter (DAF) and Detection with Discrete Fourier Transform (DDFT)	• Separate Low-rate and High-rate DDoS traffic	• High overhead • Ineffective when high and low-rate traffic are close enough
Real-time DDoS detection [84]	Detection	Complex Event Processing (CEP)	• Very effective	• False positive rate is 8 %

(*Continued*)

Table 5.2 Summary of existing countermeasures against DDoS attacks. (*Continued*)

Existing countermeasures	Mode	Operation scenario	Advantages	Disadvantages
PsyBoG [85]	Detection	Behavioral pattern of DNS	• Supports Scalability	• Effective only for DNS traffic
T-IDS [86]	Detection	Randomized Data Partitioned Learning Model (RDPLM)	• Quick identification of malicious traffic	• Time complexity and computational power is high for large data sets
Behavioral study of DNS [87]	Detection	Domain Name Generating Algorithm	• Botnet Identification	• Sampling of flow monitoring by ISP
Signature based mobile botnet detection [88]	Detection	Multi-agent, Signature-detection, Decision-action Module	• Less overhead • Lightweight detection approach for smart devices	• Ineffective against anomaly based attacks
Android based DDoS detection [89]	Detection	Feature selection and Android Asset Packaging Tools (AAPT)	• Very effective	
Stegabot detection [90, 91]	Detection	Image Entropy	• Effective in detecting stegabots in social media networks	• Scalability is not supported.

(*Continued*)

Table 5.2 Summary of existing countermeasures against DDoS attacks. (*Continued*)

Existing countermeasures	Mode	Operation scenario	Advantages	Disadvantages
Ingress–Egress Filtering [93]	Prevention	Filtering malicious packets at upstream and downstream routers	• Spoofed IP packets are easily identified	• Ineffective against legitimate IP flood.
Score based Filter [94]	Prevention	Assigning Score to incoming and outgoing packets	• Success rate is 80 %	• High overhead and processing
Weight fair throttle [95]	Prevention	Leaky bucket algorithm	• Effective against all flooding attacks	• Failed in preventing variable rate DDoS traffic
S-Flow [97]	Prevention	SDN and DCN	• Detection and prevention of attack in early phases	• Unreliable when attacks are launched from multiple SDN networks.
Floodlight based Guard system [98]	Prevention	Anti-spoofing module	• Suitable for SDN	• Single point of failure is possible
Learning Automata [99]	Prevention	Service-Oriented Architecture of IoT	• Optimized Energy and computational resources	• Unreliable false positive as well as false negative rate
Classifier DDoS system [101]	Prevention	Deep-learning accurate classifiers	• 94% accurate against simultaneous multiple attacks	• Ineffective against spoofed IP addresses

servers and filters the attack traffic from the incoming traffic flow [102]. Table 5.2 summarizes the merits and demerits of existing solution mechanisms.

5.5   Challenges and Research Directions

Though IoT supports and benefits multiple sectors, it faces more challenges than its outputs. The section focuses on addressing the critical challenges in the IoT environment in security aspects so that the new researchers in the domain explore it for a further step towards a secure IoT environment.

- Naming and Identifying the objects in the IoT environment is a bit complex. IPv4 was initially used to give IoT devices a unique address. Later, it was replaced by IPv6 because of increasing demand and spoofing problems in IPv4. Further research exploration is necessary in terms of benchmarking the naming and identifying techniques of IoT devices dynamically in the network.
- Trust, and Privacy management is the need of the hour of IoT. Its scope is more prominent than security because users are providing their private or personal information to IoT objects. Therefore privacy must be entirely ensured to the dependents of IoT. Researchers have suggested a number of strategies to provide trust and privacy, but there are still some problems. Hence it is the most crucial priority in the research domain to ensure holistic trust and privacy.
- As per estimation, by 2030, around 100 billion devices could be part of IoT. These objects collect and store an enormous amount of information. Unless we have an efficient big-data processing mechanism, managing the vast knowledge and its computation become a big issue. Hence the focus is needed in this dimension.
- Another issue in the IoT environment is authentication, followed by authorization. The usual way of authenticating the objects by username and password are replaced by access cards, retina scan, fingerprints, and voice recognition. Accessibility of resources should be given to only authenticated objects. Much effort is required in this area because this is the entry point of most of the attacks. Attackers impersonate themselves as legitimate objects in IoT and collapse the

Table 5.3 DDoS capable malwares.

Malware	DDoS-architecture	Source - code
Linux.Hydra	IRC-based	Open Source
Psybot	IRC-based	Reverse Eng.
Tsunami	IRC-based	Reverse Eng.
Kaiten	IRC-based	Reverse Eng.
Chuck Norris	IRC-based	Reverse Eng.
Zendran	IRC-based	Open Source
Aidra	IRC-based	Open Source
Bashlite	Agent–Handler	Open Source
Torlus	Agent–Handler	Open Source
XOR. DDoS	Agent–Handler	Reverse Eng.
Remaiten	IRC-based	Reverse Eng.
Mirai	Agent–Handler	Open Source

applications. Although research has attempted the solution for authentication and authorization problems in IoT [103, 104], still the loopholes persist. Thus, attention is needed in this path.

- The main reason for the threat prone environment of any Internet-based technology or network is, the focus is always on functionality than security—the manufacturers' devices for IoT with the emphasis only on providing full-fledged services at the user end without considering.

- As security practitioners, attackers are also continuously doing research on developing botnets and malwares specific to IoT. The popularity of DDoS-capable malwares is very much from 2016 onward because of dangerous malware called "Mirai" that compromised around 500,000 IoT devices and paved the way for the biggest DDoS attack of 1.2Tbps [21, 22, 105]. It is estimated that from 2012 to till date, 3 to 4 new malwares are developed by attackers that are compromising IoT devices [6]. The details of the malwares and its features are represented in Table 5.3. Hence it is very essential to develop techniques to nullify the impact of those malwares over IoT environment.

5.6 Conclusion

The impact of IoT in the upcoming years is unstoppable. This technology would be the driving force of bringing automation to the next level. Meanwhile, the security issues and loopholes are also tightly binding with IoT architectures. As a result, dangerous attacks like DDoS, botnet based attacks, etc., are causing havoc to well-developed IoT application. Unless it is dealt with needful research in the critical time, IoT becomes "Internet of Threats". Motivated by this exacerbated situation, we have articulated the security loopholes in the layered architectures of IoT. In specific, we have chosen Distributed Denial of Service (DDoS) attacks, and its menace over the IoT infrastructure is analyzed extensively along with its up-to-date taxonomy. From the detailed survey of the existing solution mechanism against DDoS over IoT environment, the general issues are identified, and critical challenges are sorted out for further research. Therefore, it is an urgent requirement to standardize the protocols compounding the security of IoT to create robust post-quantum IoT paradigm.

References

1. Internet Users. Available online: http://www.Internetlivestats.com/Internet-users/ (accessed on 07 May 2020).
2. Global Internet Usage. Available online: https://www.en.wikipedia.org/wiki/Global_Internet_usage/(accessed on 07 May 2017).
3. Oppitz, M. and Tomsu, P., *Inventing the Cloud Century: How Cloudiness Keeps Changing Our Life, Economy and Technology*, Springer, Cham, 2017.
4. Hongbo, Z., Longxiang, Y., Qi, Z., Shi, J., Ubiquitous information service networks and technology based on the convergence of communications, computing and control. *J. Commun. Inf. Netw.*, 1, 1, 98–110, 2016.
5. Yichuan, W., Yefei, Z., Xinhong, H., Wenjiang, J., Weigang, M., Game strategies for distributed denial of service defense in the Cloud of Things. *J. Commun. Inf. Networks.*, 11, 44, 143–155, 2016.
6. Irina, B., Tanczer, L., Carr, M., Blackstock, J., Regulating IoT: Enabling or Disabling the Capacity of the Internet of Things? *Risk Regul.*, 12–15, 2017;33, August. https://core.ac.uk/download/pdf/81675775.pdf

7. Zhang, C. and Green, R., Communication security in internet of thing: Preventive measure and avoid DDoS attack over IoT network. *Simul. Ser.*, 47, 3, 8–15, 2015.

8. IoT devices prediction. Available online: https://www.gartner.com/insights/ (accessed on 06 May 2020).

9. Bello, O., Zeadally, S., Badra, M., Network layer inter-operation of Deviceto-Device communication technologies in Internet of Things (IoT). *Ad. Hoc. Netw.*, 57.

10. Granjal, J. and Silva, J.S., *Security for the Internet of Things : A Survey of Existing Protocols and Open Research issues*, IEEE communications on Surveys and Tutorials, 2015.

11. Arias, O., Wurm, J., Hoang, K., Jin, Y., Privacy and Security in Internet of Things and Wearable Devices. *IEEE Trans. Multi-Scale Comput. Syst.*, 1, 2, 99–109, 2015.

12. Dragoni, N., Gieretta, A., Mazzara, M., The Internet of Hackable Things, in: *Proceedings of the 5th International Conference in Software Engineering for Defense Applications (SEDA16) Advances in Intelligent Systems and Computing*, P. Ciancarini, S. Litvinov, A. Messina, A. Sillitti, G. Succi (Eds.), Springer, 2017.

13. Yaqoob, I., Ahmed, E., Hashem, I.A.T. *et al.*, Internet of Things Architecture: Recent Advances, Taxonomy, Requirements, and Open Challenges. *IEEE Wirel. Commun.*, 24, 3, 10–16, 2017.

14. Hughes, D., Silent risk: new incarnations of longstanding threats. *Netw. Secur.*, 2016, 8, 17–20, 2016,

15. Shukla, S.K., Editorial: cyber security, IoT, block chains—risks and opportunities. *ACM Trans. Embed. Comput. Syst. (TECS)*, 16, 3, article 62, 1–2, 2017.

16. Goyal, R., Dragoni, N., Spognardi, A., Mind the tracker you wear - A security analysis of wearable health trackers. *Proc. ACM Symp. Appl. Comput.*, pp. 131–136, 2016;04-08-Apri.

17. Hoque, N., Bhattacharyya, D.K., Kalita, J.K., Botnet in DDoS Attacks: Trends and Challenges. *IEEE Commun. Surv. Tutor.*, 17, 4, 2242–2270, 2015.

18. Asosheh, A. and Ramezani, N.A., comprehensive taxonomy of DDoS attacks and defense mechanism applying in a smart classification. *WSEAS Trans. Comput.*, 7, 4, 281–290, 2008.

19. York, K., Dyn statement on 10/21/2016 DDoS attack, Dyn Blog, 2016. http://dyn.com/blog/dyn-statement-on-10212016-ddosattack/.

20. Hilton, S., Dyn analysis summary of friday october 21 attack, Dyn Blog, 2016. http://dyn.com/blog/dyn analysis-summary-offriday-october-21-attack/.

21. Angrishi, K., Turning Internet of Things(IoT) into Internet of Vulnerabilities (IoV): IoT Botnets. Published online 2017:1-17. http://arxiv.org/abs/1702.03681.

22. Klaba, O., OVH suffers 1.1 Tbps DDoS attack, in: *Tech. Rep., SC Magazine*, 2016.

23. Koshizuka, N. and Sakamura, K., Ubiquitous ID: Standards for ubiquitous computing and the internet of things. *IEEE Pervasive Comput.*, 9, 4, 98–101, 2010.
24. McDermott-Wells, P., What is Bluetooth? *IEEE Potentials*, 23, 5, 33–35, 2005.
25. Want, R., An introduction to RFID technology. *IEEE Pervasive Comput.*, 5, 1, 25–33, 2006.
26. Crosby, G.V. and Vafa, F., Wireless sensor networks and LTE-A network convergence. *Proc. - Conf. Local Comput. Networks*, 2013, LCN, pp. 731–734, October 2013.
27. Want, R., Near field communication. *IEEE Pervasive Comput.*, 10, 3, 4–7, 2011.
28. Levis P. et al. (2005) TinyOS: An Operating System for Sensor Networks. In: Weber W., Rabaey J.M., Aarts E. (eds), *Ambient Intell.*, Springer, Berlin, Heidelberg. https://doi.org/10.1007/3-540-27139-2_7.
29. Cao, Q., Abdelzaher, T., Stankovic, J., He, T., The LiteOS operating system: Towards Unix-like abstractions for wireless sensor networks. *Proc. - 2008 Int. Conf. Inf. Process Sens. Networks, IPSN 2008*, pp. 233–244, Published online 2008.
30. Xing, X.J., Wang, J.L., Li, M.D., Services and key technologies of the Internet of Things. *ZTE Commun.*, 8, 2, 2010.
31. Gigli, M. and Koo, S., Internet of Things: Services and Applications Categorization. *Adv. Internet Things*, 01, 02, 27–31, 2011.
32. Mashal, I., Alsaryrah, O., Chung, T.Y., Yang, C.Z., Kuo, W.H., Agrawal, D.P., Choices for interaction with things on Internet and underlying issues. *Ad. Hoc. Netw.*, 28, 68–90, 2015.
33. Mashal, I., Alsaryrah, O., Chung, T.Y., Yang, C.Z., Kuo, W.H., Agrawal, D.P., Choices for interaction with things on Internet and underlying issues. *Ad. Hoc. Netw.*, 28, 68–90, 2015.
34. Said, O. and Masud, M., Towards internet of things: Survey and future vision. *Int. J. Comput. Netw.*, 5, 1, 1–17, 2013. http://www.cscjournals.org/csc/manuscript/Journals/IJCN/volume5/Issue1/IJCN-265.pdf.
35. Simpson, A.K., Roesner, F., Kohno, T., Securing vulnerable home IoT devices with an in-hub security manager. *2017 IEEE Int. Conf. Pervasive Comput. Commun. Work PerCom Work 2017*, pp. 551–556, 2017;(PerLS).
36. Darwish, D.G. and Square, E., Improved Layered Architecture for Internet of Things. *Int. J. Comput. Acad. Res.*, 4, 4, 214–223, 2015. http://www.meacse.org/ijcar.
37. Madakam, S., Ramaswamy, R., Tripathi, S., Internet of Things (IoT): A Literature Review. *J. Comput. Commun.*, 03, 05, 164–173, 2015.
38. Khan, R., Khan, S.U., Zaheer, R., Khan, S., Future internet: The internet of things architecture, possible applications and key challenges. *Proc - 10th Int. Conf. Front Inf. Technol. FIT 2012*, 2012, pp. 257–260, April 2017.
39. Sethi, P. and Sarangi, S.R., Internet of Things: Architectures, Protocols, and Applications. *J. Electr. Comput. Eng.*, 2017, 9324035, 25, 2017.

40. Vivekananda Bharathi, M., Tanguturi, R.C., Jayakumar, C., Selvamani, K., Node capture attack in Wireless Sensor Network: A survey. *IEEE Int. Conf. Comput. Intell. Comput. Res. ICCIC 2012*, 2012;(i, 2012).
41. Puthal, D., Nepal, S., Ranjan, R., Chen, J., Threats to Networking Cloud and Edge Datacenters in the Internet of Things. *IEEE Cloud Comput.*, 3, 3, 64–71, 2016, doi: 10.1109/MCC.2016.63.
42. Brumley, D. and Boneh, D., Remote timing attacks are practical. *Comput. Netw.*, 48, 5, 701–716, 2005.
43. Sonar, K. and Upadhyay, H., A Survey : DDOS Attack on Internet of Things. 10, 11, 58–63, 2014.
44. Nguyen, A.T., Mokdad, L., Ben-Othman, J., Solution of detecting jamming attacks in vehicle ad hoc networks. *MSWiM 2013 - Proc 16th ACM Int. Conf. Model Anal. Simul. Wirel. Mob. Syst.*, pp. 405–410, Published online 2013.
45. Thakur, N., Introduction to Jamming Attacks and Prevention Techniques using Honeypots in Wireless Networks. *IRACST –Int. J. Comput. Sci. Inf. Technol. Secur.*, 3, 2, 2249–9555, 2013.
46. Ahmadian, Z., Salmasizadeh, M., Aref, M.R., Desynchronization attack on RAPP ultralightweight authentication protocol. *Inf. Process Lett.*, 113, 7, 205–209, 2013.
47. Prabhakar, S., Network Security in Digitalization: Attacks and Defence. *Int. J. Res. Comput. Appl. Rob.*, www.ijrcar.com. 5, 46–52, 2017, http://www.ijrcar.com/Volume_5_Issue_5/v5i512.pdf.
48. Exploit Attack in Network Layer Available online. http://searchsecurity.techtarget.com/definition/exploit/ (accessed on 07 May 2020).
49. Conti, M., Dragoni, N., Lesyk, V., A Survey of Man in the Middle Attacks. *IEEE Commun. Surv. Tutor.*, 18, 3, 2027–2051, 2016.
50. Gupta, S. and Gupta, B.B., Cross-Site Scripting (XSS) attacks and defense mechanisms: classification and state-of-the-art. *Int. J. Syst. Assur. Eng. Manage.*, 8, 512–530, 2017.
51. Sanzgiri, A. and Dasgupta, D., Classification of insider threat detection techniques. *Proc. 11th Annu. Cyber Inf. Secur. Res. Conf. CISRC 2016*, 5–8, Published online 2016.
52. Nurse, J.R.C., Erola, A., Agrafiotis, I., Goldsmith, M., Creese, S., Smart Insiders: Exploring the Threat from Insiders Using the Internet-of-Things. *Proc. - 2015 Int. Work Secur. Internet Things, SIoT 2015*, pp. 5–14, Published online 2016.
53. Canzanese, R., Kam, M., Mancoridis, S., Toward an automatic, online behavioral Malware classification system. *Int. Conf. Self-Adaptive Self-Organizing Syst. SASO*, pp. 111–120, Published online 2013.
54. Bilge, L. and Dumitras, T., Before we knew it: An empirical study of zero-day attacks in the real world. *Proc. ACM Conf. Comput. Commun. Secur. 2012*, pp. 833–844, October 2012.
55. Kaur, R. and Singh, M., A survey on zero-day polymorphic worm detection techniques. *IEEE Commun. Surv. Tutor.*, 16, 3, 1520–1549, 2014.

56. Rajarajan, G. and Ganesan, L., A decoy framework to protect server from wireless network worms. *Wirel. Pers. Commun.*, 94, 4, 1965–1978, 2017.

57. Dragoni, N., Massacci, F., Saidane, A., A self-protecting and self-healing framework for negotiating services and trust in autonomic communication systems. *Comput. Netw.*, 53, 10, 1628–1648, 2009.

58. Mirkovic, J. and Reiher, P., A taxonomy of DdoS attack and DdoS defense mechanisms. *Comput. Commun. Rev.*, 34, 2, 39–53, 2004.

59. Douligeris, C. and Mitrokotsa, A., DdoS attacks and defense mechanisms: Classification and state-of-the-art. *Comput. Netw.*, 44, 5, 643–666, 2004.

60. Tariq, U., Hong, M.P., Lhee, K.S., A comprehensive categorization of DDoS attack and DDoS defense techniques. *Lect. Notes Comput. Sci. (including Subser Lect Notes Artif. Intell. Lect Notes Bioinformatics)*, 4093 LNAI(Mic):1025–1036, 2006.

61. Hussain, A., Heidemann, J., Papadopoulos, C., A Framework for Classifying Denial of Service Attacks. *Comput. Commun. Rev.*, 33, 4, 99–110, 2003.

62. Alomari, E., Manickam S, B., Gupta, B., Karuppayah, S., Alfaris, R., Botnet-based Distributed Denial of Service (DDoS) Attacks on Web Servers: Classification and Art. *Int. J. Comput. Appl.*, 49, 7, 24–32, 2012.

63. Specht, S.M. and Lee, R.B., Distributed Denial of Service: Taxonomies of Attacks, Tools and Countermeasures. *Int. Work Secur. Parallel Distrib. Syst.*, 9, 543–550, 2004.

64. RioRey Inc, Taxonomy of DDoS Attacks, 2014. https://www.servermania. com/gallery/resources/RioRey Taxonomy DDoS Attacks 2.6 2014.pdf.

65. Kumar, K., Joshi, R.C., Singh, K., An Integrated Approach for Defending Against Distributed Denial-of-Service (DDoS) Attacks. *Iriss*, 1–6, Published online 2006.

66. Singh, E.G. and Gupta, E.M., Distributed denial-of-service. *International Journal of Computer and Electrical Engineering (IJCEE)*, 2, 2, 268–276, 2010.

67. Paxson, V., An analysis of using reflectors for distributed denial-of-service attacks. *ACMSIGCOMM Comput. Commun. Rev.*, 31, 3, 38–47, 2001.

68. Gibson, S., DRDoS:Description and Analysis of A Potent, in: *Increasingly Prevalent, and Worrisome Internet Attack*, Gibson Research Corporation, Dayton, Ohio, United States, 2002.

69. Sharafaldin, I., Lashkari, A.H., Hakak, S., Ghorbani, A.A., Developing Realistic Distributed Denial of Service (DDoS) Attack Dataset and Taxonomy, in: *2019 International Carnahan Conference on Security Technology (ICCST)*, pp. 1–8, 2019.

70. Chang, R., Defendinf against Flooding-Based Distributed Denial-of-Service Attacks: A Tutorial. *IEEE Commun. Mag.*, 40, 10, 42–51, 2002, October.

71. Zargar, S.T., Joshi, J., Tipper, D., A survey of defense mechanisms against distributed denial of service (DDOS) flooding attacks. *IEEE Commun. Surv. Tutor.*, 15, 4, 2046–2069, 2013.

72. Ranjan, S., Swaminathan, R., Uysal, M., Knightly, E., DDoS-resilient scheduling to counter application layer attacks under imperfect detection. *Proc.-IEEE INFOCOM*, pp. 1–13, Published online 2006.

73. Networks, A., The growing threat of application-Layer DDoS attacks. *Tech. Rep.*, 2011, https://dsimg.ubm-us.net/envelope/126712/324232/1298913706623_AB_ALDDoS_EN_LGQ1.pdf.

74. Gupta, B.B., Joshi, R.C., Misra, M., Defending against distributed denial of service attacks: Issues and challenges. *Inf. Secur. J.*, 18, 5, 224–247, 2009.

75. Taking charge of the IoT's security vulnerabilities (White Paper), 2017.

76. Cao, C., Guan, L., Liu, P., Gao, N., Lin, J., Xiang, J., Hey, you, keep away from my device: remotely implanting a virus expeller to defeat Mirai on IoT devices. 1–15, Published online 2017, http://arxiv.org/abs/1706.05779.

77. Sood, A.K., Zeadally, S., Bansal, R., Cybercrime at a scale: A practical study of deployments of HTTP-based botnet command and control panels. *IEEE Commun. Mag.*, 55, 7, 22–28, 2017.

78. Darwish, A., El-Gendy, M.M., Hassanien, A.E., A new hybrid cryptosystem for Internet of Things applications, in: *Multimedia Forensics and Security*, vol. 115, pp. 365–380, 2016.

79. Gupta, A. and Gupta, B., Honeynettrap: Framework to detect and mitigate ddos attacks using heterogeneous honeynet, in: *2017 International Conference on Communication and Signal Processing (ICCSP)*, IEEE, pp. 1906–1911, 2017.

80. Weiler, N., Honeypots for distributed denial-of-service attacks, 109–114, ISBN 0-7695-1748-X, 02, 2002.

81. Alharbi, S., Rodriguez, P., Maharaja, R., Iyer, P., Bose, N., Ye, Z., FOCUS: A fog computing-based security system for the Internet of Things, in: *2018 15th IEEE Annual Consumer Communications Networking Conference (CCNC)*, pp. 1–5, 2018.

82. E. Hodo *et al.*, Threat analysis of IoT networks using artificial neural network intrusion detection system, *2016 International Symposium on Networks, Computers and Communications (ISNCC)*, 1–6, 2016.

83. Toklu, S. and Simsek, M., Two-layer approach for mixed high-rate and low-rate distributed denial of service (ddos) attack detection and filtering. *Arab. J. Sci. Eng.*, 43, 12, 7923–7931, 2018.

84. da Silva Cardoso, A.M., Lopes, R.F., Magalhaes, F.B.V., Real-time ddos detection based on complex event processing for iot, in: *2018 IEEE/ACM Third International Conference on Internet-of-Things Design and Implementation (IoTDI)*, IEEE, pp. 273–274, 2018.

85. Kwon, J., Lee, J., Lee, H., Perrig, A., PsyBoG: A scalable botnet detection method for large-scale DNS traffic. *Comput. Netw.*, 97, 48–73, 2016.

86. Al-Jarrah, O.Y., Alhussein, O., Yoo, P.D., Muhaidat, S., Taha, K., Kim, K., Data Randomization and Cluster-Based Partitioning for Botnet Intrusion Detection. *IEEE Trans. Cybern.*, 46, 8, 1796–1806, 2016.

87. Dietz, C., Sperotto, A., Dreo, G. *et al.*, How to Achieve Early Botnet Detection at the Provider Level ? *10th IFIP International Conference on Autonomous Infrastructure, Management and Security (AIMS)*, pp.142–146, Munich, Germany, Jun 2016.

88. Alzahrani, A.J. and Ghorbani, A.A., SMS mobile botnet detection using a multi-agent system: Research in progress. *ACM Int. Conf. Proceeding Ser.*, Published online 2014.

89. Kirubavathi, G. and Anitha, R., Structural analysis and detection of android botnets using machine learning techniques. *Int. J. Inf. Secur.*, 17, 2, 153–167, 2018.

90. Natarajan, V., Sheen, S., Anitha, R., Detection of StegoBot: A covert social network botnet. *ACM Int. Conf. Proceeding Ser.*, pp. 36–41, Published online 2012.

91. Venkatachalam, N. and Anitha, R., A multi-feature approach to detect Stegobot: a covert multimedia social network botnet. *Multimed. Tools Appl.*, 76, 4, 6079–6096, 2017.

92. Han, F., Xu, L., Yu, X., Tari, Z., Feng, Y., Hu, J., Sliding-mode observers for real-time DDoS detection. *Proc. 2016 IEEE 11th Conf. Ind. Electron Appl. ICIEA 2016*, pp. 825–830, 2016;(51577039).

93. Ferguson, P. and Senie, D., Network ingress filtering: Defeating denial of service attacks which employ IP source address spoofing, in: *RFC 2827*, 2001.

94. Lee, Y., Lee, W., Shin, G., Kim, K., Assessing the impact of dos attacks on iot gateway, in: *Advanced Multimedia and Ubiquitous Engineering*, pp. 252–257, Springer, 2017.

95. Wisthoff, M., Ddos countermeasures, in: *Information Technology - New Generations*, pp. 915–919, Springer, 2018.

96. Keromytis, A.D., Misra, V., Rubenstein, D., SOS: secure overlay services. *In Proceedings of the 2002 conference on Applications, technologies, architectures, and protocols for computer communications (SIGCOMM '02)*, Association for Computing Machinery, New York, NY, USA, 61–72, 2002.

97. Lu, Y. and Wang, M., An easy defense mechanism against botnet-based DDoS flooding attack originated in SDN environment using sFlow. *ACM Int. Conf. Proceeding Ser.*, pp. 14–20, 2016;15-17-June.

98. Liu, J., Lai, Y., Zhang, S., FL-GUARD: A detection and defense system for DDoS attack in SDN. *ACM Int. Conf. Proceeding Ser.*, pp. 107–111, Published online 2017.

99. Misra, S., Venkata Krishna, P., Agarwal, H., Saxena, A., Obaidat, M.S., A learning automata based solution for preventing distributed denial of service in internet of things. *Proc - 2011 IEEE Int. Conf. Internet Things Cyber, Phys. Soc. Comput. iThings/CPSCom 2011*, pp. 114–122, Published online 2011.

100. Sardana, A. and Joshi, R., An auto-responsive honeypot architecture for dynamic resource allocation and QoS adaptation in DDoS attacked networks. *Comput. Commun.*, 32, 12, 1384–1399, 2009.

101. Sahi, A., Lai, D., Li, Y., Diykh, M., An Efficient DDoS TCP Flood Attack Detection and Prevention System in a Cloud Environment. *IEEE Access*, 5, c, 6036–6048, 2017.

102. Kamboj, P., Trivedi, M.C., Yadav, V.K., Singh, V.K., Detectiontechniques of ddos attacks: A survey, in: *2017 4th IEEE Uttar Pradesh Section International Conference on Electrical, Computer and Electronics (UPCON)*, IEEE, pp. 675–679, 2017.

103. Shang, W., Ding, Q., Marianantoni, A., Burke, J., Zhang, L., Securing building management systems using named data networking. *IEEE Netw.*, 28, 3, 50–56, 2014.

104. Liu, J., Xiao, Y., Chen, C.L.P., Authentication and access control in the Internet of things. *Proc. - 32nd IEEE Int. Conf. Distrib. Comput. Syst. Work ICDCSW 2012*, pp. 588–592, Published online 2012.

105. Millman, R., KrebsOnSecurity hit with record DDoS, KrebsonSecurityBlog, 2016. https://krebsonsecurity.com/2016/09/krebsonsecurity-hit-with-record-ddos/.

6

Machine Learning and Deep Learning Techniques for Phishing Threats and Challenges

Bhimavarapu Usharani

Department of Computer Science and Engineering, Koneru Lakshmaiah Education Foundation, Vaddeswaram, India

Abstract

Dependency concerning on-line applications is increasing time by using day. Due the speedy evolution of the internet users, security plays a foremost role in this internet world. Internet security threats are kept on rising due to the several vulnerabilities and numerous attacking techniques. The swindlers who take skills over the vulnerable on-line services and get admission to the information of genuine people thru these virtual features are early and late expanding. Utilizing the modern-day skills about the net, they are discovering innovative procedures according to gather confidential records regarding the customers certain as much profile identification 's, PINs, credit or debit visiting card particulars, etc. One on the near frequent cyber security risks is the phishing attack. Identifying various network related attacks, especially phishing attacks, unforeseen attacks, network hidden abnormal behavior is a technical issue. The delivery note detects numerous categories of phishing attacks or deliberates the current state concerning the art options for many phishing attacks. Security should use to prevent phishing attacks and to offer the availability and confidentiality. Many researchers developed various phishing detection systems in the past to recognize and find the intruders. In this chapter, explored the phishing attack detection using the machine learning, deep learning, and neural networks.

Keywords: Phishing threats, internet fraud, internet security, machine learning, deep learning, neural networks, spoofing, malware

Email: ushareddy@kluniversity.in

Uzzal Sharma, Parma Nand, Jyotir Moy Chatterjee, Vishal Jain, Noor Zaman Jhanjhi and R. Sujatha (eds.)
Cyber-Physical Systems: Foundations and Techniques, (123–146) © 2022 Scrivener Publishing LLC

6.1   Introduction

The net service is some over the well-known inventions, but its effect on concerning human beings is very flagrant [1]. The Internet plays a crucial role for individuals and organizations, are imparting internet trade, e-business, or functions [2]. The number of Internet customers has grown exponentially [3]. Data safety performence is an indispensable role, and the major aim is preserving the privacy, reliability, and accessibility of aid facts constructions [4]. Internet fraud in opposition to persons is developing age with the resource of length and endure emerge as a world challenge [5]. With the invention on the modern-day utilized sciences over the internet, humans are getting more than one chances as like properly so a fraud from the fraudsters and due to the fact of current loopholes between the web sites security system, data breaches are happening. By making use of pragmatic advancements, the phishes make use of its developments to extract the touchy yet non-public files over expert customers such as secret code, card number, bank credentials, etc. Spoofing is a purchaser special confrontation, and there is the want in accordance to supply protection at the consumer level. We intend at advent the ant phishing machine in accordance with choosing out the phishing URL or conscious the customers touching the safety threat. Whenever the latter URL is identified the model database is updated. There by way of imparting safety in accordance with the dependable users, then such saves the customers past the fraudsters. This demand consignment geared up as like follows. Section 6.2 summarizes a variety of phishing mechanisms identified by the literature. Related work is mentioned in Section 6.3. Section 6.4 assesses the phishing attack procedures for internet website phishing recognition. Section 6.5 gives the Assessment Information.

6.2   Phishing Threats

In this section, we examine different phishing systems utilized by the phishers.

6.2.1   Internet Fraud

The internet commercial enterprise is growing [6]. As indicated by means of the measurable reports, the volume of casualties is increasing internationally [7]. Fraudsters collect a large measure of consumer records from online organizations, for example, online web-based media profile data, search history, and internet perusing conduct, fraud of labeled and non-public records [8]. Various kinds of online fakes are electronic mail extortion [9], online sale extortion [10], and economic extortion [11]. There are quite several varieties of misrepresentation and the techniques to distinguish misrepresentation, examined in [12]. Extraordinary misrepresentation and their lessons will be examined in the accompanying segments.

6.2.1.1   Electronic-Mail Fraud

Imposters ship messages to bait authentic clients. The purpose is to collect the secret and non-public information of actual clients, who react to their messages. Table 6.1 represents various categories of Electronic-mail fraud.

Table 6.1 Categories of electronic mail frauds.

Category	Explanation
Improvement Charge	The electronic mail requests the receivers to ship a charge in increase previous than getting a benefit
Nigerian	An email from isolated areas asks the recipient to aid move cash out of the state. Spoofers obtain reliable person financial institution small print or ask for a minor charge in develop to drop out the excise to move cash
Work-at-home	An email including a note that the receiver can operate and get cash from their cost vicinity and for becoming a member of the organization, the receivers must pay in early payment.
Greeting card	An electronic mail comprising a meeting invitation which urges to connect on a hyperlink and this hyperlink comprises of malware.
Bank-loan or credit-card	An email comprises of a note for authorization for a bank loan or deposit card and requests the recipient economic institution particulars.
Service-provider	An e mail comprises of a note to persuade the recipient to compensate instantly. If Not, the individual specific company will be at stake.

(Continued)

Table 6.1   Categories of electronic mail frauds. (*Continued*)

Category	Explanation
Reward	An e mail illuminates that association is rewarding a few humans and the receivers identify is in that file and request for the receiver individual details.
Assistance	An e-mail persuades to hand over endowments to faux charitable trust and organizations.
Cancelled-fraud	An e-mail includes a hyperlink to a phishing website online to keep on going their services
CEO-fraud	An e-mail detect of misspelled expressions of a detailed business enterprise CEO guides a message to the greater experts in that employer who must cope with money to switch cash to a specified account.
Insurance-fraud	An e-mail asking the old age people want a pension or lifestyles coverage plan strategy

6.2.1.2   Phishing Extortion

Fraudsters get subtle and categorized records of real customers like secret code, card number, bank credentials, etc. via imagining as a reliable individual. The precept purpose is to introduce malware on the PCs of net clients, pastime money to tackle the problems grown due to the malware. Table 6.2 represents various categories of phishing extortion.

Table 6.2   Categories of phishing extortion.

Category	Explanation
Bogus antivirus	Pop up window educating the net customers to transfer the antivirus software
False internet site	A generation of sincere or consistent web sites is used and requesting net customers to submit private data credentials
SMS	A message may furthermore include a hyperlink which consists of malware to achieve private indicators of the net users.
Duplicate phishing	Fraudsters imitate the earlier legit message and generate a new one by using subsequent the duplicated mail and this message comprises of hyperlink within contains mischievous software.

6.2.1.3   Extortion Fraud

In blackmail misrepresentation, the ill-conceived purchasers paint the story in a way that the genuine purchasers give the amount to the spoofers within a short duration. Table 6.3 represents various categories of extortion fraud.

6.2.1.4   Social Media Fraud

By progressions with the innovation, online channels permit folks to talk about and also change data. Fraudsters are arriving at actual consumers via web-based media [83] with ease and much less exertion. The chance of misrepresentation, statistics fraud, and absence of safety for man or woman report is expanding. Table 6.4 represents various categories of social media fraud.

Table 6.3 Categories of extortion fraud.

Category	Explanation
Ransomware	Spoofers latch user's pc the use of certain package program till sufferers give amount
Extremist Intimidation	I Spoofers send a mail comprising of threating note to sufferers that the organization head will live if they give money to them
Blast Warning	Spoofers send a mail that to customers that there is an explosive in specific constructing, and only be detached by giving money to them
DDOS-Attack	Spoofers goal a specific organization, create the fake online jam. By this incident it may be either slow down or closing the net host facilities and demand the sufferer a big amount to set right the net server and the situation.
Hit man	Spoofers send a mail that they appointed a hiding person to kill the sufferer and they provide the crucial information about their personals and demand them to give a bulk amount to withdraw that specific person. These spoofers will collect all the individual's data from online media and demand for bulk amount.

Table 6.4 Categories of social media scam.

Fraud type	Description
Work Extend	Spoofers provide a work simply an alleged commercial business and request some cash for verifying the job.
Impersonation	Spoofers create a certain false summary of some web customers. They call the sufferer's buddies or household to divulge and command cash to solve.
Fraud news	Spoofers generate faux film star information, and this information carried on social media. Professional customers start using hyperlink to analyze that information, by means of that activity, spoofers collects the consistent customer's internet community personal details and their ids important points and get complete data of the genuine internet community consumer accounts.

6.2.1.5   Tourism Fraud

Genuine humans format their entire get-away bundle by using on-line like reserving tour tickets, reserving lodgings beforehand of time. Phishes carry as a confided in company to draw guiltless with their offers, and several persons have completed their tour with counterfeit appointments. Table 6.5 represents various categories of travel fraud.

Table 6.5 Categories of tourism fraud.

Category	Explanation
Concession	Spoofers send a mail that the unique person earned a trip advance to proclaim the advantage, they must compensate a trivial cost.
Voyage vouchers	Resell Spoofers send a mail that deliberate a journey because of personal reasons and urgency, cancelling the journey and choose to promote vouchers with using cheap prices
Holiday Leasing	Spoofers send a mail that small condo rooms at a unique place and they ask to hire in advance.
Points Scam	Spoofers send a mail, a particular individual earned vast journey points. As an alternative of journey, will adjust, and request the small imprint to announce the sum.

Table 6.6 Categories of excise fraud.

Category	Explanation
Bogus Inspection	Spoofers send a mail to the reliable suffragist, just like from the excise agency, and an inconsistency insist the on-the-spot charge with the chance of imprisonment or some different intimidations.
Bogus Repayment	Spoofers send a mail to trustworthy suffragist that comprises of a hyperlink to proclaim the corresponding compensation.
Flawed Compensation	Spoofers create an electronic mail on just like from the excise corporation and pay back dumped to the e-mail beneficiaries that request the suffragist to pay back the total to the organization.
Income Tax activist	Spoofers s send a mail that no want to give the excise amount to attract concerns to the upright suffragist.

6.2.1.6   Excise Fraud

Spoofers make an effect on cost bargain or cutoff time for Income Tax documenting time is approaching. Spoofers send a URL with incorrectly spelled sentences, e.g., as an alternative than the expression e-filing, send like e-filling with different expression The residents stake their account numbers, Master card, credential information to the phishes. Table 6.6 represents various categories of travel fraud.

6.2.2   Phishing

The phrase phishing was coined in 1990 and was derived from the phrase "fishing" [13]. Phishing is an endeavor that takes others' exceptional data with the resource of the use of the entrenched internet address, cyber bug, and faux web sites [14]. By phishing, unacknowledged persons send a suspicious phishing URL, and the purchaser makes use of the equal hyperlink for doing businesses operations, considering that it is a legit transaction. Unrecognized individuals acquire the individual private information of reputable customers with the resource of pretending as a relied on 1/3 birthday social gathering [15]. Unrecognized individuals send the suspicious hyperlinks or the URL by phone messages or WhatsApp messages, electronic mail, categorized commercials and suspicious forums, including the suspicious hyperlinks or the website links [16, 17]. Phishes utilize greater than a few techniques to appear as authentic with the clients with the useful resource of the use of SSL Certificate [18], the use of URL capture methods like typo squatting [19] to obtain private statistics from the customers. Female victims for phishing are larger than guy sufferers, and the phishing fatalities are greater beneath the period crew of 18–24 due to absence of focus about the unrecognized individual events [20, 21]. Many spoofing recognition strategies have been projected and these techniques depend on the sides obtained from a range bases like web crawlers [22], internet dependent techniques like Search engine net web forum [24], blacklists [25], Domain Name System data [23], hyperlinks and internet pages [26–29], case mainly based totally reasoning [30], two stage authentication approach [31, 32], detecting assault surfaces [33], pattern method [34], intrusion detection [35], similarity [36, 37]. There are many cutting-edge methods to defend from the phishing assaults like Phishnet [38], lexical primarily based completely approach [39], proactive phishing identification technique [40], and CatchPhish [41]. Machine gaining expertise of techniques current the great over the normal rule-based algorithms [13] and the phishing detection procedures are stepped ahead via

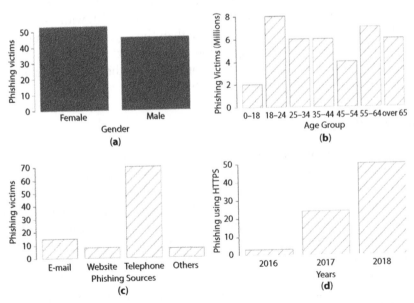

Figure 6.1 Phishing fraud [22]. (a) Gender wise phishing victims. (b) Age wise phishing victims. (c) Phishing attacks by different sources. (d) Phishing attacks using HTTPS protocol.

the pc getting to know components [2]. Many computer gaining know-hows of techniques hear on the internet form to end up conscious of phishing URLs [42–53]. There is a wide variety classifier in laptop getting to know that provides immoderate correctness for hyperlinks [54, 55] and all the machine learning algorithms set up computer gaining information of algorithms like naive Bayes and support vector machines [56]. Internet utilization is accomplishing breakthrough, so the safety tasks for online deals or networks grew to emerge as vital. Masquerading is utilized to accumulate confidential data from customers such as credit card numbers, ATM code, OTPs, etc. This study considers the awesome sorts of masquerading, one-of-a-kind varieties of online frauds, exceptional techniques for fraud recognition and comparison of quantity suspicious activities identification techniques. The forecast of the spoofing assaults is a large task due to the truth of its complexity. Gender smart spoofing sufferers are validated in Figure 6.1a, age sensible spoofing sufferers are confirmed in Figure 6.1b, diverse bases are the use of the useful resource of phishes to entice the first-rate clients are tested in Figure 6.1c and phishing assaults with the use of HTTPS protocol from 2016 to 2020 are established in Figure 6.1d.

6.3   Deep Learning Architectures

Deep learning techniques are applied in various engineering and scientific areas, where bioinformatics and computational system have comprised the initial submission areas of deep learning. Deep learning is a subcategory of machine learning and implies the request of a set of procedures called neural networks and their alternatives. Various categories of deep learning neural networks are tabulated in Table 6.7.

6.3.1   Convolution Neural Network (CNN) Models

Convolution neural networks are used to analyze and classify the images and object recognition. Different architectures of the convolution neural networks are tabulated in Table 6.8.

6.3.1.1   Recurrent Neural Network

Recurrent neural network (RNN) [72] is a classification of deep learning models and used to model time series. The main advantage of the recurrent network is it maintains a feedback loop which helps to output from the previous step and fed as input to the current step. Some RNN variants are tabulated in Table 6.9.

Table 6.7 Deep learning architectures.

Model	Description	Applications
Radial Basis Network (RBN)	A sigmoid function provides the result between 0 and 1	Event Estimate. Time series Forecast. Categorization. System Management
Deep Feed Forward Network	By adding more hidden layers, reduces overfitting and generalization	Data Firmness. Pattern Recognition. Computer Vision, Financial Forecast.
Recurrent Neural Network (RNN)	distinction to feed-forward (FF) networks. The neurons accept an input with pause in time.	Time Series Forecast. Speech Recognition. Speech Synthesis. Time Series Anomaly Recognition.
Long Short-Term Memory (LSTM)	Long memory is introduced and by using this the data can be stored for long time	Speech Recognition. Writing Recognition
Gated Recurrent Unit (GRU)	Alternative to the LSTM and gives the best results than the LSTM	Speech Signal Modeling. Natural Language Processing.
Generative Adversarial Network (GAN)	The main scenario of GAN is creating the deep fake images	Create Innovative Individual Models. Photos to Emojis. Face Maturing.
deep residual network	Precludes mortification of results,	Image Classification. Object Detection.
Deep belief network	correspond to DBNs as grouping of Restricted Boltzmann Machines (RBM) and Autoencoders (AE).	Reclamation of Files or Illustrations. Nonlinear-Dimensionality Lessening.
Deep convolutional network	Works in the opposite process of the CNN	Optical flow evaluation.
SVM	Using to perform the binary classifications.	Face Recognition. Text Classification. Writing gratitude.

Table 6.8 CNN models.

Model	Description	Parameters	Depth
LeNet	categorizes digits and to distinguish hand-written numbers spatial correlation decreases the evaluation and number of considerations.	60,000	5
Alexnet	Introduces regularization concept and provides an idea of deep and comprehensive CNN architecture	60 Million	8
VGG	Establishes active receptive field	138 Million	19
GoogleNet/ Inception-v1	Created the Multiscale Filters within the layers, applied the model of global average-pooling at final layer and sparse Connections, use of auxiliary classifiers to improve the convergence rate	4 Million	22
Resnet	reduced the error rate for deeper networks, Created the notion of residual learning.	25.6 Million	152
Inception-v3	demoralized asymmetric filters and bottleneck layer to reduce the computational cost of architectures	23.6 Million	159
Xception	Introduces the varying size filters	22.8 Million	126
WideResnet	enhances the width of ResNet and reduces its depth, enable feature reclaim	36.5 Million	28
Squeeze and Excitation Networks	Created the generic block	27.5 Million	152
PyramidalNet	Enhances the width gradually per unit	116.4 Million	200

Table 6.9 RNN variants.

Model	Description	Database
QRNN [73]	computationally effective hybrid of LSTMs and CNNs.	IMDb movie review dataset, PTB dataset, IWSLT data set
BRNN: Bidirectional recurrent neural networks [74]	contemplates all input sequences in together with the past and future for assessment of the output vector	TIMIT
MDRNN: Multidimensional RNNs [75]	expanding the pertinence of RNNs to n-dimensional data.	Air Freight, MNIST database
Deep RNN [76]	an option deeper design, which indicates to numerous deeper alternatives of an RNN	Nottingham, JSB Chorales and Muse Data datasets
Pixel RNNs [77]	discrete prospect of the vivid image element values and establishes the entire set of requirements in the image and take account of rapid two-dimensional recurrent layers and significant usage of residual connections in deep recurrent networks	MNIST, CIFAR-10 and ImageNet datasets

6.3.1.2 Long Short-Term Memory (LSTM)

Long short-term Memory (LSTM) [78] is an enhanced model of recurrent neural network (RNN) which is a good at forecasting time series events. LSTM solves the vanishing gradient problem. LSTM variants are tabulated in Table 6.10. LSTM uses the long term memory which helps to store the data for a long time.

Table 6.10 LSTM variants.

Model	Description	Database
Grid LSTM [79]	A network that is arranged in a grid of one or more dimensions. Works on vectors, sequences, or better dimensional information such as images	Hutter challenge Wikipedia dataset
Associative LSTM [80]	established on complex-valued trajectories and is closely associated to Holographic Reduced Representations and LSTM.	own dataset, English Wikipedia dataset
Siamese LSTM [81]	improve the discriminative capability of the local characteristics	Market-1501, CUHK03, VIPeR
DECAB-LSTM [82]	extensive basic LSTM by integrating an attention mechanism to study the significant part of a sentence for a known feature for the text classification	1852 biomedical publication abstracts from PubMed journals

6.4   Related Work

This section discusses the cutting-edge anti phishing techniques with the resource of the use of the algorithms of laptop learning, deep learning, and neural neighborhood strategies to take care of the phishing websites.

6.4.1   Machine Learning Approach

Table 6.11 affords a unique assessment of computer mastering method for phishing detection.

Table 6.11 Machine Learning approach.

Source	Description	Metrics	Dataset
[43]	Implements a content-based method to realize phishing net pages via the use of a laptop getting to know technique.	TPR, FPR	Phish tank, legitimate web pages
[57]	Detects phishing and affords tight security	TP, FP, authentication	Phish tank
[58]	Detects phishing URLs the use of the hybrid strategy with clustering and classification	Accuracy	Phish tank, DMOZ
[59]	Phishing detection is carried out the usage of the URL aspects and net web page ranking	Accuracy, RMSE	Phish tank, DMOZ
[60]	Detection of internet phishing the usage of the heuristic function known as area pinnacle web page similarity	Accuracy, precision, f-measure, error rate	100 login forms, clean mx
[38]	Improving the URL blacklisting by means of the usage of 2 components	Cumulative distribution	DMOZ, yahoo, spam scatter

6.4.2   Neural Network Approach

Table 6.12 offers a designated contrast of neural community method for the phishing detection system.

Table 6.12 Neural network approach.

Source	Description	Metrics	Dataset
[49]	Neural community primarily based internet site classification the use of a secure MC (Monto Carlo) algorithm	True Positive Rate, False Positive Rate, accuracy, precision, recall, f-measure	Google SEARCH
[61]	Classify the phishing UPL's the usage of the back-propagation	Accuracy, MSE	Phish tank
[62]	Detecting phishing web sites based on the URL features	True Positive, True Negative, False Positive, False Negative, RMSE, accuracy	Phish tank
[63]	Detects phishing internet pages the usage of synthetic neural community based totally on self-structuring neural networks	accuracy	Phish tank, smiles, yahoo
[64]	Fast appearing proactive phishing URL detection gadget	Accuracy, recall, precision, f-measure	Phish tank

6.4.3 Deep Learning Approach

Deep learning makes use of computers by becoming aware of algorithms dependent on neural networks utilized to function supervised, unsupervised and semi-supervised learning. Deep analyzing version gets an extended period for preparation as they involve limitless layers of neural network. By allowing the broad range of layers, the mannequin correctness and general overall implementation can be improved. Table 6.13 gives a precise evaluation of deep analyzing strategy for the Spoofing recognition system.

Table 6.13 Deep learning approach.

Source	Description	Metrics	Dataset
[65]	Detects phishing web pages the use of the MD5 approach	Md	Financial institutions spam data, phish net
[66]	Phishing internet site detection method primarily based on multidimensional points the use of deep gaining knowledge of soft-max classifier	Accuracy, FPR, FNR	tweets
[67]	Classifying phishing web sites the usage of swarm talent with modified bat and hybrid bat algorithms	accuracy, median	Phish tank, UCI
[68]	Identification of phishing web sites the usage of deep studying procedures, i.e. deep neural and stacked auto encoder	Accuracy	Phish tank

6.5 Analysis Report

According to the anti-phishing working crew (APWG) survey APWG (2020), the phishing assaults in 2020 have been 350 shares up. File much less malware extended and the crypto mining assaults go up in 2020. In 2020, an increase of 90% online fraud of far-flung spoof recognition activities was recognized. This paper converses the one-of-a-kind of online fraud. The forecast of spoofing net web sites is a quintessential assignment. A momentary critical evaluation has been done on the spoofing assaults using computing device learning, neural networks and, deep getting to be aware of methods. The figures given below illustrate the range of articles posted in modern years especially on the phishing assaults with the use of the above cited three techniques. Figure 6.2a suggests the evaluation of the three techniques from 2008 to 2020 and the extent of articles posted up to 2020 as tested in Figure 6.2b. Content-based spoofing assaults use the internet web page textual content material data, which makes use of the

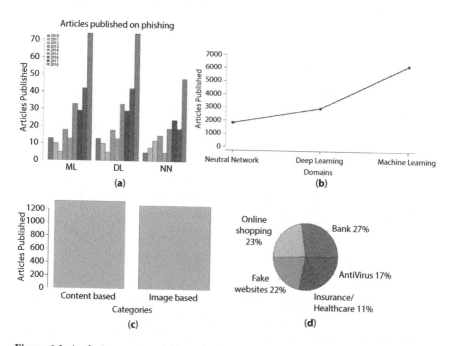

Figure 6.2 Analysis report on phishing fraud. (a) Total no. of phishing articles published using Machine Learning, Deep Learning, Neural Networks from 2008 to 2020. (b) Articles published on phishing using Machine Learning, Deep Learning, Neural Networks up to 2020. (c) Total no: of phishing articles published on category wise. (d) Total no. of phishing articles published in different sectors.

desktop gaining information of method. A spoofing website online comprises of totally snap pictures that are hard to pick out the assault. The distinction of the range of articles posted based totally on content-based and image-based spoofing assaults are in Figure 6.2c. According to the APWG file APWG (2020), the founded vicinity in 2020 is the cost sector. The second diagram suggests articles posted up to 2020 on more than a few online phishing attacks.

6.6   Current Challenges

6.6.1   File-Less Malware

File much less malware is a malware that operates on barring putting executable files on the victim's machine. Malicious code is now not file primarily based but exists in memory only. According to the APWG document APWG (2020), 77% of successful cyber assaults used file much less techniques. [30] mentioned the faux anti-virus getting into the pc with the aid of clicking the malicious URL hyperlinks.

6.6.2   Crypto Mining

Cryptomining (also referred to as crypto jacking or malicious crypto mining) is an online danger that hides on a pc or cellular units and makes use of the machine resources to collect the records of online cash transactions. [69] mentioned the dangers about online shopping, paying consignment via the usage of the single wi-fi connection interior of a construction. [70, 71] mentioned the protection chance for the transaction on open and allotted environment. McAfee Labs Threats Report cited that crypto currency malware increased by 4,000 shares in 2020.

6.7   Conclusions

In this digital age, security is quintessential not depending on security challenges. Phishing assaults are inevitable. Fraudsters strive or use a variety of potential to gather individual or monetary data of professional customers. In this paper are presented the particular of spoofing mechanisms in the internet forums. Spoofing recognition strategies that alleviate the spoofing assaults are studied.

References

1. Bujlow, T., Carela-Español, V., Sole-Pareta, J., Barlet-Ros, P., A survey on web tracking: Mechanisms, implications, and defenses. *Proceedings of the IEEE*, vol. 105, pp. 1476–1510, 2017.
2. Liu, J. and Ye, Y., Introduction to e-commerce agents: Marketplace marketplace solutions, security issues, and supply and demand, in: *E-Commerce Agents*, pp. 1–6, Springer, Springer-Verlag Berlin Heidelberg, 2001.
3. Gupta, B., Arachchilage, N.A., Psannis, K.E., Defending against phishing attacks: taxonomy of methods, current issues and future directions. *Telecommun. Syst.*, 67, 247–267, 2018.
4. Zafar, H., Human resource information systems: Information security concerns for organizations. *Hum. Resour. Manage. Rev.*, 23, 105–113, 2013.
5. Button, M., Cross-border fraud and the case for an "interfraud". *Policing: An Int. J. Police Strategies & Manage.*, 35, 285–303, 2012.
6. Sun, Z. and Finnie, G.R., *Intelligent techniques in e-commerce*, Springer, Springer-Verlag Berlin Heidelberg, 2004.
7. Whitty, M.T., Mass-marketing fraud: a growing concern. *IEEE Secur. Priv.*, 13, 84–87, 2015.
8. Guha, S., Cheng, B., Francis, P., Challenges in measuring online advertising systems, in: *Proceedings of the 10th ACM SIGCOMM conference on Internet measurement*, ACM, pp. 81–87, 2010.
9. Konte, M., Feamster, N., Jung, J., Dynamics of online scam hosting infrastructure. *International conference on passive and active network measurement*, Springer, pp. 219–228, 2009.
10. Ramesh, G., Krishnamurthi, I., Kumar, K.S.S., An efficacious method for detecting phishing webpages through target domain identification. *Decis. Support Syst.*, 61, 12–22, 2014.
11. Wei, W., Li, J., Cao, L., Ou, Y., Chen, J., Effective detection of sophisticated online banking fraud on extremely imbalanced data. *World Wide Web*, 16, 449–475, 2013.
12. Laleh, N. and Azgomi, M.A., A taxonomy of frauds and fraud detection techniques, in: *International Conference on Information Systems, Technology and Management*, Springer, pp. 256–267, 2009.
13. Stavroulakis, P. and Stamp, M., *Handbook of information and communication security*, Springer Science & Business Media, Springer-Verlag Berlin Heidelberg, 2010.
14. Wenyin, L., Huang, G., Xiaoyue, L., Deng, X., Min, Z., Phishing web page detection, in: *Eighth International Conference on Document Analysis and Recognition (ICDAR'05)*, IEEE, pp. 560–564, 2005.
15. Ma, J., Saul, L.K., Savage, S., Voelker, G.M., Learning to detect malicious urls. *ACM Trans. Intell. Syst. Technol. (TIST)*, 2, 30, 2011.

16. Garera, S., Provos, N., Chew, M., Rubin, A.D., A framework for detection and measurement of phishing attacks. *Proceedings of the 2007 ACM workshop on Recurring malcode*, ACM, pp. 1–8, 2007.

17. Al-Mhiqani, M.N., Ahmad, R., Abidin, Z.Z., Ali, N.S., Abdulkareem, K.H., Review of cyber attacks classifications and threats analysis in cyber-physical systems. *Int. J. Internet Technol. Secur. Trans.*, 9, 282–298, 2019.

18. Akhawe, D. and Felt, A.P., Alice in warningland: A large-scale field study of browser security warning effectiveness, in: *Presented as part of the 22nd {USENIX} Security Symposium ({USENIX} Security 13)*, pp. 257–272, 2013.

19. Moore, T. and Edelman, B., Measuring the perpetrators and funders of typosquatting. *International Conference on Financial Cryptography and Data Security*, Springer, pp. 175–191, 2010.

20. Sheng, S., Holbrook, M., Kumaraguru, P., Cranor, L.F., Downs, J., Who falls for phish?: a demographic analysis of phishing susceptibility and effectiveness of interventions, in: *Proceedings of the SIGCHI Conference on Human Factors in Computing Systems*, ACM, pp. 373–382, 2010.

21. Sheng, S., Magnien, B., Kumaraguru, P., Acquisti, A., Cranor, L.F., Hong, J., Nunge, E., Anti-phishing phil: the design and evaluation of a game that teaches people not to fall for phish, in: *Proceedings of the 3rd symposium on Usable privacy and security*, ACM, pp. 88–99, 2007.

22. APWG, Apwg phishing attack trends reports. https://www.antiphishing.org/resources/apwg-reports/, 2020. [Online; Accessed: 2020-12-26].

23. Eshete, B., Villafiorita, A., Weldemariam, K., Binspect: Holistic analysis and detection of malicious web pages, in: *International Conference on Security and Privacy in Communication Systems*, Springer, pp. 149–166, 2012.

24. Wenyin, L., Liu, G., Qiu, B., Quan, X., Antiphishing through phishing target discovery. *IEEE Internet Comput.*, 16, 52–61, 2012.

25. Ma, J., Saul, L.K., Savage, S., Voelker, G.M., Beyond blacklists: learning to detect malicious web sites from suspicious urls, in: *Proceedings of the 15th ACM SIGKDD international conference on Knowledge discovery and data mining*, ACM, pp. 1245–1254, 2009.

26. Marchal, S., Saari, K., Singh, N., Asokan, N., Know your phish: Novel techniques for detecting phishing sites and their targets, in: *2016 IEEE 36th International Conference on Distributed Computing Systems (ICDCS)*, IEEE, pp. 323–333, 2016.

27. Naumov, A., Vlajic, N., Roumani, H., Geotracking of webpage sources: a defence against drive-by-download attacks. *Int. J. Internet Technol. Secur. Trans.*, 4, 312–326, 2012.

28. Jain, A.K. and Gupta, B.B., A machine learning based approach for phishing detection using hyperlinks information. *J. Ambient Intelll. Humaniz. Comput.*, 10, 2015–2028, 2019.

29. Jain, A.K. and Gupta, B.B., A novel approach to protect against phishing attacks at client side using auto-updated white-list. *EURASIP Inf. Secur. J.*, 2016 9, 1–11, 2016.

30. Abutair, H., Belghith, A., AlAhmadi, S., Cbr-pds: a case-based reasoning phishing detection system. *J. Ambient Intell. Humaniz. Comput.*, 10, 2593–2606, 2019.

31. Jain, A.K. and Gupta, B.B., Two-level authentication approach to protect from phishing attacks in real time. *J. Ambient Intell. Humaniz. Comput.*, 9, 1783–1796, 2018.

32. Choukse, D., Singh, U.K., Kanellopoulos, D., An intelligent anti-phishing solution: password-transaction secure window. *Int. J. Internet Technol. Secur. Trans.*, 3, 279–292, 2011.

33. Ouchani, S. and Lenzini, G., Generating attacks in sysml activity diagrams by detecting attack surfaces. *J. Ambient Intell. Humanuz. Comput.*, 6, 361–373, 2015.

34. Xylogiannopoulos, K.F., Karampelas, P., Alhajj, R., A password creation and validation system for social media platforms based on big data analytics. *J. Ambient Intell. Humanuz. Comput.*, 11, 1, 1–21, 2019.

35. Langin, C. and Rahimi, S., Soft computing in intrusion detection: the state of the art. *J. Ambient Intell. Humanuz. Comput.*, 1, 133–145, 2010.

36. Mishra, A. and Gupta, B., Intelligent phishing detection system using similarity matching algorithms. *Int. J. Inf. Commun. Technol.*, 12, 51–73, 2018.

37. Jain, A.K. and Gupta, B.B., Detection of phishing attacks in financial and e-banking websites using link and visual similarity relation. *Int. J. Inf. Comput. Secur.*, 10, 398–417, 2018.

38. Prakash, P., Kumar, M., Kompella, R.R., Gupta, M., Phishnet: predictive blacklisting to detect phishing attacks, in: *2010 Proceedings IEEE INFOCOM*, IEEE, pp. 1–5, 2010.

39. Blum, A., Wardman, B., Solorio, T., Warner, G., Lexical feature based phishing url detection using online learning, in: *Proceedings of the 3rd ACM Workshop on Artificial Intelligence and Security*, ACM, pp. 54–60, 2010.

40. Marchal, S., Francois, J., Engel, T. *et al.*, Proactive discovery of phishing related domain names, in: *International Workshop on Recent Advances in Intrusion Detection*, Springer, pp. 190–209, 2012.

41. Rao, R.S., Vaishnavi, T., Pais, A.R., Catchphish: detection of phishing websites by inspecting urls. *J. Ambient Intell. Humaniz. Comput.*, 11, 2, 1–13, 2019.

42. Zhang, Y., Hong, J., II, Cranor, L.F., Cantina: a content-based approach to detecting phishing web sites, in: *Proceedings of the 16th international conference on World Wide Web*, ACM, pp. 639–648, 2007.

43. Xiang, G., Hong, J., Rose, C.P., Cranor, L., Cantina+: A feature-rich machine learning framework for detecting phishing web sites. *ACM Trans. Inf. Syst. Secur. (TISSEC)*, 14, 21, 2011.

44. Hadi, W., Aburub, F., Alhawari, S., A new fast associative classification algorithm for detecting phishing websites. *Appl. Soft Comput.*, 48, 729–734, 2016.

45. James, J., Sandhya, L., Thomas, C., Detection of phishing urls using machine learning techniques, in: *2013 International Conference on Control Communication and Computing (ICCC)*, IEEE, pp. 304–309, 2013.

46. Aburrous, M., Hossain, M.A., Dahal, K., Thabtah, F., Intelligent phishing detection system for e-banking using fuzzy data mining. *Expert Syst. Appl.*, 37, 7913–7921, 2010.

47. Sunil, A.N.V. and Sardana, A., A pagerank based detection technique for phishing web sites, in: *2012 IEEE Symposium on Computers & Informatics (ISCI)*, IEEE, pp. 58–63, 2012.

48. Verma, R. and Dyer, K., On the character of phishing urls: Accurate and robust statistical learning classifiers, in: *Proceedings of the 5th ACM Conference on Data and Application Security and Privacy*, ACM, pp. 111–122, 2015.

49. Feng, F., Zhou, Q., Shen, Z., Yang, X., Han, L., Wang, J., The application of a novel neural network in the detection of phishing websites. *J. Ambient Intell. Humaniz. Comput.*, 1, 1, 1–15, 2018.

50. Camastra, F., Ciaramella, A., Staiano, A., Machine learning and soft computing for ict security: an overview of current trends. *J. Ambient Intell. Humaniz. Comput.*, 4, 235–247, 2013.

51. Park, S.-T., Li, G., Hong, J.-C., A study on smart factory-based ambient intelligence context-aware intrusion detection system using machine learning. *J. Ambient Intell. Humaniz. Comput.*, 11, 4, 1–8, 2018.

52. Chen, Z., Jiang, W., Lei, M., Zhang, J., Hu, J., Xiang, Y., Shao, D., Mem: a new mixed ensemble model for identifying frauds. *Int. J. Inf. Communication Technol.*, 15, 294–303, 2019.

53. Lin, C.-C. and Wang, M.-S., Genetic-clustering algorithm for intrusion detection system. *Int. J. Inf. Comput. Secur.*, 2, 218–234, 2008.

54. Gabriel, A.D., Gavrilut, D.T., Alexandru, B., II, Stefan, P.A., Detecting malicious urls: a semi-supervised machine learning system approach, in: *2016 18th International Symposium on Symbolic and Numeric Algorithms for Scientific Computing (SYNASC)*, IEEE, pp. 233–239, 2016.

55. Verma, R. and Das, A., What's in a url: Fast feature extraction and malicious url detection, in: *Proceedings of the 3rd ACM on International Workshop on Security and Privacy Analytics*, ACM, pp. 55–63, 2017.

56. Zuhair, H. and Selamat, A., Phishing classification models: Issues and perspectives. *2017 IEEE Conference on Open Systems (ICOS)*, IEEE, pp. 26–31, 2017.

57. Cao, Y., Han, W., Le, Y., Anti-phishing based on automated individual whitelist. *Proceedings of the 4th ACM workshop on Digital identity management*, ACM, pp. 51–60, 2008.

58. Feroz, M.N. and Mengel, S., Phishing url detection using url ranking, in: *2015 IEEE international congress on big data*, IEEE, pp. 635–638, 2015.

59. Nguyen, L.A.T., To, B.L., Nguyen, H.K., Nguyen, M.H., A novel approach for phishing detection using url-based heuristic. *2014 International Conference on Computing, Management and Telecommunications (ComManTel)*, IEEE, pp. 298–303, 2014.

60. Sanglerdsinlapachai, N. and Rungsawang, A., Using domain top-page similarity feature in machine learning-based web phishing detection, in: *2010*

Third International Conference on Knowledge Discovery and Data Mining, IEEE, pp. 187 – 190, 2010.

61. Gupta, S. and Singhal, A., Phishing url detection by using artificial neural network with pso, in: *2017 2nd International Conference on Telecommunication and Networks (TE L-NET),* IEEE, pp. 1–6, 2017.

62. Nguyen, L.A.T., To, B.L., Nguyen, H.K., Nguyen, M.H., An efficient approach for phishing detection using single - layer neural network, in: *2014 International Conference on Advanced Technologies for Communications (ATC 2014),* IEEE, pp. 435 – 440, 2014.

63. Mohammad, R.M., Thabtah, F., McCluskey, L., Predicting phishing websites based on self-structuring neural network. *Neural Comput. Appl.,* 25, 443–458, 2014.

64. Bahnsen, A.C., Bohorquez, E.C., Villegas, S., Vargas, J., Gonzalez, F.A., Classifying phishing urls using recurrent neural networks, in: *2017 APWG Symposium on Electronic Crime Research (eCrime),* IEEE, pp. 1 – 8, 2017.

65. Wardman, B. and Warner, G., Automating phishing website identification through deep md5 matching, in: *2008 eCrime Researchers Summit,* pp. 1–7, IEEE, Atlanta, GA, USA, 2008.

66. Wu, T., Liu, S., Zhang, J., Xiang, Y., Twitter spam detection based on deep learning, in: *Proceedings of the Australasian Computer Science Week Multiconference,* ACM, p. 3, 2017.

67. Vrbancic, G., Fister Jr., I., Podgorelec, V., Swarm intelligence approaches for parameter setting of deep learning neural network : Case study on phishing websites classification, in: *Proceedings of the 8th International Conference on Web Intelligence, Mining and Semantics,* ACM, p. 9, 2018.

68. Aksu, D., Turgut, Z., Ustebay, S., Aydin, M.A., Phishing analysis of websites using ¨ classification techniques, in: *International Telecommunications Conference,* Springer, pp. 251–258, 2019.

69. Maghdid, S.A., Maghdid, H.S., HmaSalah, S.R., Ghafoor, K.Z., Sadiq, A.S., Khan, S., Indoor human tracking mechanism using integrated onboard smartphones wi-fi device and inertial sensors. *Telecommun. Syst.,* 71, 3, 1–12, 2018.

70. Zhang, M., Yao, Y., Jiang, Y., Li, B., Tang, C., Accountable mobile e-commerce scheme in intelligent cloud system transactions. *J. Ambient Intell. Humaniz. Comput.,* 9, 1889–1899, 2018.

71. Carlin, D., O'kane, P., Sezer, S., Burgess, J., Detecting cryptomining using dynamic analysis, in: *2018 16th Annual Conference on Privacy, Security and Trust (PST),* IEEE, pp. 1–6, 2018.

72. Zeiler, M.D. and Fergus, R., Visualizing and understanding convolutional networks, in: *European conference on computer vision,* Springer, pp. 818–833, 2014.

73. Xie, S., Girshick, R., Dollar, P., Tu, Z., He, K., Aggregated residual transformations for deep neural networks, in: *Proceedings of the IEEE conference on computer vision and pattern recognition,* pp. 1492–1500, 2017.

74. Szegedy, C., Vanhoucke, V., Ioffe, S., Shlens, J., Wojna, Z., Rethinking the inception architecture for computer vision. *Proceedings of the IEEE conference on computer vision and pattern recognition*, pp. 2818–2826, 2016.

75. Szegedy, C., Ioffe, S., Vanhoucke, V., Alemi, A., Inception - v4, inception-resnet and the impact of residual connections on learning, 1, 1, 1–12 2016. arXiv.

76. Chollet, F., Xception: Deep learning with depthwise separable convolutions. *Proceedings of the IEEE conference on computer vision and pattern recognition*, pp. 1251–1258, 2017.

77. Zagoruyko, S. and Komodakis, N., Wide residual networks, 1, 1, 1–15, 2016. arXiv.

78. Hu, J., Shen, L., Sun, G., Squeeze-and-excitation networks, in: *Proceedings of the IEEE conference on computer vision and pattern recognition*, pp. 7132–7141, 2018.

79. Kim, J., Han, D., Kim, J., Deep pyramidal residual networks, in: *CVPR 2017 IEEE Conference on Computer Vision and Pattern Recognition. IEEE Computer Society and the Computer Vision Foundation (CVF)*, 2017.

80. Kuen, J., Kong, X., Wang, G., Tan, Y.-P., Delugenets: deep networks with efficient and flexible cross-layer information inflows, in: *Proceedings of the IEEE International Conference on Computer Vision Workshops*, pp. 958–966, 2017.

81. Bradbury, J., Merity, S., Xiong, C., Socher, R., Quasi-recurrent neural networks, 1, 1, 1–11, 2016. arXiv.

82. Schuster, M. and Paliwal, K.K., Bidirectional recurrent neural networks. *IEEE Trans. Signal Process.*, 45, 11, 2673–2681, 1997.

83. Kumar, A., Chatterjee, J.M., Díaz, V.G., A novel hybrid approach of SVM combined with NLP and probabilistic neural network for email phishing. *Int. J. Electr. Comput. Eng.*, 10, 1, 486, 2020.

7

Novel Defending and Prevention Technique for Man-in-the-Middle Attacks in Cyber-Physical Networks

Gaurav Narula[1]*, Preeti Nagrath[1], Drishti Hans[2] and Anand Nayyar[3,4]

[1]*Computer Science Engineering Department, Bharati Vidyapeeth's College of Engineering, New Delhi, India*
[2]*Electrical and Electronics Engineering Department, Bharati Vidyapeeth's College of Engineering, New Delhi, India*
[3]*Graduate School, Duy Tan University, Da Nang, Vietnam*
[4]*Faculty of Information Technology, Duy Tan University, Da Nang, Vietnam*

Abstract

Cyber security is now a global and heated debate. Man-in-the-Middle Attack is a type of cyber-attack in which an unauthorized person enters the online network between the two users, avoiding the sight of both users. The recent Chinese cyber-attack has prompted India to ban 59 Chinese apps, the issue is acute, and the system is likely to be threatened/hacked by this malware without adequate authentication security, this can cause a lot of potential data loss. This paper is mainly aimed at understanding the term 'man in middle attacks', along with various techniques such as rogue access points, Address Resolution Protocol (ARP) spoofing, Domain Name Server (DNS) and multicast Domain Name Server (mDNS) spoofing etc. The authors devised algorithms for detection and prevention of any potential data loss from such attacks. The algorithms devised were implemented on virtual servers and machines to replicate the real time scenarios. The scripts developed successfully defended the deployed virtual machines from the Man in the Middle Attacks. Also, it was observed that the user was also alerted if an attack was happening so that the vulnerability can be secured in the future. The main purpose behind this topic is to make readers aware of the title of the paper and to be beware of cyber-attacks.

*Corresponding author: gnarula438@gmail.com

Uzzal Sharma, Parma Nand, Jyotir Moy Chatterjee, Vishal Jain, Noor Zaman Jhanjhi and R. Sujatha (eds.)
Cyber-Physical Systems: Foundations and Techniques, (147–178) © 2022 Scrivener Publishing LLC

Keywords: ARP spoofing, DNS spoofing, SSL (Secure Sockets Layer), access point, man in the middle attacks

7.1 Introduction

A cyber-physical (CPS) system is a computer system in which a computer-based algorithm controls a process. Physical and software elements in cyber-physical structures are deeply consolidated, able to act on a range of spatial and temporal levels, displaying many more special modes of action, as well as individual communication with others. Smart grids, stand-alone automotive systems, medical supervision, industrial control systems, automation and automatic pilot avionics are some of the examples of CPS. All these systems communicate with networks, and these connections can be intercepted by people in man in the middle attacks, and the safety of these systems can be affected.

In 1992 the National Aeronautics and Space Administration (NASA) first proposed the concept of cyber-physical systems (CPSs), and it was detailed by Baheti and Gill [1], respectively. Now, in the next phase of the Industrial Revolution [2], they became the core technology, and a number of works to show their value have been done, such as the Top-Eight Intelligence Technologies [3], German Industry 4.0 [4], US Industrial Internet [5], Artemis [6] and CPS European Roadmap and Strategy [7].

CPS is widely applied in industrial control systems, advanced communication, smart grids [8], transportation systems [9] and social vehicle networks [10, 11]. In order to track and control processes [13, 14], computing, communication and control (3C) technologies [12] are incorporated into CPS, and their overall structure is shown in Figure 7.1. A CPS may arise, depending on the outline. It can be split into three layers: layer of perception execution, layer of data transfer, and layer of application control [15, 16]. The perception execution layer consists of mainly physical components like sensors, etc. User services are provided by the application control layers which consist of various services for users. An intermediary for transfer of data between these two layers is data transmission layer which consists of a communication array for smooth transfer of data.

The MITM is a cryptographic and computer security attack in which the attacker secretly relies on, and may be intercepting, messages between two parties that believe they are communicating directly with each other. An example of an MITM attack is an active wake-up call where the attacker contacts the victim independently and discovers that they are talking to each other directly through a private network, while the attacker is monitoring

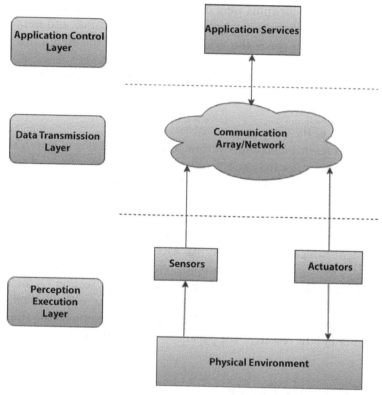

Figure 7.1 Different layers in a cyber-physical network.

the whole conversation. All relevant messages passing between the two victims must be intercepted and new injections made by the attacker. It is simple in some cases; for example, an intruder may insert itself in a non-encrypted Wi-Fi port as a man in the receiving portfolio [17].

MITM attacks can be avoided or detected using two methods: authentication and detection of manipulations. Authentication ensures that a specific message comes from a valid source. Tamper detection is the only sign that the message has been changed.

The main objectives of this paper are:

1. Understanding what Man in the Middle attacks are, analyzing its different types and techniques used in each one if it.
2. Developing techniques and algorithms to detect the attacks and prevent them from stealing any data or harming the client.

3. Various algorithms were developed that were implemented in form of scripts on virtual servers and machines and were attacked to check the working efficiency of the algorithms proposed.
4. Deploy Test websites to validate the DNS spoofing attack prevention technique.

Organization of the Chapter

Section 7.2 presents a literature review regarding studies and research presented by various researchers in past years about different types of analysis on Man in the middle attacks and cyber-physical systems and how different techniques are used to bypass the security in these systems. Section 7.3 first discusses the various techniques that are implemented in different layers of the cyber-physical system and also various attacks on a particular layer of such systems which involve attacks like ARP (Address Resolution Protocol) Spoofing, DNS Spoofing, SSL Stripping, etc. deployed by the attackers in such systems and networks to implement such attacks. Section 7.4 discusses the proposed algorithms to prevent the attacks along with the real time deployment of the scripts. Section 7.5 presents the results achieved from the algorithms and the research. The paper concludes with Section 7.6.

7.2   Literature Review

Zegzhda *et al.* [18] discussed in their article how powerful rogue access points can be and how popular they are becoming as a method to attack clients. Even having WEP (Wired Equivalent Privacy), WPA (Wi-Fi Protected Access), and WPA2 security protocols, no protocol is there to check the AP (Access Point) and the enterprise version makes it easier to add another access point due to availability of multiple APs. They also analyzed that there are multiple ways by which a Rogue AP can be setup.

Yang *et al.* in their paper discussed how man in the middle attacks are used widely to gain potential information. In detail the authors discussed how evil twin attacks, a version of rogue access point attack, are used widely now-a-days. They mainly classified the attack in two different categories, one of which monitors the Radio Frequencies while the other monitors the traffic on the network [19].

Ramachandran and Nandi discussed in their paper how ARP spoofing attacks are imminent and how it is a main and foremost attack to implement man in the middle attack. They also discussed various already implemented techniques to detect the attack, what are the lags in the existing techniques and how important it is to detect the attack and prevent it from happening [20].

Nam *et al.* [21] in their paper suggested how to mount attacks on ARP poisoning, like DoS (Denial of Service), Spoofing and other MITM attacks, by means of ARP poisoning. He also talks about various tries to address the problem of poisoning ARPcache. Dynamic ARP (DAI) inspection conducted on the Ethernet switch may prevent spoofing and poisoning of the ARP but requires the network manager to manually configure the network and will not protect the network part of the Can-incapable DAI Ethernet switch.

Maksutov *et al.* [22] addressed that, people transmit data across the network, which is of great benefit. Shopping in online stores, paying the fine and booking a ticket in the theater—all these include transmitting private data through the network, such as passport or credit card details. They studied how DNS spoofing can affect and rob these data, and what role SSL stripping plays in this.

Wander *et al.* [23] analyzed the strength of DNS attacks happening worldwide and how these attacks affect the security of a country and compromise confidential information. They analyzed despite various measures, how attackers steal information using different techniques. Also, they discussed DNS injection which is used to bring firewalls down giving access to private information. They mentioned how these attacks affect third parties and individuals. They also discussed how particular domains are targeted from which users are targeted to gain access over the whole network thus proving how social engineering is effective in such attacks.

In their chapter, Prowell and others discussed how deadly cyberattacks can be like man in the middle attacks, and what strategies are now used to execute various variations of the same attack to circumvent security protocols, and how potential data is lost every second to these attacks [24].

Khalif *et al.* proposed a new man in the middle attack on hardware devices. They have introduced a new PCIe attack vector based on man-in-the-middle hardware. This device allows for real-time data processing, data-replay, and a shadow-copy affected copy technique [25].

Sandhya and Devi proposed a method to implement man in middle attacks in Bluetooth networks, thus increasing the area of attack but reducing the attack range [28].

Deng in the paper discussed how DoS attacks are done in cyber-physical systems, what are the effects on the system and proposed a method to prevent such kind of attacks [29].

Li *et al.* [30] reviewed the intensity of attacks that happen on cyber-physical systems and how it interferes with proper functioning of the system and what were some of the drastic attacks that happened and why it is important to develop methods to prevent such attacks.

All the researchers conclude that the intensity of attacks on the cyber-physical system is increasing day by day. The protection measures used in the systems are not capable of defending against such attacks like ARP Poisoning, DNS Spoofing, DDoS attacks, etc. These allow an attacker to exploit an application to reveal sensitive data such as technical details of the application, developer comments, environment, or user-specific data. An attacker may use this sensitive data to exploit the target application, its hosting network, or its users. The authors addressed these issues to develop some scripts to defend against these attacks.

7.3　Classification of Attacks

Currently, three kinds of CPS network attacks are based on Figure 7.1.

1. Network attack on the perception execution layer
2. Network attack on results, i.e.

   a. Network attack on the transmission layer
   b. Network attack on the application control layer [15].

7.3.1　The Perception Layer Network Attacks

There are various sensor and actuator nodes in the perception execution layer where physical components are data received and controls are transmitted from the control center. Most nodes in this layer are deployed in an unsafe environment. So, it's safe to be a victim of the assailant.

Work on network assault in the layer of perception mainly focuses on safety issues for sensors and actuators. In essence, the perceptual execution layer contains four types of network attack: Actuator Enabled (AE Attack), Actuator Disability (AD attack), Sensor Erasure (SE Attack) and Sensor Insertion (SI-Attack) Attack [31, 41]. Unless the sensor or actuator is targeted, plant information or instructions to be implemented may be flawed. Therefore, the device may be damaged in an unstable state. Other common attacks are attacks by manipulation, powerful attacks on pole dynamics, covert attacks and powerful attacks.

7.3.2   Network Attacks on the Application Control Layer

This layer consists of different user program applications and some controllers. This layer makes a decision based on the data received from the data transmission layer, it will execute some commands and it would give the results to the physical unit of the network i.e. the perception execution layer via the intermediary data transmission layer. The actuators perform the relevant operations on the basis of information received.

Personal data of users including their usage habits of the network is stored in this later. An attacker can simply inject a script to kill the database or can gain unauthorized access to the system via a reverse shell which can severely affect the application control layer, also jeopardising user privacy. A single security strategy is difficult to satisfy the security needs of these layers as it is based on multiple applications systems thus requiring different security layers to protect the user's data.

7.3.3   Data Transmission Layer Network Attacks

In order for data to be transmitted between these two levels, the transmission layers include the perception execution and application control layers. A network of contacts is the central carrier network of the data relay layer. Through communication networks like the Internet, a private network or a LAN (Local Area Network), this layer is used to transmit data between them. These communication networks consist of various vulnerable points as they have access to the equipment's, the system design and several security procedures this presenting with certain risks to the CPSs.

The layer has the ability to process big data and handle it. It is possible to transmit large amounts of data across the data transmission layer of the network, so the CPS will be vulnerable to network attacks.

When an intruder is hard to attack the data transmission layer, the attacker may alter the information transmitted on the network channel freely after the attacker passes the data channel successfully. Man-in-the-middle attacks [32], one of the most effective network attacks against a data layer, observe, hide and even change information transmitted from one computer to another through communications channels [33]. In other words, an attacking party collects false information and then pushes the CPS into an unstable state that harms the system.

DoS (Denial-of-Service) [34–36] is an attack to reduce resources which exploits protocol/software errors in the network or too many unprofitable requests to redirect assets of an object for the Send Attack. Finally, the server or network of contacts cannot be provided with services [37].

In CPSs, malicious software uses a DoS attack to consume contact bandwidth to prevent the controller and the actuator from communicating information. DoS attacks are mostly triggered by malicious attacks. These attacks would interrupt the communication between the controller and the actuator, so the controller cannot receive the data input in time. The routing and server resources will be consumed by large numbers of invalid service requests [37], finally deteriorating and even collapsing outputs. No message is sent or sent on the channel during a DoS attack.

7.3.3.1   Rogue Access Point

In essence, the rogue access point is an access point linked to the CPS network, without anyone knowing it. The individual is not fully mindful of his presence there. This is a kind of scenario, especially if no one interacts with it and manages it perfectly, that can create a type of back door. With considerable security concerns, it is an access point. This is because the wireless access point can be very easily plugged in. If a network user does not execute a protocol to control access to a network, it is very easy to attach extra workstations and access points to a network.

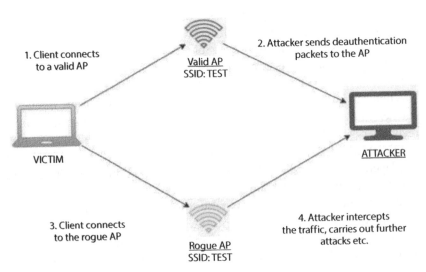

Figure 7.2 Attacker creating a rogue access point with the same SSID and forcing the user to connect to it by DE authenticating the user from the valid access point.

The attacker usually names the access point to be hacked, and it is shown in Figure 7.2 with various packets because there are many access points in the company, customers and machines that cannot connect to that access point, So the hacker sets its access point with the same name so that things are not suspicious, and the hacker becomes the middleman when customers enter and can now steal information and control the entire network.

The danger is that unauthorized wireless access points may be used outside of the organization to leak sensitive data, including passwords and cardholder information. The local administrator does not approve this, but works on the network anyway. This can be installed by a naïve user who has no malicious intent or who may be purposely installed for testing or for some other purpose by internal IT staff. A hacker who is supposedly attempting to carry out an attack can also mount it. For outsiders, a rogue access point offers a wireless backdoor channel into the private network. It can bypass firewalls and other security devices on the network and open up attacks on the network. In any event, a rogue access point may pose a serious safety danger or even a personal home network to large corporations because anyone who reaches this access point uses private networks, what can be downloaded, and even misleads the user. Inform the hackers of websites of hazardous information. It may also lead the user to a website which would cause him/her without the user to download the malicious software.

7.3.3.2   ARP Spoofing

Spoofing of ARP is a kind of network assault where an incorrect message is sent to a local area network by a malicious user/hacker. It is applied to the MAC (Media Access Control) address of an intruder, along with the IP address (Internet Protocol) of a valid network device or server. The attacker can start collecting any data for that IP address when the attacker's MAC address is associated with a valid IP address. ARP spoofing may allow inter-transit, modification or even interception of transit data by malicious parties. ARP spoofing attacks can only occur on local area networks that have protocols of address resolution. A typical network connecting hackers and victims to the same gateway is shown in Figure 7.3. The network is scanned for attacks on IP addresses using a basic network scanner. If found, the hacker robs the gateway by retaining the IP address of the victim and telling the victim that he or she has the IP address of the gateway, as shown in Figure 7.4. The hacker becomes the middleman after this spoof, and all requests and answers start to flow through the hacker, as shown in Figure 7.5. The attack can be transmitted to all devices connected to the network, too.

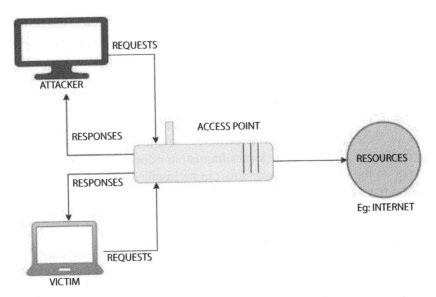

Figure 7.3 Diagram showing a typical network with two different devices connected to an access point.

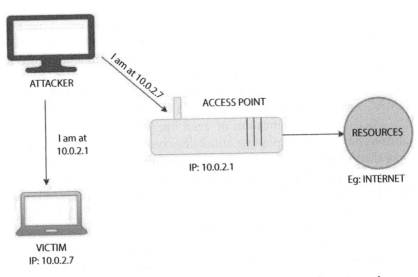

Figure 7.4 Diagram showing attacker spoofing the access point as the victim and spoofing the victim as access point placing itself in the middle of the connection.

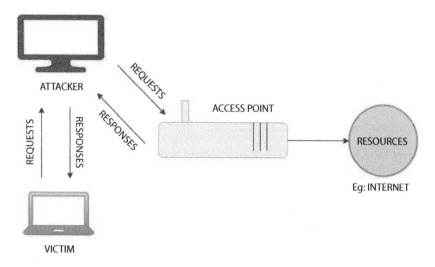

Figure 7.5 A spoofed network with attacker as man in the middle hijacking every request and response made by the victim.

For enterprises, the results of ARP spoofing attacks may have significant repercussions. In its most fundamental implementation, ARP spoofing attack is used by the extraction of confidential information to take control over the entire CPS network. Furthermore, to simplify other attacks, ARP spoofing attacks are also used, such as:

- Service-related attacks: DoS attacks mostly use ARP spoofing to connect multiple IP addresses to the same target MAC address. The destination traffic is then sent to the MAC address of the destination for several different IP addresses, which is then overloaded with traffic.
- Session hijacking: ARP spoofing can be used by Session Hijacking to steal session IDs, giving private systems and attackers access to data.
- Change contact, such as pushing a malicious file or website to the workstation.

7.3.3.3   DNS Spoofing

Clients have the IP address linked with the domain name on the DNS resolutioner/server. They take addresses from human-readable sites, for example abc.com, and convert them into machine-readable IP addresses. Your operating system would search for a DNS resolver if a user is interested in

| Bing.com | A | 204.79.197.200 |
| Facebook.com | A | 194.44.21 |

DNS SERVER

Figure 7.6 A typical DNS server with records stored to resolve domain names to their IPs along with certificates.

accessing a website. As shown in Figure 7.6, the DNS solver responds to IP address and the web explorer takes that address and starts loading the website.

The user requests the IP address from the DNS server by assigning it a domain name, receives the IP address in return, and routes the user to that same IP address, as seen in Figures 7.7 and 7.8. Domain Name System (DNS) Spoofing is an attack that redirects internet traffic to a bogus website that matches its intended destination using the changed DNS record.

When users are asked to sign in (which they believe) to their account, allowing the perpetrator the ability to steal their access credentials and other confidential information.

Furthermore, a malicious website is also used to install a worm or virus on a user's computer, providing long access to the attacker and the data he or she stores. The DNS cache server can be poisoned by DNS cache

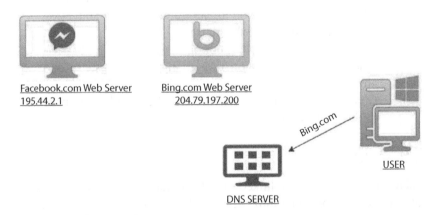

Facebook.com Web Server
195.44.2.1

Bing.com Web Server
204.79.197.200

Bing.com

USER

DNS SERVER

Figure 7.7 Diagram showing how every request made by any user is first redirected to the DNS server to resolve the IP of that domain.

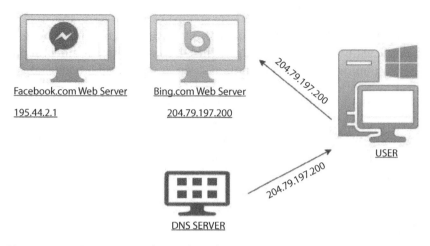

Figure 7.8 DNS server responding with a redirection request to the user for the requested domain and user redirected to the server of that domain.

attackers by a request for a DNS resolver, a request for a DNS resolver, and then pressured to react when a name server queries the DNS resolver. This is possible because UDP instead of TCP is used by DNS clients, and because there is actually no validation of DNS information. Usually, by ARP spoofing, the first attacker to carry out this assault will be a middleman. If this

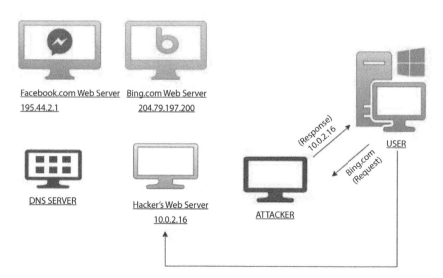

Figure 7.9 Attacker using DNS spoofing to redirect any request by the user to its own web server and thus gaining potential information using spoofed pages.

attack is successful, user requests are spoiled by the attacker and stopped from flowing to the DNS domain, as seen in Figure 7.9, the attacker begins their site with a spoof of those pages. The UDP or datagram protocol allows all communicators to start communication and perform a handshake to check system identity instead of using TCP. In addition, it is a UDP that allows all the communication parties in this process. UDP does not ensure a connection is open, that the receiver will be pleased to receive or that the sender will be who it believes to be. This is why the UDP is susceptible to forging. By forging header data, an attacker can send a message over UDP and claim to be a reaction from a legitimate server. Instantly, the customer is routed to the spoof page rather than to the official website. Now since it is an intruder's server, stealing all the information entered into it is straightforward.

7.3.3.4   mDNS Spoofing

A protocol that uses, but utilises otherwise, the same API as Unicast DNS system is Multicast DNS (mDNS). Each of the machines on the LAN stores their respective DNS record list (such as A, MX, PTR, SRV, etc.), and is named if both the IP address of the PC and the recording are to be known from the mDNS client. With its IP address, the PC responds.

Unless the attack is performed on a network where DNS requests cannot be sniffed at and eventually modified by attackers, mDNS spoofing attacks

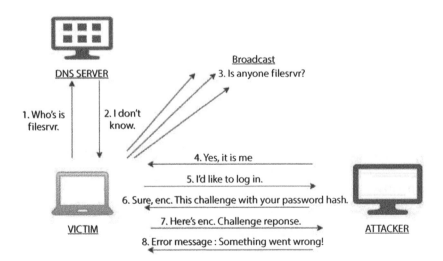

Figure 7.10 mDNS spoofing attack by capturing every broadcast request and spoofing the user into believing that the attacker is the file server.

are likely because it makes a difference. No matter what kind of transportation. mDNS spoofing attacks impact several items like not just iTunes, Firefox, Xbox 360, different routers, most printers, and more. Figure 7.10 demonstrates that the request is transmitted when no server is identified and the attacker with the mDNS spoofing attack convinces the user that it is the file server because it has collected all requests on each server and hence the hacker has become a man in the middle of it. Now that can escalate this situation into any attack.

MDNS can be queried at a multicast address by an mDNS enabled client. In return, all clients listening to that address will answer with their name. Today, if we have two same-name clients, they are always the first, they win. For example, if your word processing program tries to print a document by searching for printer. Local, a false response to that DNS query is easy for attackers to upload, enabling them to search for a printer that has a different IP address. Gives directions. Thus, the local name is essentially stolen/poisoned for a period of time.

This method of attack is not as successful on a WiFi network as it is easier to fire DNS packets and to forge DNS answers, so mDNS attacks are very useful in occasions. A case of this kind happens when you estimate. Since most devices support MDNS to one degree or another, attackers can learn a variety of useful objects, such as user-friendly versions and tool forms, administrative URLs and user email addresses, support information, etc.

7.3.3.5 SSL Stripping

SSL/TLS is a static protocol that is used to share confidential data. This protocol is used, for example, for sharing private documents, such as banking and email communications. The protocol is protected through the creation of an encrypted connection between two parties (typically a client application and a server). This protocol is also used by browsers and web servers when a secure connection is required. In most circumstances, the following accidents occur when a stable link is established:

1. An unsecured HTTP request is submitted by the user.
2. The server responds via HTTP and forwards the user to a secure protocol (HTTPS).
3. A secure HTTPS request is submitted by the user, and the secure session begins.

SSL striped or down gradable attacks on websites that are capable of removing the safety measures imposed by Secure Socket Layer (SSL) certificates are attacks on HTTPS (Hypertext Transfer Protocol Protected) sites. SSL stripping is a technique which reduces your HTTPS—Hypertext Transfer Protocol connection from a secure HTTP, which makes the connection unsafe and makes your data easy to handle. The attacker redirects the attacker to a secure HTTP to strip SSL. The HTTPS protocol receives a user request to the server. The attacker would then establish an HTTPS connection between him and the server and, as a bridge, unsecured connections with the user.

The SSL strip benefits from accessing SSL sites for the majority of users. Most visitors connect to a web page that redirects to the SSL page with a 302 redirect or through a link to a non-SSL domain. For instance, if the user wants to buy a product and enter the URL www.abc.com in the address bar the browser connects to the attached device and the server awaits the response. In short, the assailant sends the victim's application on the online store server in the SSL strip and receives HTTPS secured payment tab. For starters, https://www.abc.com. At this point the intruder is fully controlled by the secure payment page. It downgrades and returns it to the HTTPS browser of the victim. You have now redirected your web to http://www.abc.com. From now on, all the data from the victim will be sent in plain text format and interrupted by the intruder. In the meantime, the server on the website should assume that it has successfully created a stable link on the machine of the victim, but not to the attacker.

The KRACK attack ultimately showed that the media connecting companies with the Internet cannot rely blindly on the consumer. It shows that encryption, even though the website requires HTTPS, can be completely removed. After the SSL strip attack was successfully performed, victim information is sent in plain text format and is avoidable by anyone, including the attacker. This violates integrity and confidentiality of PIIs, such as login passwords, bank accounts, sensitive business records, and other information that is publicly identified. The possibility of this vulnerability is obvious and it will have different consequences for your digital presence.

7.4   Proposed Algorithm of Detection and Prevention

7.4.1   ARP Spoofing

Generally, man in the middle attacks happen by changing a property of the system like the MAC address of the router, server address or even the access point. For the detection of such attacks special scripts can be made which will monitor the device while it is running for any such change and alert the user and prevent any data loss to the attacker.

```
C:\Users\IEUser>arp -a

Interface: 192.168.0.110 --- 0x6
  Internet Address         Physical Address        Type
  192.168.0.1             04-95-e6-62-d6-f0        dynamic
  192.168.0.102           40-a3-cc-ed-84-e2        dynamic
  192.168.0.255           ff-ff-ff-ff-ff-ff        static
  224.0.0.22              01-00-5e-00-00-16        static
  224.0.0.251             01-00-5e-00-00-fb        static
  224.0.0.252             01-00-5e-00-00-fc        static
  239.255.255.250         01-00-5e-7f-ff-fa        static
  255.255.255.255         ff-ff-ff-ff-ff-ff        static
```

Figure 7.11 ARP table of a typical network with 192.168.0.1 as the gateway and other devices connected to the network.

```
C:\Users\IEUser>arp -a

Interface: 192.168.0.110 --- 0x6
  Internet Address         Physical Address        Type
  192.168.0.1             40-a3-cc-ed-84-e2        dynamic
  192.168.0.102           40-a3-cc-ed-84-e2        dynamic
  192.168.0.255           ff-ff-ff-ff-ff-ff        static
  224.0.0.22              01-00-5e-00-00-16        static
  224.0.0.251             01-00-5e-00-00-fb        static
  224.0.0.252             01-00-5e-00-00-fc        static
  239.255.255.250         01-00-5e-7f-ff-fa        static
  255.255.255.255         ff-ff-ff-ff-ff-ff        static
```

Figure 7.12 ARP table of a spoofed network with two different IP 192.168.0.1 and 192.168.0.102 having the same MAC address depicting the attacker's IP as 192.168.0.102.

ARP attacks generally alter the ARP table of the system. In a network,

1. No two IP addresses can have the same MAC address.
2. When connected to a network the MAC address of the gateway cannot change until and unless the network changes.

Figure 7.11 shows the ARP table of a typical network. Figure 7.12 shows the ARP table of a spoofed network.

For detection, avoidance and avoidance of ARP spoofing attacks, the following approaches are recommended:

- Filtering packets: packet filters scan packets when sent over the network. Packet filters Packet filters are useful in ARP spoofing protection because they can filter and block packets with contradictory source address data (packets from outside the network that show source addresses from inside the network and vice versa).
- Stop untrustful relationships: organisations should maintain at least processes that are trust-dependent. Confidence relationships only depend on the IP address for authentication, so that attackers are able to spoof ARP attacks much easier.
- Tools to detect spoofing of ARP: Applications that support organisations in tracking attacks from Spoofing ARP are available for most applications. These programmes work before the transmission and authentication of data sent and authenticated.
- The use of encrypted network protocols is to prevent data encryption attacks before transmission and data are handled by the ARP bolster, such as Transport Layer Protection (TLS), Secure SSH, HTTP Secure and other secure networking protocols.

For prevention, the script developed works on the theory that when one connects to a new network, the ARP table of the system is updated to store the MAC address of the gateway. This table gets updated each time a user connects to a new network. This new record is then monitored over by the script. As soon as the attacker tries to poison the user into MITM attack, the MAC address following that IP address will automatically get changed. As the IP is being monitored over, as soon as the change happens it is notified to the user in the form of an alert box, also asking them to disconnect from the network they are being connected to and thus prevents any information from flowing through to the attacker. Figure 7.13 depicts the algorithm used to develop the script.

Figure 7.14 shows that the user is being alerted that there was an ARP attack and then he/she is asked if they want to disconnect from the network as shown in Figure 7.15. If the user clicks on OK, then the user gets disconnected to protect the information as shown in Figure 7.16. But if for some reason the user decides to continue with the network, then a warning sign is shown, and no further action will be taken as according to Figure 7.17.

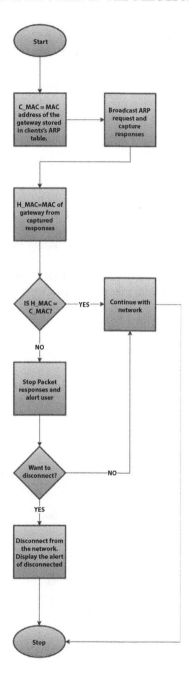

Figure 7.13 The ARP detection script explained using a detailed algorithm with all choices taken from the user.

Figure 7.14 A test web page was developed, when the attacker tries to become man in the middle the alert is shown that the user is under attack to prevent loss of potential information.

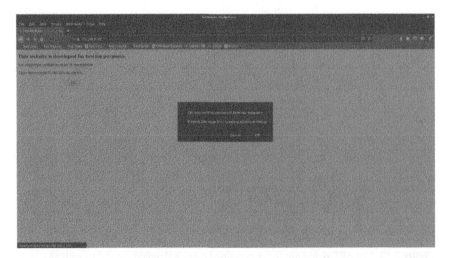

Figure 7.15 Script asking the user if he/she wants to disconnect from the network as they are under ARP spoofing attack.

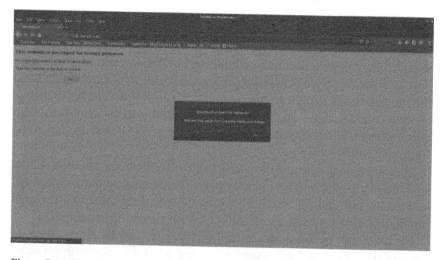

Figure 7.16 User disconnected from the attacked network on choosing to disconnect, preventing any information loss.

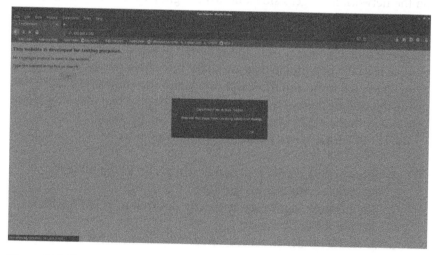

Figure 7.17 No action taken even under ARP attack as the user decided to continue even after alerting.

Also, the script monitors the ARP table for same MAC address as sometimes the poisoning is done through different gateway, and as no two IP addresses can have same MAC address, so as soon as the poisoning is done, the MAC address of two IP's become same as shown in Figure 7.14 and the script once again alerts the user as above asking with the same protocol.

7.4.2   Rogue Access Point and SSL Stripping

Usually, there are legal APs for hotels, colleges and companies, and an intruder may have access to a cellular network. Here, the attacker's purpose is to provide friends with network access. Instead of exchanging keys, the intruder links the AP to the current AP, allowing friends to exchange allowed contacts. Since many wired identification systems focus on switch port use rules, wireless traffic that does not detect RAP that appears to be legitimate will be observed.

This is not only a security concern, but it also limits the business model for hotels that offer wireless connectivity. This is because the attacker will now be an ISP and sell the link, which is part of the Mac OS, through Internet sharing (or users can install Open App on Linux machines).

For detection of Rogue access points, the user can be made aware of some of the facts that these access points are generally open with no security key as compared to other protected APs with WEP/WPA/WPA2/WPA2PSK (Wi-Fi Protected Access2 PreShared Key) protection. Also, on the network manager's side a network login page can be administered in which each user should have different login information. And HSTS (Hypertext transfer protocol Strict Transport Security) should be forced on the above said login page. Thus, the authors developed a script which helps to force HTTPS on the login page, so all the information transferred will be in an encrypted form, and the script developed also runs on the user's side giving them alerts if they try to access a HTTP page so that they should not continue with their sign in as the information can be stolen.

The HTTPS force script works in the following way:

1. It has an SSL certificate checker which checks for authenticity of the certificates on the flow.
2. The network login page is strictly directed to HTTPS with 301 permanently moved.
3. A HSTS header is served under base domain for HTTPS requests.
4. Also, all subdomain directives and predictive are specified.
5. All subdomains of the login page are then again covered with SSL certificates.

The script works in the way that if during a network connection the user is displayed a login page over HTTP instead of HTTPS then the user gets alerted. The script monitors the browser for the SSL certificates as shown in the algorithm in Figure 7.18.

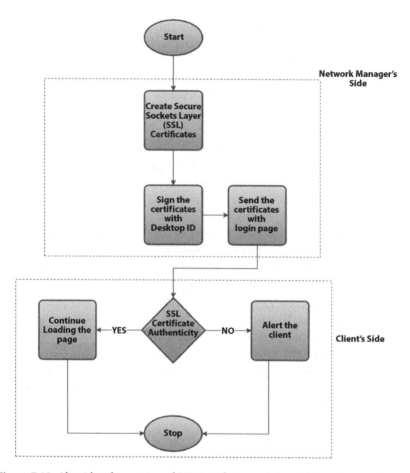

Figure 7.18 Algorithm for creation of SSL Certificates and its validation to prevent rogue access point from doing any damage.

7.4.3   DNS Spoofing

DNS spoofing is a serious threat. Fortunately, there are several simple measures you can take that provide effective protection against DNS spoofing.

1. Using Transport Encryption
   You should at least be able to detect DNS spoofing attacks if your links are secured by transport encryption. Since the malicious host does not have the security certificate that the real host will have, when the connection is created, the browser and email client can submit warnings. It provides

you an opportunity to terminate the connection and introduce additional security measures.

2. Encrypt DNS traffic

If the data transmission is secured by transport encryption, the connection to the DNS server is still vulnerable and is called the weakest link. On the user side, though, there are dedicated implementations for DNS request encryption. Furthermore, DNS servers must also support DNS encryption-related authentication technologies for this to function.

3. Using virtual private networks

Using virtual private networks (VPNs) can also help guard against DNS spoofing, in addition to transport security and protecting DNS service connections. All the links are routed into an encrypted tunnel while using a VPN. You should bear in mind, though, that the IP address of the DNS server will still be stored in most VPN programs. The VPN's defence against DNS spoofing would become inadequate if it is a malicious address.

4. Using a public DNS resolver network

Using a public DNS resolver is one of the most important security precautions you24 can take against DNS spoofing. The following advantages are offered by the use of public DNS solvers:

o High-speed DNS responses: thousands of servers worldwide are powered by massive DNS resolver networks. The physically nearest servers are still used for name resolution thanks to Anycast routing, which is reflected in shorter response times.

o High data protection and confidentiality level: Many Internet service providers sell data generated by DNS traffic from their users. Usually, these common public resolutions store little or no user data, giving a high degree of data protection and confidentiality.

o Censorship imposes no measures: Laws of state censorship are applicable only inside national borders. Usually, Internet service providers work within the homes of their customers and are expected to enforce state censorship. However, without contemplating state-governed censorship, a resolute network based abroad will serve its networks worldwide.

- ○ Supports current norms of security: Specializing in responding to DNS requests, wide public DNS resolver networks. Using current security protocols like DNSSEC, DoH, DoT and DNSCrypt, they are also trailblazers.
- ○ Blocks malicious domains: Since they hold a blacklist of established malicious domains, using public DNS resolver networks will help protect against ransomware [39] and phishing. Trying to enter these domains would result in the redirection of the user to the alert page.

But all these have their limitations and can be broken or by passed easily so, as in DNS spoofing, as the attacker redirects to the spoofed page, the developed script checks for authenticity of the redirected page by first checking the domain name as generally the spoofed domain doesn't exactly match the exact domain of the page. So, if there is any change then it again alerts the user that it isn't an authenticated web page as shown in Figure 7.19. After which the user can decide to test its server for DNS spoofing attack. The spoofing attack can be tested using overloading the request server. The script so developed is used in such a manner that it sends an adequate number of requests over a very less period. If the server crashes readily then it is not a real server but a spoofed one and the user is alerted about it, but if the server doesn't crash then it is of no problem. It works on the

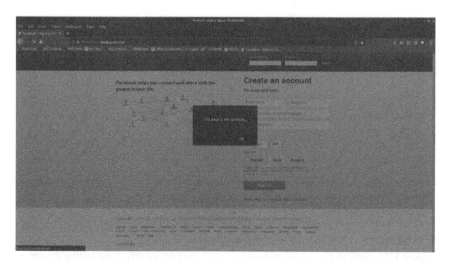

Figure 7.19 A spoofed login page of Facebook.com but the domain contains three o's which are generally neglected by any user the script alerted the domain was not authentic thus preventing information loss.

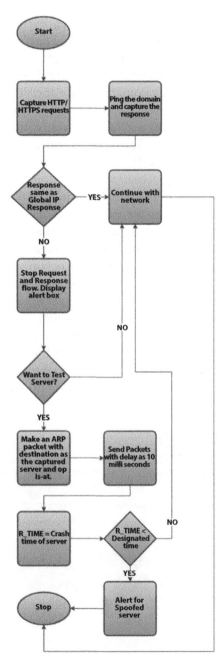

Figure 7.20 Steps implemented in detection of DNS spoofing script and testing the server for the spoof based on crashing time.

theory that a company server is configured to handle multiple requests at a single time whereas this feature is not available in a hacker's or an individual's server. So, then the crash time is noted and if that time is less than the given time, it means that the user is being DNS Spoofed and is alerted at that time as shown in the algorithm developed in Figure 7.20.

7.5   Results and Discussion

Oppliger *et al.* [26] in their article discussed how all the methods to provide security against SSL/TLS attacks fail to provide security with the advanced attacks. They also argued how these sessions even running on SSL fail to provide security by impersonation of tokens. Zheng *et al.* [27] analyzed various ARP spoof detection techniques and classified them based on which part of attack they stopped to protect the system. But these techniques are not yet effective as they work on specific parts which make them vulnerable to other attacks.

Authors developed novel scripts that check for different variations of cyberattacks mainly man in the middle attacks like ARP Poisoning, DNS Spoofing, SSL Stripping, each of which scripts runs in the background preventing a specific type of attack and if any of the attacks happen, the user is alerted at that time only to take any necessary actions to prevent potential data loss. Though the method of attacking is being advanced day by day, these scripts provide a general and novel way to prevent these attacks from happening instead of already existing applications to prevent the attack which were focused on a specific type of attack thus, not very successful in defending the network and machines.

7.6   Conclusion and Future Scope

Although with growing dependence on wireless technology, the threats are rising day by day and it is impossible to stop the attacks altogether but detection of these in early stages can prevent potential data loss. For each attack a different method is designed which monitors the specific component which is affected by that attack which helps in detection of such attacks. Such as ARP poisoning can't be done without having two same IPs in the ARP table, any method of implementing ARP will result in the same MAC address of two different IPs (Internet Protocols), so monitoring the base component helps to detect the attack in any form.

Every attack has a different script, and these can be packaged into a single application which will try to prevent the attacks altogether. Authors tried to replicate real time scenarios and it was achieved using virtual machines and the scripts were tested on them. It was found that they are working properly, and all the figures attached in the paper are the tests performed on these machines. This led to a conclusion that even if the attacks cannot be prevented; if the user can be educated enough and these scripts are used properly data loss can be prevented.

Social networking has become an inevitable catchline among teenagers as well as today's older generation. In recent years, there has been observed remarkable growth in social networking sites, especially in terms of adaptability as well as popularity both in the media and academia [38, 40, 41]. The sharing of sensitive information can be spoofed or changed using different MITM attacks. Thus, the scripts developed by the authors can be used in such online social networks on users' end to increase the security and privacy. Also, with the boom in the internet age with the ongoing pandemic the need to secure individual and commercial devices from such attacks is the most important concern and the scripts developed thus can be integrated in the security systems implemented in the PC and laptops thus providing a sense of privacy and security.

References

1. Baheti, R. and Gill, H., Cyber-physical systems. *Impact Control Technol.*, 12, 161–166, Mar. 2011.
2. Ge, H., Yue, D., Xie, X.P., Deng, S., Hu, S.L., Analysis of cyber physical systems security issue via uncertainty approaches. *Proc. Adv. Comput. Methods Life Syst. Model. Simulation*, pp. 421–431, 2017.
3. Liu, Y., Peng, Y., Wang, B., Yao, S., Liu, Z., Review on cyber-physical systems. *IEEE/CAA J. Autom. Sin.*, 4, 1, 27–40, 2017.
4. Kagermann, H., Change through digitization-value creation in the age of Industry 4.0, in: *Management of Permanent Change National Academy of Science and Engineering*, pp. 23–45, Springer, Berlin, Germany, 2015.
5. Annunziata, M. and Evans, P.C., *The industrial Internet@ work*, General Electric White Paper, 2013.
6. *Advanced Research and Technology for Embedded Intelligence and Systems*, ARTEMIS Industry Association, 2007.
7. Schätz, B., Törngren, M., Passerone, R., Pfeifer, H., Bensalem, S., McDermid, J., Sangiovanni-Vincentelli, A., Cengarle, M.V., CyPhERS-cyber-physical European roadmap and strategy.pp 1-48 Fortiss GmbH, Munich, Germany, Tech. Rep, 611430, 2015.

8. Rana, M.M., Li, L., Su, S.W., Cyber-attack protection and control of microgrids. *IEEE/CAA J. Autom. Sin.*, 5, 2, 602–609, Mar. 2018.

9. Teixeira, A., Shames, I., Sandberg, H., Johansson, K.H., A secure control framework for resource-limited adversaries. *Automatica*, 51, 135–148, Jan. 2015.

10. Wang, X., Ning, Z., Zhou, M., Hu, X., Wang, L., Zhang, Y. *et al.*, Privacy-preserving content dissemination for vehicular social networks: Challenges and solutions. *IEEE Commun. Surv. Tutor.*, 21, 2, 1314–1345, 2nd Quart, 2019.

11. Xie, Y., Liu, L., Li, R., Hu, J., Han, Y., Peng, X., Security-aware signal packing algorithm for CAN-based automotive cyber-physical systems. *IEEE/CAA J. Autom. Sin.*, 2, 4, 422–430, Oct. 2015.

12. Lee, E.A., Cyber physical systems: Design challenges. *Proc. 11th IEEE Int. Symp. Object Compon. -Oriented Real-Time Distrib. Comput. (ISORC)*, pp. 363–369, May 2008.

13. Shi, J., Wan, J., Yan, H., Suo, H., A survey of cyber-physical systems. *Proc. Int. Conf. Wireless Commun. Signal Process. (WCSP)*, pp. 1–6, 2011.

14. Mo, Y., Kim, T.H.-J., Brancik, K., Dickinson, D., Lee, H., Perrig, A. *et al.*, Cyber–physical security of a smart grid infrastructure. *Proc. IEEE*, vol. 100, pp. 195–209, Jan. 2012.

15. Lu, T., Xu, B., Guo, X., Zhao, L., Xie, F., A new multilevel framework for cyber-physical system security. *Proc. 1st Int. Workshop Swarm Edge Cloud*, pp. 1–2, 2013.

16. Liu, Y., Peng, Y., Wang, B., Yao, S., Liu, Z., Review on cyber-physical systems. *IEEE/CAA J. Autom. Sin.*, 4, 1, 27–40, Jan. 2017.

17. Callegati, F., Cerroni, W., Ramilli, M., Man-in-the-Middle Attack to the HTTPS Protocol. *IEEE Secur. Priv.*, 7, 1, 78–81, 2009.

18. Callegati, F., Cerroni, W., Ramilli, M., Man-in-the-Middle Attack to the HTTPS Protocol. *IEEE Secur. Priv. Mag.*, 7, 1, 78–81, 2009.

19. Yang, C., Song, Y., Gu, G., Active User-Side Evil Twin Access Point Detection Using Statistical Techniques. *IEEE Trans. Inf. Forensics Secur.*, 7, 5, 1638–1651, 2012.

20. Ramachandran, V. and Nandi, S., Detecting ARP Spoofing: An Active Techniqu. *Inf. Syst. Secur. Lect. Notes Comput. Sci.*, 3803, 239–250, 2005.

21. Nam, S., Kim, D., Kim, J., Enhanced ARP: preventing ARP poisoning-based man-in-the-middle attacks. *IEEE Commun. Lett.*, 14, 2, 187–189, 2010.

22. Maksutov, A.A., Cherepanov, I.A., Alekseev, M.S., Detection and prevention of DNS spoofing attacks. *2017 Siberian Symposium on Data Science and Engineering (SSDSE)*, 2017.

23. Wander, M., Boelmann, C., Schwittmann, L., Weis, T., Measurement of Globally Visible DNS Injection. *IEEE Access*, 2, 526–536, 2014.

24. Prowell, S., Kraus, R., Borkin, M., Man-in-the-Middle, in: *Seven Deadliest Network Attacks*, pp. 101–120, 2010.

25. Khelif, M.A., Lorandel, J., Romain, O., Regnery, M., Baheux, D., Barbu, G., Toward a hardware man-in-the-middle attack on PCIe bus. *Microprocessors and Microsystems*, vol. 77, p. 103198, 2020.

26. Oppliger, R., Hauser, R., Basin, D., SSL/TLS session-aware user authentication – Or how to effectively thwart the man-in-the-middle. *Comput. Commun.*, 29, 12, 2238–2246, 2006.

27. Zheng, M., Yang, S., Piao, X., Sun, W., Research on ARP Spoof Detection Strategies in Unreliable LAN. *Hum. Centered Comput. Lect. Notes Comput. Sci.*, 8944, 216–225, 2015.

28. Sandhya, S. and Devi, K.S., Contention for Man-in-the-Middle Attacks in Bluetooth Networks. *2012 Fourth International Conference on Computational Intelligence and Communication Networks*, 2012.

29. Deng, C., Distributed Resilient Control for Cyber-Physical Systems under Denial-of-Service Attacks. *2019 23rd International Conference on Mechatronics Technology (ICMT)*, 2019.

30. Li, F., Yan, X., Xie, Y., Sang, Z., Yuan, X., A Review of Cyber-Attack Methods in Cyber-Physical Power System. *2019 IEEE 8th International Conference on Advanced Power System Automation and Protection (APAP)*, 2019.

31. Carvalho, L.K., Wu, Y.-C., Kwong, R., Lafortune, S., Detection and mitigation of classes of attacks in supervisory control systems. *Automatica*, 97, 121–133, Nov. 2018.

32. Comer, D.E. and Droms, R.E., *Computer Networks and Internets*, Prentice-Hall, Upper Saddle River, NJ, USA, 2003, [online] Available: https://dl.acm.org/doi/book/10.5555/861590.

33. Lima, P.M., Alves, M.V.S., Carvalho, L.K., Moreira, M.V., Security against network attacks in supervisory control systems, in: *IFAC-PapersOnLine*, vol. 50, pp. 12333–12338, Jul. 2017.

34. Wood, A.D. and Stankovic, J.A., Denial of service in sensor networks. *Comput. J.*, 35, 10, 54–62, Oct. 2002.

35. Xu, W., Ma, K., Trappe, W., Zhang, Y., Jamming sensor networks: Attack and defense strategies. *IEEE Netw.*, 20, 3, 41–47, May/Jun. 2006.

36. Liu, S., Liu, X.P., El Saddik, A., Denial-of-Service (dos) attacks on load frequency control in smart grids. *Proc. IEEE PES Innov. Smart Grid Technol. Conf. (ISGT)*, pp. 1–6, Feb. 2013.

37. Srikantha, P. and Kundur, D., Denial of service attacks and mitigation for stability in cyber-enabled power grid. *Proc. IEEE Power Energy Soc. Innov. Smart Grid Technol. Conf. (ISGT)*, pp. 1–5, Feb. 2015.

38. Le, D.N., Kumar, R., Mishra, B.K., Chatterjee, J.M., Khari, M. (Eds.), Cyber Security in Parallel and Distributed Computing: Concepts, Techniques, in: *Applications and Case Studies*, John Wiley & Sons, USA, 2019.

39. Tandon, A. and Nayyar, A., A comprehensive survey on ransomware attack: a growing havoc cyberthreat, in: *Data Management, Analytics and Innovation*, pp. 403–420, 2019.

40. Jain, R., Jain, N., Nayyar, A., Security and privacy in social networks: data and structural anonymity, in: *In Handbook of Computer Networks and Cyber Security*, pp. 265–293, Springer, Cham, 2020.
41. Vasaki, P., Jhanjhi, N.Z., Humayun, M., Fostering Public-Private Partnership: Between Governments and Technologists in Developing National Cybersecurity Framework, in: *Employing Recent Technologies for Improved Digital Governance*, pp. 237–255, IGI Global, USA, 2020.

8

Fourth Order Interleaved Boost Converter With PID, Type II and Type III Controllers for Smart Grid Applications

Saurav S.* and Arnab Ghosh

Department of Electrical Engineering, National Institute of Technology Rourkela, Rourkela, India

Abstract

Switched mode power converters are an important component in interfacing renewable energy sources to smart grids and microgrids. The voltage obtained from power conversion is usually full of ripples. In order to minimize the ripple in the output, certain topological developments are made. Increasing the energy storage elements and interleaving them for 180° phase shift reduces the ripple in the circuit. This is made possible by controlling the converters using Type II and III controllers and the results are compared with PID controller. The performance is analyzed and compared in Simulink environment. Transient and steady state analysis is done for better understanding of the system.

Keywords: Interleaved fourth order boost converter, higher order converters, Type II and III controllers, PID controller, smart grid interface, k-factor approach

8.1 Introduction

In the evolving age of cyber physical systems, several technologies and algorithms have been developed for automation where human effort is minimum. One example of such system is the smart grids. Smart grids are evolving faster to accommodate the growing energy demands. These grids are well-equipped with systems which can select the power sources

---

Corresponding author: sauravjan24@gmail.com

Uzzal Sharma, Parma Nand, Jyotir Moy Chatterjee, Vishal Jain, Noor Zaman Jhanjhi and R. Sujatha (eds.) *Cyber-Physical Systems: Foundations and Techniques,* (179–208) © 2022 Scrivener Publishing LLC

considering various real time loses in the system. In order to fully utilize the power from different sources, these equipments must reduce the losses to minimum. Smart grids and microgrids play a major part in renewable energy applications. These systems are employed to harness the energy obtained from natural sources such as sun, wind, etc. [1]. In order to effectively utilize the power generated from these sources, an efficient dc-dc power converter has to be designed [2–4]. These dc–dc converters are used depending on the application like increasing or reducing the obtained voltage depending on the load, MPPT (Maximum Power Point Tracking) [5] tracking, regulated DC voltage and battery charging applications.

There are several innumerable topologies which exist in the current research literatures which are developed to address this problem [6]. Many topologies including the higher order topologies and the tristate converters which are used to address the research problems. Higher order converters are basically required for reducing the ripple in the circuit, as it has more energy storing elements than normal dc–dc power converters [7, 8]. Interleaved converters have also been researched extensively and their construction is in such a way that the energy storing elements and the switches are parallel to one another [9]. So basically, interleaved converter is also a form of higher order converter. This is done specially to reduce the ripples as well as the size and loses of ripples in the output filter. There are other topological modifications such as tristate boost converters which also has an extra mode and degree mode of freedom which have been proven to remove the non-minimum phase in the boost converter [10]. In this chapter the discussion is about higher order boost converters. Just like other boost converters the interleaved boost converter also has a pole in the right half of the s-plane [11]. As a result of this non-minimum phase, the closed loop bandwidth is restricted [12]. The restriction of closed loop bandwidth leads to slower response of the system. The order of the converter is more and when PID controller is used, difficulty lies in controlling the output voltage during line and load regulation and also amidst parametric uncertainties. So, the PID controller can be tuned to Type II or Type III controller based on the applications [13].

The discussion in this chapter is entitled to two phases interleaved [14–17] fourth order boost converter [18] each of which is fourth order. The characteristics of the interleaved converters apply here as well. The two phases are 180° out of phase with each other. This converter is modeled and controlled using Type II and III controllers [19–25]. The results obtained are compared with PID controller and with each other and a conclusion is derived from the comparison.

Here in this chapter, state space modeling which is more convenient is used to model the power converter, and it is derived in Sections 2.1 and 2.2. The state space averaging techniques and the small signal analysis are discussed in Sections 2.3 and 2.4 respectively through which the transfer functions of the plant are derived. After modeling is done, various controllers suited for the converters are analyzed and discussed in Section 8.3. The responses of the designed power converter are analyzed and the result obtained from the simulation is compared for the two types of controllers designed in Section 8.4. Section 8.5 is the conclusion derived from this virtual simulation conducted.

8.2   Modeling of Fourth Order Interleaved Boost Converter

8.2.1   Introduction to the Topology

The fourth order Interleaved Boost converter (FIBC) consists of two Fourth order boost converters which are connected in parallel with respect to energy storing elements and switches as shown in Figure 8.1. The total number of energies storing elements are seven, of which there are four inductors (L_1, L_2, L_3, L_4) and three capacitors (C_1, C_2, C_3). There are also two controlled switches which are basically MOSFETs (S_1 and S_2) and two uncontrolled switches which are the diodes (D_1 and D_2). When comparing it with regular Fourth order Boost converter in Figure 8.2, it has three

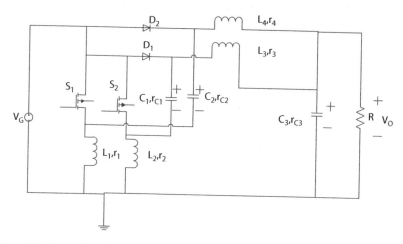

Figure 8.1 General configuration of fourth order interleaved boost converter.

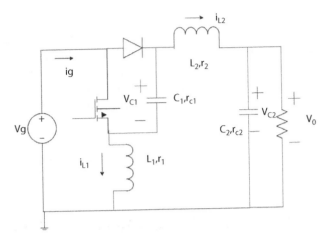

Figure 8.2 General configuration of fourth order boost converter.

extra energy storing elements in the middle with the exception of an output capacitor. Thus, it can be said as a parallel combination of two Fourth order boost converters except the source voltage (V_g), load (R) and output capacitor (C_3) are unique.

8.2.2   Modeling of FIBC

There are four modes of operation when the Fourth order interleaved circuit diagram is considered. It has two controlled switches (in this case MOSFET S1 and S2) and two uncontrolled switches (the two diodes D1 and D2). The different modes and the corresponding steady state equations are discussed for every mode of operation.

8.2.2.1   Mode 1 Operation (0 to d_1Ts)

In this mode the MOSFET S_1 is On, the diode D_1 is Off, the MOSFET S_2 is On and the diode D_2 is On. The equivalent circuit diagram following this mode of operation is shown below:

By applying KVL and KCL in Figure 8.3 we get the following equations,

$$\dot{i}_{L1} = \frac{V_g}{L_1} - \frac{i_{L1}r_1}{L_1} \tag{8.1}$$

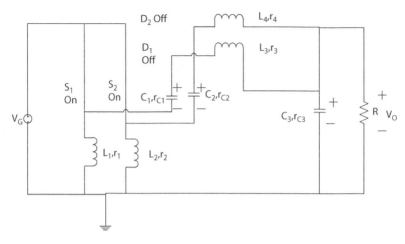

Figure 8.3 Mode 1 operation of FIBC.

$$\dot{i}_{L2} = \frac{V_g}{L_2} - \frac{i_{L2}r_2}{L_2} \tag{8.2}$$

$$\dot{i}_{L3} = \frac{V_g}{L_3} - \frac{V_{C1}}{L_3} - \frac{V_{C3}}{L_3} - \frac{i_{L3(r_{C1+r3})}}{L_3} - \frac{R(i_{L3}+i_{L4})r_{C3}}{(R+r_{C3})L_3} + \frac{V_{C3}r_{C3}}{(R+r_{C3})L_3} \tag{8.3}$$

$$\dot{i}_{L4} = \frac{V_g}{L_4} - \frac{V_{C2}}{L_4} - \frac{V_{C3}}{L_4} - i_{L4}\frac{(r_{C2}+r_4)}{L_4} - \frac{Rr_{C3}(i_{L3}+i_{L4})}{(R+r_{C3})L_4} + \frac{V_{C3}r_{C3}}{(R+r_{C3})L_4} \tag{8.4}$$

$$\dot{V}_{C1} = \frac{i_{L3}}{C_1} \tag{8.5}$$

$$\dot{V}_{C2} = \frac{i_{L4}}{C_2} \tag{8.6}$$

$$\dot{V}_{C3} = \frac{(i_{L3}+i_{L4})R}{(R+r_{C3})C_3} - \frac{V_{C3}}{C_3(R+r_{C3})} \tag{8.7}$$

The above equations (Eqs. (8.1)–(8.7)) obtained from mode 1 are converted into state space form and the representation is given below:

$$\dot{x_1} = A_1 x + B_1 V_g \tag{8.8}$$

$$y_1 = C_1 x + D_1 V_g \tag{8.9}$$

Here,

$$A_1 = \begin{bmatrix} \frac{-r_1}{L_1} & 0 & 0 & 0 & 0 & 0 & 0 \\[2mm] 0 & \frac{-r_2}{L_2} & 0 & 0 & 0 & 0 & 0 \\[2mm] 0 & 0 & \frac{-(Rr_{C_1} + Rr_3 + r_{C_3}r_{C_1} + r_3 r_{C_3} + Rr_{C_3})}{(R+r_{C_3})L_3} & \frac{-Rr_{C_3}}{(R+r_{C_3})L_3} & \frac{-1}{L_3} & 0 & \frac{-R}{(R+r_{C_3})L_3} \\[2mm] 0 & 0 & \frac{-Rr_{C_3}}{(R+r_{C_3})L_4} & \frac{-(Rr_{C_2} + Rr_4 + r_{C_3}r_{C_2} + r_4 r_{C_3} + Rr_{C_3})}{(R+r_{C_3})L_4} & 0 & \frac{-1}{L_4} & \frac{-R}{(R+r_{C_3})L_4} \\[2mm] 0 & 0 & \frac{1}{C_1} & 0 & 0 & 0 & 0 \\[2mm] 0 & 0 & 0 & \frac{1}{C_2} & 0 & 0 & 0 \\[2mm] 0 & 0 & \frac{R}{(R+r_{C_3})C_3} & \frac{R}{(R+r_{C_3})C_3} & 0 & 0 & \frac{-1}{(R+r_{C_3})C_3} \end{bmatrix}$$

$$B_1 = \begin{bmatrix} \frac{1}{L_1} & \frac{1}{L_2} & \frac{1}{L_3} & \frac{1}{L_4} & 0 & 0 & 0 \end{bmatrix}$$

$$C_1 = \begin{bmatrix} 0 & 0 & \frac{Rr_{C_3}}{(R+r_{C_3})} & \frac{Rr_{C_3}}{(R+r_{C_3})} & 0 & 0 & \frac{R}{(R+r_{C_3})} \end{bmatrix}$$

$$D_1 = [0]$$

8.2.2.2 Mode 2 Operation (d_1Ts to d_2Ts)

In this mode the MOSFET S1 is On, the diode D_1 is OFF, the MOSFET S_2 is OFF and the diode D_2 is On. The equivalent circuit diagram following this mode of operation is shown below:

By applying KVL and KCL in Figure 8.4 we get the following equations,

$$\dot{i}_{L1} = \frac{V_g}{L_1} - \frac{i_{L1}}{L_1} \tag{8.10}$$

$$\dot{i}_{L2} = \frac{V_g}{L_2} - \frac{i_{C2}}{L_2} \tag{8.11}$$

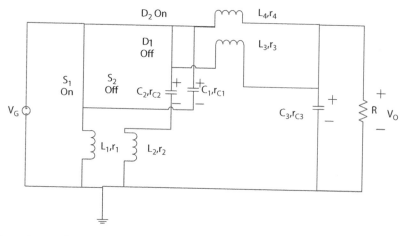

Figure 8.4 Mode 2 operation of FIBC.

$$\dot{i}_{L3} = \frac{V_g}{L_3} - \frac{V_{C1}}{L_3} - \frac{V_{C3}}{L_3} - i_{L3}\frac{(r_{C1} + r_{C3})}{L_3} - \frac{i_{C3}r_{C3}}{L_3} \tag{8.12}$$

$$\dot{i}_{L4} = \frac{V_g}{L_4} - \frac{V_{C3}}{L_4} - \frac{i_{L4}r_4}{L_4} - \frac{i_{C3}r_{C3}}{L_4} \tag{8.13}$$

$$\dot{V}_{C1} = \frac{i_{L3}}{C_1} \tag{8.14}$$

$$\dot{V}_{C2} = \frac{i_{L2}}{C_2} \tag{8.15}$$

$$\dot{V}_{C3} = \frac{(i_{L3} + i_{L4})R}{(R + r_{C3})C_3} - \frac{V_{C3}}{(R + r_{C3})} \tag{8.16}$$

The above equations (Eqs. (8.10)–(8.16)) obtained from mode 1 are converted into state space form and the representation is given below:

$$\dot{x}_2 = A_2 x + B_2 V_g \tag{8.17}$$

$$y_2 = C_2 x + D_2 V_g \tag{8.18}$$

Here,

A_2

$$
=
\begin{bmatrix}
\dfrac{-r_1}{L_1} & 0 & 0 & 0 & 0 & 0 & 0 \\[2mm]
0 & \dfrac{-(r_2+r_2)}{L_2} & 0 & 0 & 0 & \dfrac{-1}{L_2} & 0 \\[2mm]
0 & 0 & -\dfrac{(Rr_{C3}+Rr_{C1}+Rr_3+r_{C3}r_3)}{L_3(R+r_{C3})} & -\dfrac{Rr_{C3}}{(R+r_{C3})L_3} & -\dfrac{1}{L_3} & 0 & -\dfrac{R}{(R+r_{C3})L_3} \\[2mm]
0 & 0 & -\dfrac{Rr_{C3}}{(R+r_{C3})L_4} & -\dfrac{(Rr_{C3}+Rr_{C2}+Rr_4+r_{C3}r_4)}{L_4(R+r_{C3})} & 0 & 0 & -\dfrac{R}{(R+r_{C3})L_4} \\[2mm]
0 & 0 & \dfrac{1}{C_1} & 0 & 0 & 0 & 0 \\[2mm]
0 & \dfrac{1}{C_2} & 0 & 0 & 0 & 0 & 0 \\[2mm]
0 & 0 & \dfrac{R}{(R+r_{C3})C_3} & \dfrac{R}{(R+r_{C3})C_3} & 0 & 0 & -\dfrac{1}{(R+r_{C3})}
\end{bmatrix}
$$

$$B_2 = B_1$$
$$C_2 = C_1$$
$$D_2 = D_1$$

8.2.2.3   Mode 3 Operation ($d_2 Ts$ to $d_3 Ts$)

This mode is exactly the same as mode 1. The equivalent circuit diagram following this mode of operation is shown below:

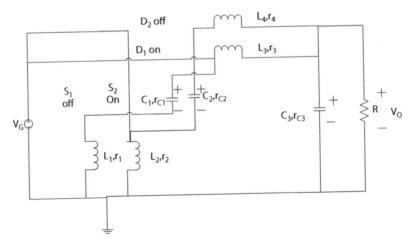

Figure 8.5 Mode 3 operation of FIBC.

By applying KVL and KCL in Figure 8.5 we get the following equations,

$$\dot{i}_{L1} = \frac{V_g}{L_1} - \frac{i_{L1}r_1}{L_1} \tag{8.19}$$

$$\dot{i}_{L2} = \frac{V_g}{L_2} - \frac{i_{L2}r_2}{L_2} \tag{8.20}$$

$$\dot{i}_{L3} = \frac{V_g}{L_3} - \frac{V_{C1}}{L_3} - \frac{V_{C3}}{L_3} - \frac{i_{L3}(r_{C1}+r_3)}{L_3} - \frac{R(i_{L3}+i_{L4})r_{C3}}{(R+r_{C3})L_3} + \frac{V_{C3}r_{C3}}{(R+r_{C3})L_3} \tag{8.21}$$

$$\dot{i}_{L4} = \frac{V_g}{L_4} - \frac{V_{C2}}{L_4} - \frac{V_{C3}}{L_4} - i_{L4}\frac{(r_{C2}+r_4)}{L_4} - \frac{Rr_{C3}(i_{L3}+i_{L4})}{(R+r_{C3})L_4} + \frac{V_{C3}r_{C3}}{(R+r_{C3})L_4} \tag{8.22}$$

$$\dot{V}_{C1} = \frac{i_{L3}}{C_1} \tag{8.23}$$

$$\dot{V}_{C2} = \frac{i_{L4}}{C_2} \tag{8.24}$$

$$\dot{V}_{C3} = \frac{(i_{L3}+i_{L4})R}{(R+r_{C3})C_3} - \frac{V_{C3}}{(R+r_{C3})} \tag{8.25}$$

The above equations (Eqs. (8.19)–(8.24)) obtained from mode 3 are converted into state space form and the representation is given below:

$$\dot{x}_3 = A_3x + B_3V_g \tag{8.26}$$

$$y_3 = C_3x + D_3V_g \tag{8.27}$$

Here,

$$A_3 = A_1$$

$$B_3 = B_1$$

$$C_3 = C_1$$

$$D_3 = D_1$$

8.2.2.4   Mode 4 Operation (d_3Ts to Ts)

In this mode the MOSFET S1 is Off, the diode D1 is On, the MOSFET S2 is On and the diode D2 is Off. The equivalent circuit diagram following this mode of operation is shown below:

By applying KVL and KCL in Figure 8.6 we get the following equations,

$$\dot{i}_{L1} = \frac{V_g}{L_1} - \frac{V_{C1}}{L_1} - \frac{i_{L1}(r_{C1}+r_1)}{L_1} \tag{8.28}$$

$$\dot{i}_{L2} = \frac{V_g}{L_2} - \frac{i_{L2}r_2}{L_2} \tag{8.29}$$

$$\dot{i}_{L3} = \frac{V_g}{L_3} - \frac{i_{L3}(Rr_3 + r_{C3}r_3 + Rr_{C3})}{(R+r_{C3})L_3} - \frac{i_{L4}Rr_{C3}}{(R+r_{C3})} \tag{8.30}$$

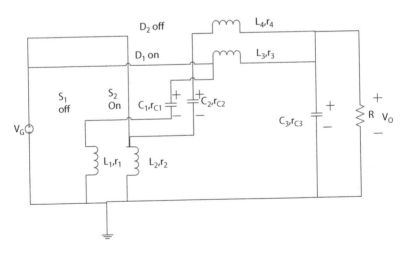

Figure 8.6 Mode 4 operation of FIBC.

$$\dot{i}_{L4} = \frac{V_g}{L_4} - \frac{V_{C2}}{L_4} - \frac{RV_{C3}}{(R+r_{C3})L_4} - \frac{i_{L3}Rr_{C3}}{(R+r_{C3})L_4} - i_{L4}\frac{(Rr_{C2}+Rr_4+r_{C3}r_{C2}+r_{C3}r_4)}{(R+r_{C3})L_4}$$

$$(8.31)$$

$$\dot{V}_{C1} = \frac{i_{L1}}{C_1}$$

$$(8.32)$$

$$\dot{V}_{C2} = \frac{i_{L4}}{C_2}$$

$$(8.33)$$

$$\dot{V}_{C3} = \frac{(i_{L3}+i_{L4})R}{C_3(R+r_{C3})} - \frac{V_{C3}}{C_3(R+r_{C3})}$$

$$(8.34)$$

The above equations (Eqs. (8.28)–(8.34)) obtained from mode 2 are converted into state space form and the representation is given below:

$$\dot{x_4} = A_4 x + B_4 V_g$$

$$(8.35)$$

$$y_4 = C_4 x + D_4 V_g$$

$$(8.36)$$

Here,

$$A_4 =$$

$$\begin{bmatrix}
-\frac{(r_{C1}+r_1)}{L_1} & 0 & 0 & 0 & \frac{-1}{L_1} & 0 & 0 \\
0 & -\frac{r_2}{(R+r_{C3})L_4} & 0 & 0 & 0 & 0 & 0 \\
0 & 0 & -\frac{(Rr_{C3}+Rr_3+r_{C3}r_3)}{(R+r_{C3})L_3} & -\frac{Rr_{C3}}{(R+r_{C3})L_3} & 0 & 0 & -\frac{R}{(R+r_{C3})L_3} \\
0 & 0 & -\frac{Rr_{C3}}{(R+r_{C3})L_4} & -\frac{(Rr_{C2}+Rr_4+r_{C3}r_{C2}+r_{C3}r_4+Rr_{C3})}{(R+r_{C3})L_4} & 0 & 0 & -\frac{R}{(R+r_{C3})L_4} \\
\frac{1}{C_1} & 0 & 0 & 0 & 0 & 0 & 0 \\
0 & 0 & 0 & \frac{1}{C_2} & 0 & 0 & 0 \\
0 & 0 & \frac{R}{(R+r_{C3})C_3} & \frac{R}{(R+r_{C3})C_3} & 0 & 0 & -\frac{1}{(R+r_{C3})C_3}
\end{bmatrix}$$

$$B_4 = B_1$$
$$C_4 = C_1$$
$$D_4 = D_1$$

8.2.3 Averaging of the Model

State space averaging is done to ensure that the four modes of operation happen during a single clock cycle. The four state space matrices in Eqs. (8.8–8.9), (8.17–8.18), (8.26–8.27) and (8.35–8.36) are averaged according the formula given below in Eqs. (8.37–8.42).

$$\dot{x} = Ax + BV_g \qquad (8.37)$$

$$y = Cx + DV_g \qquad (8.38)$$

Where

$$A = A_1 d_1 + A_2 d_2 + A_3 d_3 + A_4 d_4 \qquad (8.39)$$

$$B = B_1 d_1 + B_2 d_2 + B_3 d_3 + B_4 d_4 \qquad (8.40)$$

$$C = C_1 d_1 + C_2 d_2 + C_3 d_3 + C_4 d_4 \qquad (8.41)$$

$$D = D_1 d_1 + D_2 d_2 + D_3 d_3 + D_4 d_4 \qquad (8.42)$$

$$A = \begin{bmatrix} \dfrac{-(r_1 + r_{C3}(d))}{L_1} & 0 & 0 & 0 & \dfrac{-d}{L_1} & 0 & 0 \\ 0 & \dfrac{-r_2 + r_{C3}d}{L_2} & 0 & 0 & 0 & \dfrac{-d}{L_2} & 0 \\ 0 & 0 & \dfrac{-((Rr_3 + r_3 r_{C3} + Rr_{C3}) + d(R + r_{C3})r_{C2})}{(R + r_{C3})L_3} & \dfrac{-Rr_{C3}}{(R + r_{C3})L_3} & \dfrac{-(1 + d')}{L_3} & 0 & \dfrac{-R}{(R + r_{C3})L_3} \\ 0 & 0 & \dfrac{-Rr_{C3}}{(R + r_{C3})L_4} & \dfrac{-((Rr_4 + r_4 r_{C3} + Rr_{C3}) + (d)(R + r_{C3})r_{C2})}{(R + r_{C3})L_4} & 0 & \dfrac{-(1 + d')}{L_4} & \dfrac{-R}{(R + r_{C3})L_4} \\ \dfrac{d}{C_1} & 0 & \dfrac{(1 + d')}{C_1} & 0 & 0 & 0 & 0 \\ 0 & \dfrac{d}{C_2} & 0 & \dfrac{(1 + d')}{C_2} & 0 & 0 & 0 \\ 0 & 0 & \dfrac{R}{(R + r_{C3})C_3} & \dfrac{R}{(R + r_{C3})C_3} & 0 & 0 & \dfrac{-1}{(R + r_{C3})C_3} \end{bmatrix}$$

$$B = \begin{bmatrix} \dfrac{1}{L_1} & \dfrac{1}{L_2} & \dfrac{1}{L_3} & \dfrac{1}{L_4} & 0 & 0 & 0 \end{bmatrix}$$

$$C = \begin{bmatrix} 0 & 0 & \dfrac{Rr_{C3}}{(R + r_{C3})} & \dfrac{Rr_{C3}}{(R + r_{C3})} & 0 & 0 & \dfrac{R}{(R + r_{C3})} \end{bmatrix}$$

$$D = [0]$$

8.2.4 Small Signal Analysis

The transfer functions are obtained by adding perturbations to the instantaneous values of state variables and control variable.

$$x = (X + \hat{x})$$

$$d = (D + \hat{d})$$

where D, X are the steady state values and $\hat{d}$ *and* $\hat{x}$ are the perturbations (small signal).

After substituting the small signal values in the above generated state space equations, we get,

$$\dot{\hat{x}} = (A_1 + A_2 + A_3 + A_4)D\hat{x} + B\hat{u} + (A_1 + A_3 - A_2 - A_4)x\hat{d} \quad (8.43)$$

Input to output transfer function (I2O) is obtained by substituting $\hat{d} = 0$ and Control to output transfer function (C2O) is obtained by substituting $\hat{u} = 0$ respectively in Eq. (8.43).

The transfer functions are obtained as given below;

I2O is given by:

$$\frac{\hat{y}(s)}{\hat{u}(s)} = C(sI - A)^{-1}B + D \qquad (8.44)$$

C2O is given by:

$$\frac{\hat{y}(s)}{\hat{d}(s)} = C(sI - A)^{-1}P + D$$

$$(8.45)$$

where, $P = (A_1 + A_3 - A_2 - A_4)X$

Table 8.1 Converter parameters.

Parameter	Value
Vg	20 V
R	20 Ω
V_O	50 V
r_1, L_1, r_2, L_2	0.055 Ω, 250 μH
r_3, L_3, r_4, L_4	0.035 Ω, 110 μH
r_{C1}, r_{C2}, C_1, C_2	0.1 Ω, 22 μF
r_{C3}, C_3	0.1 Ω, 220 μF

Table 8.1 represents the values for converter parameters to be substituted in Eqs. (8.44) and (8.45) to form a transfer function. The switching frequency is assumed to be 80 KHz. By substituting these values, we get the following transfer function.

Input to Output Transfer function:

$$G_{Vg}(s)$$
$$= \frac{1809s^6 + 8.443 \times 10^7 s^5 + 1.862 \times 10^{11} \times s^4 + 3.119 \times 10^{15} s^3 - 1.884 \times 10^{18} s^2 - 1.585 \times 10^{23} s - 5.98 \times 10^{25}}{s^7 + 3.933 \times s^6 + 1.365 \times 10^6 s^5 + 3.12 \times 10^{11} s^4 + 4.51 \times 10^{15} s^3 + 3.353 \times 10^{18} s^2 + 6.311 \times 10^{20} s - 3.137 \times 10^{19}}$$

Control to output Transfer function:

$$G_{Vd}(s)$$
$$= \frac{-90.45s^6 + 2.014 \times 10^8 s^5 + 8.542 \times 10^{12} s^4 - 2.129 \times 10^{16} s^3 + 5.12 \times 10^{20} s^2 - 2.679 \times 10^{24} s - 1.093 \times 10^{27}}{s^7 + 3.933 \times s^6 + 1.365 \times 10^6 s^5 + 3.12 \times 10^{11} s^4 + 4.51 \times 10^{15} s^3 + 3.353 \times 10^{18} s^2 + 6.311 \times 10^{20} s - 3.137 \times 10^{19}}$$

From Figure 8.7 we can see that the root locus depicts the presence of zeros and poles in the C2O transfer function. As observed from the figure, there exists a zero in the RHP of the imaginary axis (s-plane). This represents the non-minimum behavior of the transfer function of boost converters. This right half plane zero exist only in the C2O transfer function and not in the I2O transfer function as seen from Figure 8.8. This non minimum behavior can be observed from the bode plot in Figure 8.9. Around the cut off frequency, the non-minimum nature can be observed from the bode diagram.

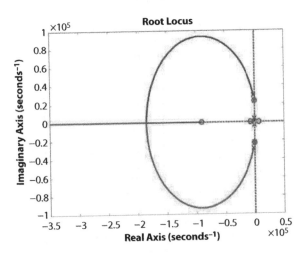

Figure 8.7 Root locus of G_{vd}.

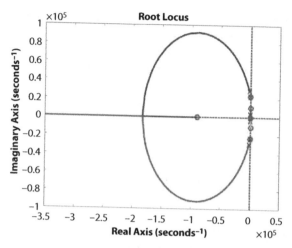

Figure 8.8 Root locus of G_{vg}.

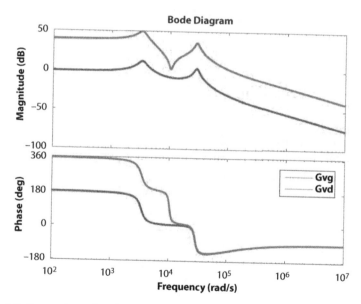

Figure 8.9 Comparison of Bode plots of the two transfer function of FIBC.

8.3   Controller Design for FIBC

8.3.1   PID Controller

This controller is taken as a reference for the comparison of the Type II and III controllers. This is the most popular controller used in the industry and the comparison of this controller with the rest of the discussed topics provides a reasonable explanation. The PID controller consists of three terms Proportional, Integral and derivative parts. These are represented in the form of an expression in frequency domain (Eq. (8.47)). It is given by

$$C(s) = \frac{K_P s + K_I + K_D s^2}{s} \tag{8.46}$$

$$C(s) = K_P + \frac{K_I}{s} + K_D s \tag{8.47}$$

By using Ziegler–Nicholas tuning method we get the values for the three PID parameters in Eq. (8.47) and the transfer function is given by,

$$C(s) = 2.67 \times 10^{-7} \times \frac{(s + 5.12 \times 10^3)(s + 5.12 \times 10^3)}{s}$$

8.3.2   Type II Controller

This controller is nothing but a lead circuit combined with an integrator. The main focus of this controller is that it gives a higher phase boost ($\emptyset_{max}$) of up to 90°. In this regard, the controller is designed in such a way as to obtain a desired phase margin of around 60°. The general representation of a type II controller is given in Eq. (8.48).

$$G_C(s) = \frac{w_{p0}\left(1 + \dfrac{s}{w_z}\right)}{s\left(1 + \dfrac{s}{w_p}\right)} \tag{8.48}$$

Where w_p, w_z are the pole and zero locations of this controller. Tuning of the controller parameter is a very important criteria for the design of any controller. Here k-factor approach is used for the tuning of the controller parameters. Here k is the ratio of pole location to zero location. This value of k is defined according to the frequency domain design criteria. In this design example, a phase margin of about 60° is considered for this controller. The amount of phase boost to achieve a phase margin of 60° is the required phase boost (Ø) in this design. K is given by Eq. (8.49).

$$k = tan\left(\frac{\varnothing}{2} + 45°\right)$$

(8.49)

The Pole location is given by Eq. (8.50).

$$f_{pole} = k \times f_{cut-off} = tan\left(\frac{\varnothing}{2} + 45°\right) \times f_{cut-off}$$

(8.50)

The value of Ø is noted from the Figure 8.9. The frequency at which the Ø is calculated is the cut-off frequency. Correspondingly, the frequency of maximum phase is given by Eq. (8.51).

$$f_{\varnothing maximum} = \sqrt{f_{pole} \times f_{zero}}$$

(8.51)

The zero frequency location is given by Eq. (8.52).

$$f_{zero} = \frac{f_{pole}}{tan\left(\frac{\varnothing}{2} + 45°\right)}$$

(8.52)

After finding the pole and zero location, the transfer function becomes,

$$G_c(s) = 3.9097 \times \frac{(s+596)}{(s+461)}$$

8.3.3 Type III Controller

This controller is nothing but the combination of an integrator and lead-lead circuit. The main focus of this controller is that it gives a maximum phase boost ($\varnothing_{max}$) of 180°. In this regard, the controller is designed in such a way as to achieve a phase margin of around 90°. The general representation of a Type III controller is given by Eq. (8.53)

$$G_c(s) = \frac{w_{p0}\left(1 + \dfrac{s}{w_{z1}}\right)\left(1 + \dfrac{s}{w_{z2}}\right)}{s\left(1 + \dfrac{s}{w_{p1}}\right)\left(1 + \dfrac{s}{w_{p2}}\right)} \qquad (8.53)$$

Where w_{z1}, w_{z2}, w_{p1}, and w_{p2} are the zeros and poles of this controller's transfer function respectively. Similar to Type II controller, here also the same approach is used for tuning the controller parameter for this controller's transfer function. K is defined in a similar way for this controller also. It is given in Eq. (8.54).

$$\sqrt{k} = tan\left(\frac{\emptyset}{2} + 45°\right) \qquad (8.54)$$

Where $\emptyset$ is the phase boost required to maintain the desired phase margin.

The pole location is given by Eq. (8.55).

$$f_{pole1}(f_{pole2}) = \sqrt{k} \times f_{cut-off} = tan\left(\frac{\emptyset}{2} + 45°\right) \times f_{cut-off} \qquad (8.55)$$

The value of $\emptyset$ is noted from the magnitude-frequency plots of the converter's transfer function. The corresponding frequency of phase boost ($\emptyset$) is called the cut off frequency ($f_{cut-off}$). The value of frequency of max. phase boost ($\emptyset_{max}$) is given by Eq. (8.56).

$$f_{\emptyset maximum} = \sqrt{f_{pole1}(f_{pole2}) \times f_{zero1}(f_{zero2})} \qquad (8.56)$$

From the above calculated values, we can arrive at the zero location frequency is given from Eq. (8.57).

$$f_{zero1}(f_{zero2}) = \frac{f_{pole1}(f_{pole2})}{tan\left(\dfrac{\emptyset}{2} + 45°\right)} \qquad (8.57)$$

After finding the pole and zero location of this controller, the transfer function is given by,

$$G_c(s) = 3.0857 \times \frac{(s+2341)(s+8.09)}{s(s+11.9)(s+1110)}$$

8.4   Computational Results

The system performance of FIBC is realized with the three controllers and the results are compared with conventional PID controllers for better analysis. The simulation is done in the MATLAB environment. The results obtained are satisfactory when compared with ordinary Fourth Order Boost converter when operated with the same controllers.

The step response of FIBC along with Type II controller is plotted in the Figure 8.10. The bode diagram as well as the root locus plot of the system is depicted in Figures 8.11 and 8.12. From these plots, it is inferred that the converter with Type II controller settles in 7 msec. The rise time is found to be 4.2 msec. This results in the faster convergence of the system when compared with PID controller. The PID controller's settling time for the same

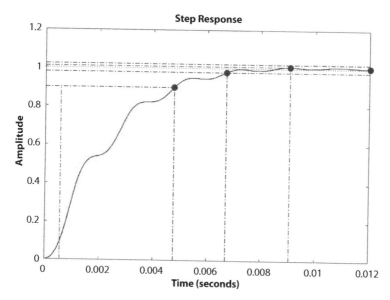

Figure 8.10 Response of FIBC with Type II controller.

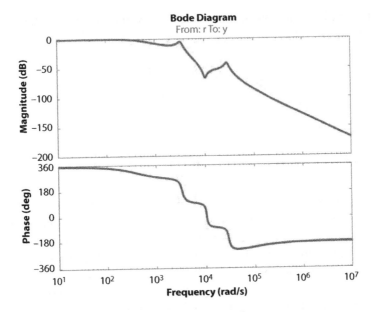

Figure 8.11 Bode diagram of FIBC with Type II controller.

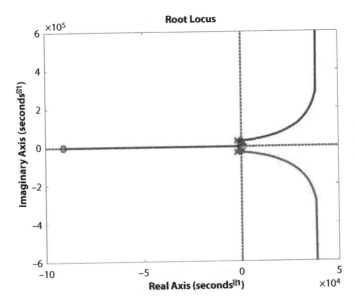

Figure 8.12 Root locus of FIBC with Type II controller.

converter is approximately 10 msec and the rise time is approximately 5 msec. The step response involving PID controller tuned with the classical design formula is shown in Figure 8.13.

It can be inferred from the above plots that the Type III controller (Figure 8.14) settles faster when compared with the other two controllers. The settling time is observed to be less than 5 msec and the rise time is 2.5 msec. Thus, we can conclude that the Type III controller exhibits faster response when compared with all other controllers discussed here

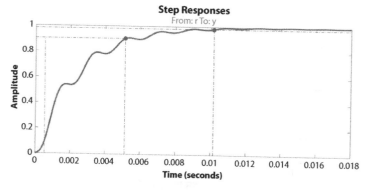

Figure 8.13 Response of FIBC with PID controller.

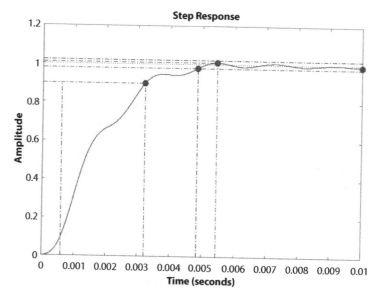

Figure 8.14 FIBC with Type III controller.

(Figure 8.15). This FIBC is in fact, faster than the ordinary Fourth order Boost converter without interleaving operation (Figure 8.16). The comparison of the transient response of the three controllers in closed loop with the converter is plotted in the Figure 8.17. The comparison of the closed

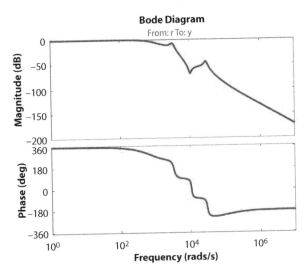

Figure 8.15 FIBC with Type III controller- magnitude and phase plot.

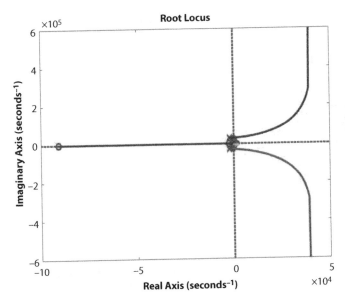

Figure 8.16 Root locus of FIBC with Type III controller.

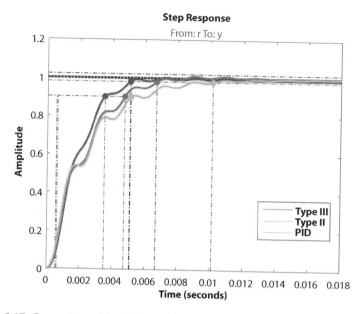

Figure 8.17 Comparison of the different controllers in closed loop operation.

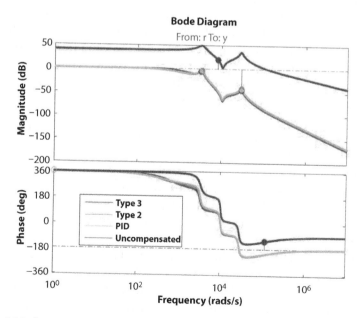

Figure 8.18 Comparison of the bode response of different controllers in closed loop.

Table 8.2 Comparison of different controllers in closed loop performance.

Parameter	PID controller	Type-II controller	Type-III controller
Rise time	0.0052 s	0.004 s	0.0025 s
Settling time	0.01 s	0.007 s	0.0048 s
Maximum peak overshoot	0%	0%	0%
Gain margin	9.1 dB	12.5dB	9.79 dB
Phase margin	59°	62.8°	80°
Steady state error	0.0	0.0	0.0

loop bode response with different controllers are also shown in the Figure 8.18. From this plot we can observe the phase boost achieved in closed loop system when compared with the uncompensated system.

From Table 8.2, it is noted that the Type III controller performs well with FIBC. It is worth noted that this performance reflects both in frequency domain as well as time domain.

Comparison of the Different Controller's Responses During Steady State

As we can observe from Figures 8.19 and 8.20 reference tracking is carried by the addition or subtraction of 50% of the desired output voltage. This is done to ensure that the designed controller has good tracking tolerance despite the system being designed for a specific voltage. Here, it is observed from the above graphs that the system involving Type III controller settles faster when compared with the other two controllers even though the changes are very small.

Line regulation is one of the important criteria in analyzing the robustness of the system. It is done by checking the tolerance of the changes in input voltage by at least 10% of the actual input voltage. It can be observed from Figure 8.21 that the three controllers behave almost identical when this change is applied. The oscillation occurs for few milliseconds and it eventually settles down. This lies within the approvable range in the literatures.

In Figure 8.22 changes in the load in terms of load voltage are observed. This is identical to changing the load at the output in simulation environment. Here, a part of the voltage (−50%) is added to the existing load voltage. The output is seen disturbed for a few milliseconds before it settles

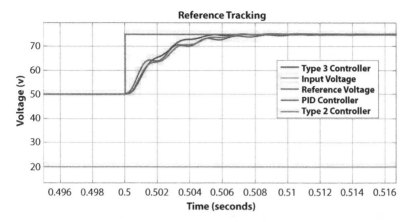

Figure 8.19 Comparison of the three different controllers when 50% of reference voltage is added.

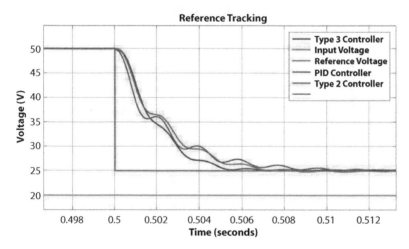

Figure 8.20 Comparison of the three different controllers when 50% of reference voltage is subtracted.

down to the reference value. It is evident from this Figure that the oscillations in Type III settles faster when compared with the Type II and PID controllers.

Figure 8.23 depicts the ripple in the output of this converter. Its value is approximately 0.3 V. The percentage ripple is 0.6%. This is very less when compared with the normal fourth order boost converter which is close to

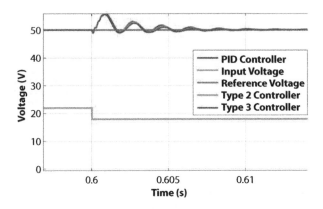

Figure 8.21 Comparison of the changes in 10% of input voltage for different controllers in closed loop.

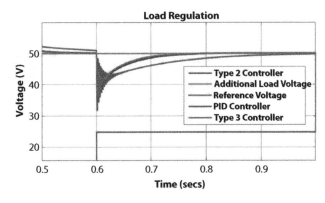

Figure 8.22 Comparison of the load regulation by adding additional load voltage in the circuit (–50% of load voltage).

1.5%. This percentage of ripple changes as the duty ratio is varied. The percentage of ripple varies inversely with the duty ratio.

8.5   Conclusion

It is observed that the discussed converter is stable and agrees with the reference voltage. It is clear from the graphs that converter is underdamped initially and after approximately 7 msec it settles down. in the case of Type

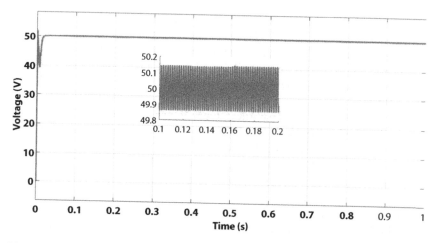

Figure 8.23 Ripple in the output of FIBC.

II controller and in approximately 5 msec for a Type III controller. The rise time also reduces considerably when compared with PID and Type II controller. The simulation results are according to the desired value and is improved in terms of quicker response and source fluctuations. The steady state responses of the simulation results proves that the controller is stable and robust as well. The reference tracking and regulation subjected to disturbances does not alter the nature of the output voltage although certain fluctuations are present at the time of impact after which it settles down to the desired value. Thus, this converter can be effectively used in smart grids for compensation in the supply voltage due to any irregularities in the supply voltage. FIBC can be used in smart grids or microgrids to aide in harnessing the potential of renewable energy with minimum losses.

References

1. Liu, X. and Su, B., Microgrids—An integration of renewable energy technologies, in: *2008 China International Conference on Electricity Distribution*, IEEE, pp. 1–7, 2008.
2. Erickson, R.W. and Maksimovic, D., *Fundamentals of Power Electronics*, Springer Science & Business Media, USA, 2007.
3. Ogata, K., *Modern Control Engineering*, Prentice Hall, USA, 2010.
4. Sivakumar, S., Jagabar Sathik, M., Manoj, P.S., Sundararajan, G., An assessment on performance of DC–DC converters for renewable energy applications. *Renew. Sust. Energ. Rev.*, 58, 1475–1485, 2016.

5. Hohm, D.P. and Ropp, M., Comparative study of maximum power point tracking algorithms. *Prog. Photovolt.: Res. Appl.*, 11, 1, 47–62, 2003.

6. Vijayakumari, A., Warner, B.R., Devarajan, N., Topologies and control of grid connected power converters, in: *2014 International Conference on Circuits, Power and Computing Technologies [ICCPCT-2014]*, IEEE, pp. 401–410, 2014.

7. Veerachary, M. and Saxena, A.R., Design of robust digital stabilizing controller for fourth-order boost DC–DC converter: A quantitative feedback theory approach. *IEEE Trans. Ind. Electron.*, 59, 2, 952–963, 2011.

8. Babu, C.S. and Veerachary, M., Predictive valley current control for two inductor boost converter, in: *Proceedings of the IEEE International Symposium on Industrial Electronics, 2005. ISIE 2005*, vol. 2, IEEE, pp. 727–731, 2005.

9. Banerjee, S., Ghosh, A., Rana, N., An improved interleaved boost converter with PSO-based optimal type-III controller. *IEEE J. Emerg. Sel. Top. Power Electron.*, 5, 1, 323–337, 2016.

10. Rana, N., Kumar, M., Ghosh, A., Banerjee, S., A novel interleaved tri-state boost converter with lower ripple and improved dynamic response. *IEEE Trans. Ind. Electron.*, 65, 7, 5456–5465, 2017.

11. De Nardo, A., Femia, N., Nicolo, M., Petrone, G., Spagnuolo, G., Power stage design of fourth-order DC–DC converters by means of principal components analysis. *IEEE Trans. Power Electron.*, 23, 6, 2867–2877, 2008.

12. Hoagg, J.B. and Bernstein, D.S., Nonminimum-phase zeros-much to do about nothing-classical control-revisited part II. *IEEE Control Syst. Mag.*, 27, 3, 45–57, 2007.

13. Papadopoulos, K.G., Papastefanaki, E.N., Margaris, N.I., Optimal tuning of PID controllers for type-III control loops, in: *2011 19th Mediterranean Conference on Control & Automation (MED)*, IEEE, pp. 1295–1300, 2011.

14. Rahavi, J.S.A., Kanagapriya, T., Seyezhai, R., Design and analysis of interleaved boost converter for renewable energy source, in: *2012 International Conference on Computing, Electronics and Electrical Technologies (ICCEET)*, IEEE, pp. 447–451, 2012.

15. Kumar, G.V.B. and Palanisamy, K., Interleaved Boost Converter for Renewable Energy Application with Energy Storage System, in: *2019 IEEE 1st International Conference on Energy, Systems and Information Processing (ICESIP)*, IEEE, pp. 1–5, 2019.

16. Henn, G.A.L., Silva, R.N.A.L., Praca, P.P., Barreto, L.H.S.C., Oliveira, D.S., Interleaved-boost converter with high voltage gain. *IEEE Trans. Power Electron.*, 25, 11, 2753–2761, 2010.

17. Kamtip, S. and Bhumkittipich, K., *Design and analysis of interleaved boost converter for renewable energy applications*, Rajamangala University of Technology Thanyaburi, 2011.

18. Saurav, S. and Ghosh, A., Design and Analysis of PID, Type II and Type III controllers for Fourth Order Boost Converter, in: *2021 7th International Conference on Electrical Energy Systems (ICEES)*, IEEE, pp. 323–328, 2021.

19. Ghosh, A., Banerjee, S., Sarkar, M.K., Dutta, P., Design and implementation of type-II and type-III controller for DC–DC switched-mode boost converter by using K-factor approach and optimisation techniques. *IET Power Electron.*, 9, 5, 938–950, 2016.

20. Ghosh, A. and Banerjee, S., A comparative performance study of a closed-loop boost converter with classical and advanced controllers using simulation and real-time experimentation. *Int. Trans. Electr. Energy Syst.*, 30, 10, e12537, 2020.

21. Ghosh, A. and Banerjee, S., A comparison between classical and advanced controllers for a boost converter, in: *2018 IEEE International Conference on Power Electronics, Drives and Energy Systems (PEDES)*, IEEE, pp. 1–6, 2018.

22. Ghosh, A. and Banerjee, S., Control of Switched-Mode Boost Converter by using classical and optimized Type controllers. *J. Control Eng. Appl. Inform.*, 17, 4, 114–125, 2015.

23. Ghosh, A. and Banerjee, S., Design and implementation of Type-II compensator in DC-DC switch-mode step-up power supply, in: *Proceedings of the 2015 Third International Conference on Computer, Communication, Control and Information Technology (C3IT)*, IEEE, pp. 1–5, 2015.

24. Almusaylim, Z.A. and Zaman, N., A review on smart home present state and challenges: linked to context-awareness Internet of Things (IoT). *Wirel. Netw.*, 6, 3193–3204, 2019.

25. Chatterjee, J.M., Kumar, R., Khari, M., Hung, D.T., Le, D.N., Internet of Things based system for Smart Kitchen. *Int. J. Eng. Manuf*, 8, 4, 2.9, 2018.

9

Industry 4.0 in Healthcare IoT for Inventory and Supply Chain Management

Somya Goyal

Department of Computer and Communication Engineering, Manipal University Jaipur, India

Abstract

Industry 4.0 is a set up reality that seems to fulfil various necessities of the clinical field with expansive assessment is going around there. Radio Frequency Identification (RFID) advancement not simply offers following capacity to discover stuff, supplies and people persistently, yet furthermore gives capable and exact permission to clinical data for prosperity specialists. In any case, the reality of RFID assignment in clinical administrations is far behind earlier presumption. This work proposes to pass on Radio repeat conspicuous evidence (RFID) development to follow and administer an enormous number of clinical supplies. RFID advancement using radio waves can be utilized to scrutinize and get information taken care of on a mark attached to a thing, for instance, clinical administrations supplies. Before IR 4.0, the route toward following stock incorporated a lot of troublesome work. Noticing stock truly is a significant test. One huge clarification is that clinical facilities purchase a combination of things from suppliers and store a lot of things on the spot for express techniques. Second, things' pass dates ought to be solidly noticed, while the inadequacy of stock can incite a lot of time spent on coordinating stock checks. Therefore, RFID marking advancement close by IIoT is being proposed to be used for stock and SCM the heads in clinical consideration. Better arranged RFID systems with negligible exertion are required to grow affirmation of RFID in clinical administrations.

Keywords: Smart asset tracking, RFID, healthcare, IIoT, SCM

Email: somyagoyal1988@gmail.com

Uzzal Sharma, Parma Nand, Jyotir Moy Chatterjee, Vishal Jain, Noor Zaman Jhanjhi and R. Sujatha (eds.)
Cyber-Physical Systems: Foundations and Techniques, (209–228) © 2022 Scrivener Publishing LLC

9.1   Introduction

The rising Industry 4.0 finds application in the healthcare sector. The implementation of IoT technology allows using radio-frequency identification (RFID) for smart inventory management and SCM in healthcare organizations [1, 2]. RFID enables real-time traceability, identification, and location data for resources. RFID & IoT find application in cost-effective tracking of objects in hospitals. Radio frequency identification identifies the location of inventory assets using radio-frequency electromagnetic fields. The hospital items are tagged with special RFID tags [3]. RFID readers are installed in hospital corridors, rooms, and in the premises. IoT plays a crucial part for carrying the data which is collected by RFID readers.

9.1.1   RFID and IoT for Smart Inventory Management

IoT enabled smart inventory management and SCM work as explained below (as in Figure 9.1) with three major components namely RFID tags, RFID reader and IoT infrastructure. Hospital inventory assets are equipped with tags. RFID tags are attached to the boxes containing medicines, etc. RFID readers are installed in the hospital rooms and corridors to send the info about the location of assets. A doctor or assistant to the doctor tracks the assets with a mobile or web app (see Figure 9.2). Whenever something is desired, the IoT system locates the item and informs the user [4]. Radio Frequency Identification (RFID) is finding applications in hospital inventory management and SCM. It allows the medical staff to locate and manage the medical devices and material quickly and easily [5]. It allows tracking the medical devices, medicines, and other material goods in warehouses of hospitals during the shipping from vendor and storage in warehouse.

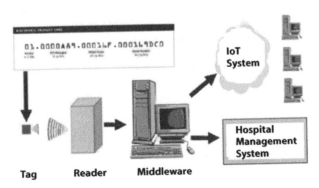

Figure 9.1 Basic components of RFID based system.

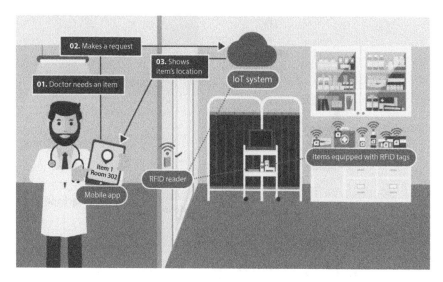

Figure 9.2 IoT and RFID for hospital inventory control.

Nowadays, where nearby progression, thriving is the fundamental issue for a solid life, it additionally has gotten urgent to administrate and deal with the clinical advantages industry, especially keeping up the patient history, stock record, workers record, and different other has become a dreary and complex undertaking. IoT gives the hard and fast one-time exhaustive arrangement all around coordinated, and careful methodology for exact control of managerial cycles RFID based clinical office the heads framework. In the present authentic world, the clinical thought industry is persistently looking for the assistance of the farthest down the line advancement to ad lib their working environments and holds a certifiable edge to their flourishing associations. Healthcare 4.0 allows the unfathomably gainful, deliberate, current yet easy to use clinical focus the board application with RFID.

Presently, the utilization and advantages of RFID have been investigated in the medical care area [6]. RFID is able to catch information naturally. In contrast with scanner tag filtering, it doesn't need line-of-sight with reader. A RFID framework regularly comprises of a tag, reader, and a product application. Information gathered from the reader is then to a data set introduced on a worker. Clients would then be able to recover the information utilizing an application introduced on the worker [7]. The entire working is based on the RFID tag and RFID reader pair, the backend server which is rich of all RFID enabled assets' data and the interconnecting IoT network support as shown in Figure 9.3.

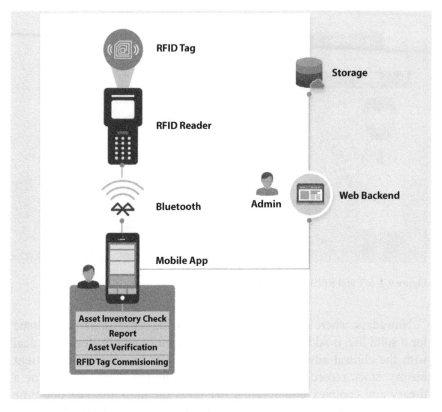

Figure 9.3 Working principle of RFID enabled tracking.

The point of this investigation is to investigate the advantages and boundaries of actualizing RFID innovation in the medical care area. The chapter is organized as follows. Section 9.2 discusses the promising benefits and barriers in the implementation of IoT based RFID inventory control and SCM in healthcare industry. Section 9.3 brings case studies where RFID has implemented for inventory management. Section 9.4 discusses the proposed methodology for hospital management using RFID. Finally, the work is concluded with remarks on future scope in Section 9.5.

9.2 Benefits and Barriers in Implementation of RFID

This section brings into the light the benefits and barriers in the implementation of RFID.

9.2.1   Benefits

The IoT with RFID extends the ability to locate the hospital inventory items; to gather information about medical material, medicine, devices and helps the entire hospital administration in multiple ways [8].

9.2.1.1   Routine Automation

Automation replaces manual asset tracking and avoids slow human speed, errors, extra paperwork.

9.2.1.1.1   Drug Supply Automation

If a specific medication is about to vanish, then an IoT enabled system can automatically order for the same. It is shown with the help of flow diagram in Figure 9.4. In the figure, the transfer of medicines is shown from Hospital B to Hospital A. It is clear that Hospital A is running short of some medicines, which are surplus with Hospital B. Hence, Hospital B sells automatically to Hospital A without hassle with the help of RFID

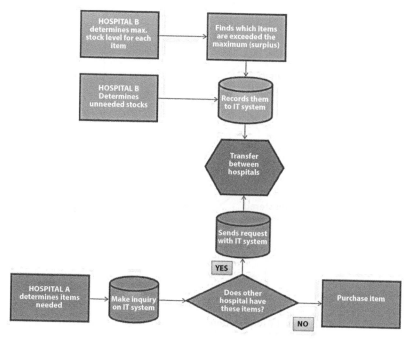

Figure 9.4 Automation of drug-supply.

enabled smart inventory management. In this way, the wastage of drug can be controlled and simultaneously the need of requiring can be satisfied.

9.2.1.1.2 Equipment Utilization Report Generation

This relates to how different departments are utilizing hospital items can be reported in order to identify shortage of assets or underrated assets.

9.2.1.1.3 Automated Attendance Monitoring

The entire staff of hospital can be given RFID enabled ID cards, with which their personal and work details can be stored in more effective way. The ID card can also be used for automated attendance marking system. It helps to save time in making and fetching the attendance of individual employee. It also enhances the effectiveness of payroll system (as in Figure 9.5).

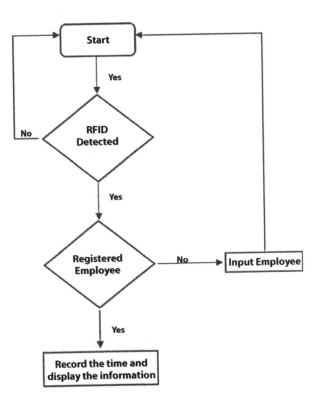

Figure 9.5 Automated employee attendance.

9.2.1.2 Improvement in the Visibility of Assets and Quick Availability

Health-workers spend most of their time looking for necessary items. With the IoT based system, the localization of devices and equipment becomes easier and fast, ultimately reduces the overall search and access time, especially if the assets do belong to different teams and departments. It speeds up and maintains the quality of hospital inventory management. Ting *et al.* [9] deployed RFID to generate automated warning signal in case IV fluid level falls below a threshold. It demonstrates that quick action is desirable in healthcare work and time cannot be wasted in searching for the assets or passing the information.

9.2.1.3 SCM-Business Benefits

RFID labels empower ongoing correspondence and keen SCM with RFID assists with improving the business estimation of clinic. Gigantic number of stock things are kept put away in emergency clinic working rooms. It is vital for monitor acquisition of things and clear perceivability is alluring in the inventory network. It assists with decreasing the unapproved stock. Continuous following of products all through the store network is the primary advantage of RFID innovation. Ongoing following of conveyance time empowers Just-in-Time (JIT) assembling and retailing. JIT encourages emergency clinic buying gatherings to settle on essential choices [10]. The advantages incorporate improved following of high-esteem things/

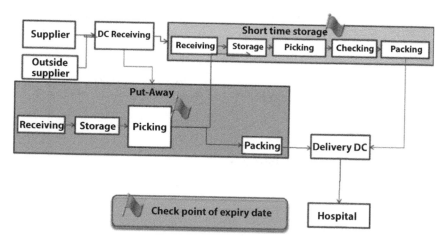

Figure 9.6 Automation of SCM in Healthcare 4.0.

resources, improved creation arranging and keen reviews for compelling planning, stock perceivability, exactness, and productivity at each stage, decreased shrinkage and transportation mistakes in the store network, and innovation principles which drive down expenses through economies of scale demonstrated in Figure 9.6.

9.2.1.4   Automated Lost and Found

Every device or item is installed with RFID tag, in this situation if an item leaves some designated area without authorization then an automated notification can be generated for hospital security system regarding the potential lost and found case. The complete flow chart is given in Figure 9.7. All the equipment needs to be tagged with RFIDs. The billing system is

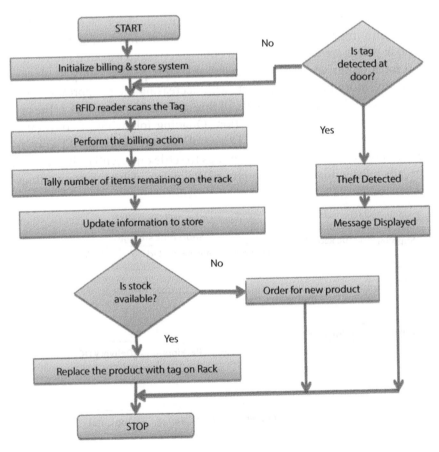

Figure 9.7 Working of automated theft detection system.

based on RFID reader. If the billing counter detects the appropriate RFID, then billing is done. If the tag is detected at the door, then theft will be detected. In this way, the security of equipment and sensitive reports can be achieved with RFIDs.

9.2.1.5 Smart Investment on Inventory

Perishable inventory storage and management is very expensive in healthcare industry. The product can be dangerous to use, after the expiration date. In such situation, a smart centralized distribution center for hospital with multiple vendors in connection is desirable. Automated reports on hospital autilization helps to reduce the expenses on not required equipment the rental cost or, the purchase cost, and maintenance cost [11].

9.2.1.6 Automated Patient Tracking

The patients can be tracked using RFIDs which allow maintaining all their records updated and easily accessible to the nurse/doctors for treatment purposes. The patients are provided with RFID enable wrist bands, by which their location is updated to the cloud constantly, whenever required can be accessed in quick way via apps by the authorized staff of the hospital. This scenario is depicted in Figure 9.8.

Figure 9.8 Tracking patients using RFIDs.

9.2.2   Barriers

IoT enabled RFID has proven promising in inventory management and SCM for healthcare industry, but still it faces some barriers in implementation of RFID based system [12].

9.2.2.1   *RFID May Interfere With Medical Activities*

RFID tags work using microwaves and may interfere with the functionality of medical devices like pacemakers. Passive tags may not influence medical processes, but active tags emit radio waves and hence, can interfere with radiology machines.

9.2.2.2   *Extra Maintenance for RFID Tags*

Hospital inventory items need sensitization on regular basis, and disinfection which may destroy RFID tags. Hence, extra maintenance is required.

9.2.2.3   *Expense Overhead*

Expenses increase due to heavy investment in tags and IoT infrastructure. Costs overhead involve maintenance cost and training costs.

9.2.2.4   *Interoperability Issues*

Hardware and software platforms for IoT implementation have not been standardized. It may cause interoperability issues.

9.2.2.5   *Security Issues*

Unauthorized access to the digital information carried by the IoT systems may cause misuse, or disclosure of sensitive information. There may be third-party unauthorized interception of the tag information [13].

These are the benefits and barriers in the implementation of IoT based inventory and SCM managements. In the next section, the case studies of IoT based RFID for inventory management of hospitals are discussed.

9.3   IoT-Based Inventory Management—Case Studies

This segment brings the contextual investigations of execution of IoT based stock control and SCM at emergency clinics. Tsai *et al.* [14] detailed a RFID framework executed in clinic for following the clinical gear with ensured quick access and successful control and better upkeep. A shrewd application is interface to collaborate with the framework. It fundamentally diminished the entrance time and quest time for hardware. Emergency clinic stock administration has become key segment to adapt to expanding medical services costs in industrialized nations [15].

BJC HealthCare (BJC.org) [16] implementing RFID based Smart Inventory control system at Progress West Hospital. The distribution centre is installed with RFID based IoT technology to automate the SCM of Medical products—both the reception and stocking of products—are installed with RFID tags. The reported success results are tabulated as Table 9.1.

RFID and IoT help to leave blunder inclined manual emergency clinic resource the executives behind making the cycle more steady and successful. Robotized resource following is significant not exclusively to clinical hardware yet additionally to an extraordinary assortment of the stock utilized by each medical clinic like hand-gloves, tissues or towels, coverings, etc. [17].

The rundown of operational and business benefits is somewhat great:

- localizing medical services hardware dissipated across various offices and even emergency clinics.
- Reducing medical clinic stock volumes and improving resource accessibility.
- Identifying shaky areas in medical clinic measures.
- Reducing and forestalling resource misfortune and burglary.
- Improving interests in new resources.

It additionally has the right to specify that shrewd resource following requirements a comparing foundation—hardware for RFID following and

Table 9.1 Success results of implementing IoT inventory system at BJC healthcare.

S.n.	Particular	Value
1.	Reduction in Direct inventory	23%
2.	Reduction in Consigned inventory	10%
3.	Additional inventory reduction	32%
4.	Production expiration	<1%
5.	Inventory holding cost reduction	$7,800
6.	Freight savings (annualized)	$49,000
7.	Bulk buy savings (one-time)	$2.1 million

a protected IoT framework. The framework gives information gathering, putting away, preparing and examination (counting progressed investigation) and empowers medical clinic staff and organization to lead resource the board with exceptional portable and web applications.

9.4   Proposed Model for RFID-Based Hospital Management

The proposed model for managing hospitals in hi-tech way using RFID tracking is automation of hospital management system using RFID and IoT. The complete solution to hospital management is proposed to be provided including pharmacy, inventory, patients, equipment and other major arcade (see Figure 9.9).

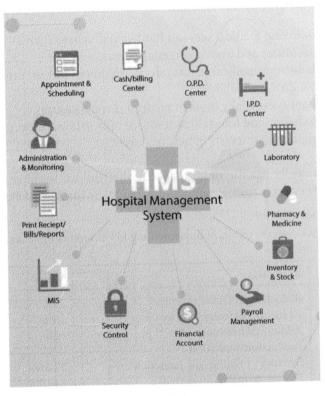

Figure 9.9 Automated complete solution to manage hospital.

Clinical center associations across the world are finding reasonable ways to deal with decrease the overall load of the administrative division of the clinical consideration industry so they can focus in on fundamental expecting the progression of their organizations while keeping a track on various limits and undertakings. The proposed architecture is layered comprising of five layers (see Figure 9.10). The bottom layer is data capturing layers. The middle layer is data processing layer. The top two layers are dedicated to the workflow and application.

The bottom layer comprises of RFID tags and readers. The processing layer gathers and processes the data for usage. The top layers enable the access to the system using web application or mobile applications.

To provide total solution to the managerial tasks at hospitals, RFID and IoT [19, 20] are devoted to revolution in healthcare 4.0. The basic working principle of RFID and IoT is given in Figure 9.11. The objects are tagged with RFIDs, readers are installed at proper places, and reported data is made available at backend. At the backend, server analyses the data and respond to the queries raised by applications or users.

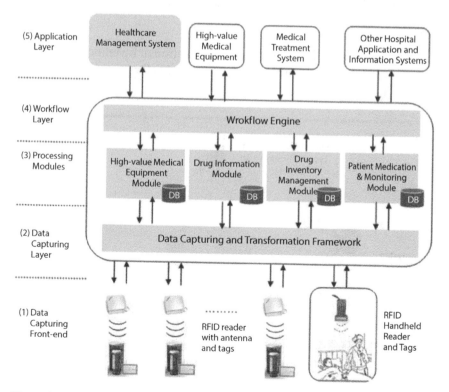

Figure 9.10 Architecture of proposed model.

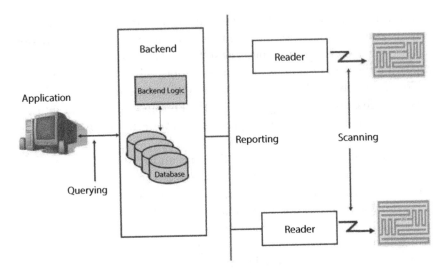

Figure 9.11 Working principle of proposed model.

Supported Features by the Proposed solution to Hospital management system:

- The proposed solution allows automation of Inventory management and Pharmacy management in all respects (shown in Figure 9.12).

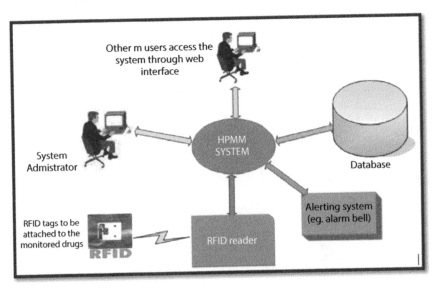

Figure 9.12 Automation of inventory and pharmacy management.

- Automation of payroll management
- Tracking of Patients and their information automatically.
- Maintaining the patients record like arrival, treatment, assigned doctors, prescriptions, billing info easily and automatically (shown in Figure 9.13).

Patients are most important entity in the hospital management. It is achieved using RFID enabled wrist band and IoT infrastructure. RFID are installed to store all the details of patients, including the medical history, arrival time, medications, prescriptions, and all essential information can be readily available via application to the authorized users.

- Tracking and identification of all entities including visitors, patients, objects, drugs, equipment, specimens, blood and other test samples (shown in Figure 9.14).

In this way, the proposed system provides all in one feature to the hospital management. For the sake of simplicity in implementation, the system is divided into three modules as shown in Figure 9.15. The first module comprises of RFID tags and readers at physical level. The second module entails the middleware including the data level services and network level services. It also includes the central database sub-module. The third module generates responses to any action, or any query made by application or by the user.

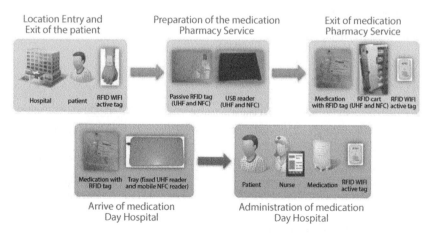

Figure 9.13 Tracking of Patients and Localization using RFIDs.

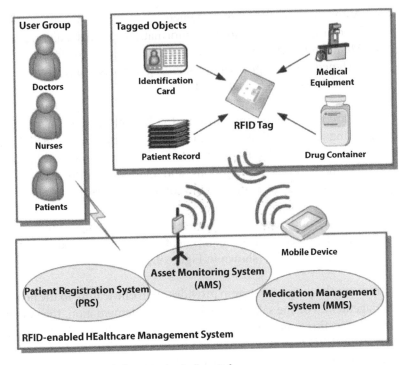

Figure 9.14 Tracking of all entities in the hospital.

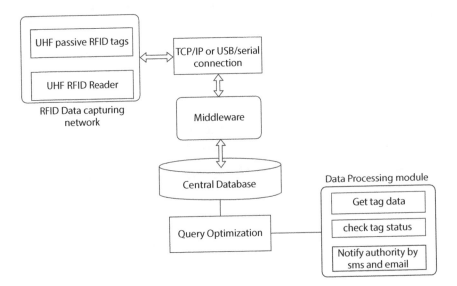

Figure 9.15 Modules in proposed system.

The proposed model is complete solution to all essential requirements of hospital management. The next section concludes the study with special references to the future prospects of this work.

9.5   Conclusion and Future Scope

This work recognizes the favorable circumstances and limits in the utilization of IoT based stock control and SCM for clinical center industry taking in idea the critical relevant examinations. It is recognized that the cost of clinical idea is rapidly raising and with high-regard resources standard it is crucial to manage supplies. Restricting waste through better stock after may widen commitment and supply capacity. RFID applications used to manage clinical associations supplies may help balance cost because of waste. Further assessment concerning the cost of utilization and potential undertaking records will help relationship with improving perspective on RFID potential. A couple of concerns are related to security and affirmation which are also ought to have been explored. RFID gathering needs broad site evaluation and testing going before use. The potential for radio intermittent impediment by current clinical stuff can occur and have unsettling effect the advancement of data information. There are distinctive express challenges that have been recorded including interface and relentlessness issues reliant on the environment in which the plan is sorted it out. Subsequently, get-together of RFID progression needs broad testing of possible radio intermittent impedance to current clinical equipment.

Considering the current making open, significant tendencies and squares to RFID affirmation were discussed. Great conditions recollected refreshes for efficiencies in patient thought and patient flourishing, improvements in patient and asset following, and expanded provider satisfaction. Checks included money related, explicit, definitive, insurance, and security challenges. Procedures to beat checks should focus in on wide money related appraisal of threat benefits, cautious testing of movement before use, arranging of staff on progress going before execution, and attestation of the requirement for fitting utilization of security attempts. RFID progression can improve profitability and security of patient thought which has positive repercussions for nursing practice. Further assessment is needed in RFID security, radio intermittent squares, and cost-reasonableness [18].

References

1. Smith, A.D., RFID Applications in Healthcare Systems From an Operational Perspective. *IJSS*, *6*, 2, 1–28, 2019.
2. Goyal, S., Bhatia, P.K., Parashar, A., Cloud-Assisted IoT-Enabled Smoke Monitoring System (e-Nose) Using Machine Learning Techniques, in: *Smart Systems and IoT: Innovations in Computing. Smart Innovation, Systems and Technologies*, vol. 141, pp. 743–754, Springer, Singapore, 2020, https://doi.org/10.1007/978-981-13-8406-6_70.
3. Carmen León-Araujo, M., Gómez-Inhiesto, E., Acaiturri-Ayesta, M.T., Implementation and Evaluation of a RFID Smart Cabinet to Improve Traceability and the Efficient Consumption of High Cost Medical Supplies in a Large Hospital. *J. Med. Syst.*, *43*, 6, 178, 2019.
4. Gómez, F.S., Escobar, N.S., Vázquez, J., RFID+ Wi-fi system to control the location of biomedical equipment within hospital areas and linked to an intelligent inventory. *Health Technol.*, *10*, 2, 479–483, 2020.
5. Tsai, M.H., Pan, C.S., Wang, C.W., Chen, J.M., Kuo, C.B., RFID medical equipment tracking system based on a location-based service technique. *J. Med. Biol. Eng.*, *39*, 1, 163–169, 2019.
6. Camacho-Cogollo, J.E., Bonet, I., Iadanza, E., RFID technology in healthcare, in: *Clinical Engineering Handbook*, pp. 33–41, Academic Press, 2020. Copyright © 2020 Elsevier Inc.
7. Seol, S., Lee, E.-K., Kim, W., Indoor mobile object tracking using RFID. *Futur. Gener. Comput. Syst.*, *76*, 443–451, 2017.
8. Paaske, S., Bauer, A., Moser, T., Seckman, C., The Benefits and Barriers to RFID Technology in Healthcare. *Online J. Nurs. Inform. (OJNI)*, *21*, 2, 1–17, 2017.
9. Ting, S.H., Wu, C.K., Luo, C.H., Design of dual mode RFID antenna for inventory management and IV fluid level warning system. *Int. J. Antennas Propag.*, 2017, 1–7, 2017.
10. Iannone, R., Lambiase, A., Miranda, S., Riemma, S., Sarno, D., Cost savings in hospital materials management: look-back versus look-ahead inventory policies. *Int. J. Serv. Oper. Manage.*, *22*, 1, 60–85, 2015.
11. Coustasse, A., Meadows, P., Hall, R., Hibner, T., Deslich, S., Utilizing radio frequency identification technology to improve safety and management of blood bank supply chains. *Telemed. e-Health*, *21*, 11, 938–945, 2015.
12. Wamba, S.F., Anand, A., Carter, L., A literature review of RFID-enabled healthcare, applications and issues. *Int. J. Inf. Manage.*, *33*, 5, 875–891, 2013.
13. Rosenbaum, B.P., Radio Frequency Identification (RFID) in healthcare: Privacy and security concerns limiting adoption. *J. Med. Syst.*, *38*, 3, 1–6, 2014.
14. Tsai, M.-H., Pan, C.-S., Wang, C.-W., Chen, J.-M., Kuo, C.-B., RFID medical equipment tracking system based on a location-based service technique. *J. Med. Biol. Eng.*, *39*, 163, 2019. https://doi.org/10.1007/s40846-018-0446-2.

15. Volland, J., Fügener, A., Schoenfelder, J., Brunner, J.O., Material logistics in hospitals: A literature review. *Omega*, 69, 82–101, 2017.

16. https://www.cardinalhealth.com/content/dam/corp/web/documents/case-study/cardinal-health-changing-the-game-case-study.pdf (accessed on 10 January 2021).

17. Ahmmad, K. and Peebles, D., Inventory management applications for healthcare supply chains. *Int. J. Supply Chain Manage.*, 6, 3, 1–7, 2017.

18. Chong, A.Y., Liu, M.J., Luo, J., Keng-Boon, O., Predicting RFID adoption in healthcare supply chain from the perspectives of users. *Int. J. Prod. Econ.*, 159, 66–75, 2017. Retrieved March 25, 2016.

19. Almulhim, M., Islam, N., Zaman, N., A lightweight and secure authentication scheme for IoT based e-health applications. *IJCSNS*, 19, 1, 107–120, 2019.

20. Kumar, A., Payal, M., Dixit, P., Chatterjee, J.M., Framework for realization of green smart cities through the Internet of Things (IoT), in: *Trends in Cloud-Based IoT*, pp. 85–111, 2020.

10

A Systematic Study of Security of Industrial IoT

Ravi Gedam* and Surendra Rahamatkar†

Amity University Chhattisgarh, Raipur, India

Abstract

During the Industry 4.0 era, Internet-of-Things (IoT) played the leading role in the first industrial revolution, comparable to steam energy. IoT offers the possibility to merge the connection between machine-to-machine (M2M) and Realtime manufacturing data collection. The implementation of IoT in the industry therefore improves dynamic optimization, control and decision-making powered by data. Domain suffered, however, due to interoperability problems. In the absence of communication standards, large numbers of IoT devices link to the Internet. The heterogeneity in IoT ranges from high to low (device connectivity, network connectivity, communication protocols) (services, applications, and platforms). In order to understand the interoperability problems and current solutions to help IoT's smart manufacturing, the project examines the current state of the industrial IoT (IIoT) ecosystem. On the basis of a literary analysis, interoperability problems at IIoT were divided into four levels: technical, syntactic, semanticized and organization. With regard to each interoperability standard, existing interoperability solutions have been grouped and evaluated. In the sense of promoting industrial interoperability, nine reference architectures have been compared. The study identified the patterns and challenges of interoperability research.

Keywords: Industrial IoT, smart manufacturing, Industry 4.0, interoperability

---

**Corresponding author*: gedam.hemraj@s.amity.edu
†*Corresponding author*: srahamatkar@rpr.amity.edu

Uzzal Sharma, Parma Nand, Jyotir Moy Chatterjee, Vishal Jain, Noor Zaman Jhanjhi and R. Sujatha (eds.)
Cyber-Physical Systems: Foundations and Techniques, (229–256) © 2022 Scrivener Publishing LLC

10.1   Introduction

During the last decade, numerous smart physical objects (so called "things") have been connected and communicate through the internet and form the global network of connected devices called the Internet of Things (IoT). According to Cisco's forecast, 500 billion devices are expected to be connected to the Internet by 2030 [1]. The smart physical devices usually contain sensors 1that can sense, collect, and communicate data, and/or actuators that can react to internal and external control signals. The features of connected devices enable IoT applications to monitor, aggregate, analyze, deliver business insights, increase efficiency, and provide more informed decisions. The IoT technologies are permeating ubiquitously in a wide range of applications in multiple domains and revolutionizing almost all aspects of society, such as healthcare, agriculture, transportation, weather forecasting, smart home and smart city, etc. For industry, IoT [34, 35] provides the potential to combine machine-to-machine (M2M) interaction, real time data collection, and big data analyzation within the field of manufacturing. This would further enhance dynamic optimization, control, and data-driven decision making [2].

A cyber-physical system (CPS) is a mechanical system where physical components (mechanical systems, electrical systems, human operators, etc.) and cyber components (communication, computation, control, etc.) are deeply intertwined, and different components interact with each other to exchange information [3]. There is tremendous adoption of CPSs in manufacturing industry, occasionally referred to as cyber-physical production system (CPPS). A CPPS usually consists of a physical shop-floor coupled with a digital twin, which uses the monitoring data collected from the shop-floor to build a digital replica as a "twin" of the physical shop-floor. Therefore, CPPS supports more informed decision making by combining the knowledge from both available physical shop floor conditions and big data analysis.

The concepts of IoT and CPS have distinct origins, with IoT mainly emerging from an information and communication technology (ICT) perspective, while CPS has primarily emerged from system engineering and control [4]. Despite their origins from different domains, there are overlaps between the concepts of IoT and CPS, since they both are concerned about connecting & interacting with the physical objects and with digital entities to realize functionality and to enhance performance. The industrial Internet of Things (IIoT) and CPS together are key enablers for accelerating the ongoing digital business transformation in the so called fourth

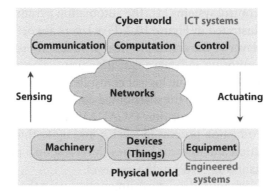

Figure 10.1 Components model showing a unified perspective of IoT and CPS.

industrial revolution (Industry 4.0) [2]. Figure 10.1 presents a unified perspective of IoT and CPS. The lower half of the figure represents the physical part of the IoT/CPS, which usually includes machinery, equipment, and smart devices. These devices capture the data about the physical state of the engineered system and send it via networks for further use. The upper half of the figure represents the virtual realm of the ICT systems, where the core functionality is communication, computation and control (3C). The data collected from various sources are fused and analysed to support overall decision making. Control decisions can be made, and actuating signals can be sent via networks to actuate effectors on the physical state. In another words, CPS/IoT aims to integrate the physical world with the digital world by using Internet as media to communicate and exchange information.

10.2   Overview of Industrial Internet of Things (Smart Manufacturing)

Modern industrial manufacturing has experienced three revolutions so far. Dating back to late 18th century, the use of steam power and waterpower enabled the transition from traditional hand production to mechanized manufacturing factories. The second revolution leads a phase of rapid industrialization in mass manufacturing using assembly lines in early 20th century. The third industrial revolution enables automation and was powered by the development of electronics and information technology in the 1970s. Today's manufacturing automation systems are mainly shaped during the third industrial revolution. The hierarchical ISA-95 architecture is currently the *de facto* architectural style for building industrial production and control systems [4]. The automation pyramid of the ISA-95 architecture is illustrated in Figure 10.2. Five layers are defined by ISA-95, from the lowest layer of the actual physical production process to the first layer of status monitoring and data acquisition using sensors/actuators and controlling with programmable logical controller (PLC). The information collected from level 1 goes to the distributed control system (DCS), supervisory control and data acquisition (SCADA) which realize supervisory control of the production process in level 2, and up to third level of manufacturing execution and towards business level resource planning (enterprise resource planning - ERP) in the top level.

In 2011, the Germany federal government first used the term "Industrie 4.0" in a technical strategy to promote the computerization of traditional industries, such as manufacturing. Subsequently, the term "Industry 4.0" is usually used to describe the ongoing fourth industrial revolution. Similar to Germany's "Industrie 4.0" which promoted the digitalization revolution in Europe, "smart manufacturing" is yet another term with a similar essence. This latter term was introduced by the United States National Institute of Standards and Technology (NIST). Despite the dissimilar terms used by different initiatives from several nations, all the terms have a similar essence of supporting the transition to smart manufacturing and can be all described under the umbrella of the fourth industrial revolution. To simplify the usage of different terminologies, this project uses "Industry 4.0" and "smart manufacturing" to refer to the current worldwide digitalization revolution in manufacturing industry.

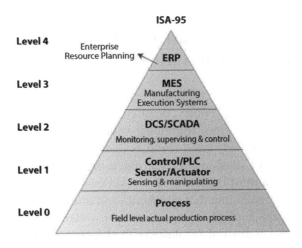

Figure 10.2 The traditional automation hierarchy of ISA-95.

Smart manufacturing includes a set of technologies, among which the major components are IoT, CPS, cloud computing, fog computing, and machine learning. As previously mentioned, the technological foundation of smart manufacturing is IoT and CPS, which together aim to integrate the physical world with the digital world by enabling seamlessly information exchange and communication through the network infrastructure. The adoption of IoT and CPS concepts in manufacturing has evolved control systems from their classic centralized hierarchy to a more open decentralized approach with the possibility of information exchange between multiple applications and systems. To present an overview of smart manufacturing, several key terms and enabling technology will be introduced in the following subsection, with more detailed insight about de facto industrial communication standard OPC UA in Section 10.2.2.

10.2.1 Key Enablers in Industry 4.0

Over the last decades, a lot of new terms have emerged within Industry 4.0. As already mentioned in the previous sections, all these paradigms are built around the concept of CPS through digitalization and integration between engineered systems and ICT systems. In this section, some key terms and enabling technology in smart manufacturing are briefly introduced:

Cloud Manufacturing: Cloud manufacturing was first introduced in [34] by Xun Xu. It utilizes cloud computing and shifts the focus from production-oriented manufacturing towards service-oriented manufacturing. Cloud manufacturing can be defined as "a model for enabling ubiquitous, convenient, on-demand network access to a shared pool of configurable manufacturing resources (e.g., manufacturing software tools, manufacturing equipment, and manufacturing capabilities) that can be rapidly provisioned and released with minimal management effort or service provider interaction".

Predictive Maintenance: Maintenance of machine components and manufacturing systems are usually based on diagnosis and prognosis. Diagnosis relates to the detection and identification of fault, while prognosis refers to the prediction of possible failures or forecasting of likely outcomes. In the context of manufacturing, prognosis is realized by calculating the remaining useful life (RUL) of machine tools or systems. Predictive maintenance (or condition-based maintenance) refers to maintenance

Process: Process before a detected fault and includes the steps of data acquisition, data processing, and maintenance decision making. Predictive maintenance is enabled by cloud manufacturing and massive data analysis.

According to Mourtzis and Vlachou, maintenance accounts for as much as 60 to 70% of a production lifecycle's total costs. Comparing to traditional periodically performed scheduled maintenance or corrective maintenance after detection of a fault, predictive maintenance significantly increases product quality, system safety, and maintenance efficiency while minimizing machinery downtime and possible loss due to equipment or system failures.

Fog/Edge Computing: To expand the capabilities of cloud computing, fog computing (also known as edge computing) was introduced as a distributed architecture that bridges the connected things to the cloud. Fog computing moves the storage, computation, and networking services from the cloud of the edge of the network. In the context of smart manufacturing, fog computing allows flexibility to be located at different levels. The benefits of adopting fog computing in manufacturing include many aspects. For example, fog nodes support real-time services for latency-sensitive applications by storing data close to the data sources. By storing data locally, fog computing can also enhance security and reduce network loads compared to sending everything directly to the cloud. Fog computing can also enhance data fusion and advanced analytics by sharing computational power at the network's edge.

10.2.2   OPC Unified Architecture (OPC UA)

Open Platform Communications Unified Architecture (OPC UA) is a data exchange protocol designed for manufacturing and automation communications. It was introduced as a successor of the classic Object Linking and Embedding (OLE) for Process Control (OPC) model, which is a client/server communication model first designed in 1996 by Microsoft as a Microsoft Windows COM/DCOM (Distributed Component Object Model) bounding to standardize communication between software components in industrial environment. The OPC classic specifications, namely OPC Data Access (OPC DA), OPC Alarms &Events (OPC AE), and OPC Historical Data Access (OPC HDA), provide separate definitions for accessing process data, alarms and events, and historical data [5]. IT spread widely in the automation industry through the past decades.

As the technology evolves, the OPC foundation introduced platform independent OPC UA Service-Oriented Architecture (SOA) a decade ago. OPC UA does not rely on Microsoft OLE nor DCOM technology as classic OPC does. Therefore, OPC UA is operating system independent and hardware platform independent. It is designed to be backward compatible with OPC classic specifications yet offers more capabilities.

The OPC UA specifications are layered and independent of the underlying transport protocols and computing technology, which opens the possibilities of mapping to future technologies. Figure 10.3 presents the OPC UA stack. As for transport layer, OPC UA TCP, SOAP/HTTP, OPC UA HTTPS, and Web Sockets are supported for the users to choose from. To provide a secure channel layer, several security protocols can be personalized to secure a communication channel to realize application level security. Three data encodings are defined: OPC UA Binary, OPC UA XML, and OPC UA JSON.

The OPC UA system is based on the client–server architecture. Applications use the OPC UA Client API and/or Server Application Programming Interface (API) to exchange messages. The client/server API handles the request and response messages between the servers and clients. It isolates the OPC UA application code from the underlying communication entity. In the most recent OPC UA specifications, the OPC UA PubSub model has been added – and supports either a broker mode or a brokerless mode in order to support message exchange in several scenarios that do not require the system components to acknowledge each other.

In OPC UA, address space provides a standard way for servers to represent objects to clients. In address space, every entity is represented as a node. OPC UA defines eight non-extensible node classes: Object, Variable, Method, View, ObjectType, VariableType, ReferenceType, and dataType. A node is uniquely identified by a NodeId and is described by a set of attributes and connected to other nodes by references.

Security is a major concern of OPC UA. A suite of controls is provided to address security at different levels. Encryption and OPC UA provides

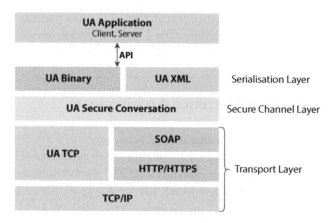

Figure 10.3 OPC UA stack overview.

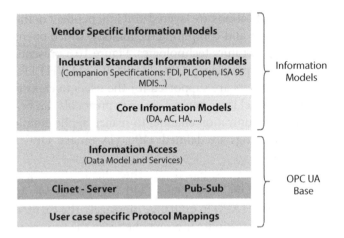

Figure 10.4 OPC UA information modeling framework.

a security model where security settings can be configured by the user to meet different security requirements. Encryption and signatures assure integrity and confidentiality at the transport layer. The security mechanism of the communication layer is to establish a secure channel utilizing X.509 to provide application layer authentication. The application layer manages the authorization and authentication of the servers and clients.

Another important feature of OPC UA is that it offers an information model to represent structure, behavior, and semantics. The multi-lever information modeling framework of OPC UA is shown in Figure 10.4. The OPC classic specifications can be extended with industry standards. With close collaboration with many standards organizations from different domains (for example, MTconnect, ISA-95, PLCopen, IEC6186, …), the OPC Foundation created different OPC UA information models to support semantic interoperability. The UA information models can also be extended by users to create personalized vendor information models.

10.3   Industrial Reference Architecture

Numerous reference models and architectures have been developed to fulfil the highly dynamic requirements of IIoT. Most reputable ICT vendors have developed their own commercial cloud IoT platforms based on public cloud approach, to name a few: AWS IoT by Amazon, Azure IoT suit by Microsoft, Google Cloud IoT by Google, Prefix IIoT by GE Digital and Watson Internet of Things by IBM.

The following part of this section gives a summary of several popular emerging IoT frameworks for industrial applications. Note that the frameworks are presented in alphabetical order, hence there is no ranking.

10.3.1   Arrowgead

The EU Arrowhead project started in 2013 and recently continued as a part of the ongoing EU project called Productive 4.0. The resulting Arrowhead framework is a SOA based framework for building scalable and interoperable IoT-based automation systems. In Arrowhead, a service can be implemented to use a number of SOA protocols, such as MQTT, CoAP, XMPP and OPC UA.

Arrowhead features a local cloud approach as its key concept to provide core automation services in a protected manner. A minimal local cloud includes three mandatory systems: service registry and discovery system, orchestration system, and authentication and authorization system. These systems enable data exchange between two applications within a local cloud. To serve all the automation demands, simultaneously interactions between multiple clouds are required. The GateKeeper handles the communication between these local clouds. Additional automation systems and services are also available, such as plant description, QoS manager, event handler, and translation.

10.3.2   FIWARE

FIWARE is an open source framework of a set of standards for context data management to support the development of smart solutions beyond

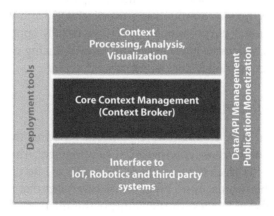

Figure 10.5 The FIWARE principle components.

IoT use cases. Figure 10.5 shows the principle components of FIWARE. The core feature of FIWARE is the handling and management of context information. The FIWARE Context Broker is the main component used to achieve this feature. Around this broker there is a suit of complementary FIWARE components available.

Next Generation Services Interface (NGSI) is a standardized API for RESTful interactions between the Context Broker and other components. The NGSI API defines a data model, a context data interface, and a context availability interface. The current specifications of FIWARE reference data models are NGSI-v2 and NGSI-LD. For IoT use cases, FIWARE describe a FIWARE I0T architecture, which consists of the Orion Context Broker (OCB) and IoT Agents. IoT Agents bridge between NGSI and typical IoT protocols, such as HTTP/MQTT, LWM2M, LoRaWAN, and OPC UA. The specifications of the FIWARE APIs and reference implementations of FIWARE components are publicly available for developers to use.

10.3.3   Industrial Internet Reference Architecture (IIRA)

IIRA is an open architecture published by Industrial Internet Consortium (IIC) for IIoT systems regardless of specific their domains. It has four viewpoints: Business, Usage, Functional, and Implementation. Three typical examples of architecture patterns are introduced: three-tier architecture pattern, gateway-mediated edge connectivity and management architecture pattern, and layered databus pattern. However, concrete open source implementations of this architecture are lacking. In their connectivity framework, DDS, OPC UA, MQTT, CoAP, and HTTP are the recommended connectivity standards. Among the standards, OPC UA is regarded as originated from the manufacturing industry while MQTT and CoAP are based on telecommunication vertical. DDS and Web service are regarded as general-purpose; hence, they are usually applied to multiple domains. IIRA addresses interoperability by introducing core gateways to connect the recommended core standards.

10.3.4   Kaa IoT Platform

Kaa is an open source middleware platform based in the US and it is designed for multipurpose enterprise IoT development. The concept of the Kaa platform is to break the features of the platform into different components, or in other words, into a range of microservices that are functionally packaged in Docker images. The flexibility of this microservice architecture helps the Kaa platform support plug and play when implementing different use cases; therefore, reducing development time and cost. The core features of Kaa include device management, communication, data collection, data visualization, and configuration management. Kaa adopts MQTT as its default protocol while also offering possibilities of future CoAP bindings. Kaa currently supports transport using plain MQTT, MQTTS, and MQTT over Websocket.

10.3.5   Open Connectivity Foundation (OCF)

OCF is an American international industry group promoting interoperability for industrial connectivity. The core specification is based on a RESTful architecture and adopts a specific transport protocol suite (CoAP over UDP over IPv6). OCF has a Concise binary object representation (CBOR) based on the JSON data model as the default encoding scheme.

An implementation of the OCF specification called IoTvity and a lightweight version IoTvity Lite are available [6]. The ancestor of IoTivity is another open source software framework called AllJoyn, which was initially designed for industrial lighting and smart homes. Detailed specifications of the OCF core and tutorials about IoTivity tools are available online for developers. With a fixed transport protocol suite and a rather fixed structure, OCF is more of a technical standard for a developer than a general-purpose industrial reference architecture.

10.3.6   Reference Architecture Model Industrie 4.0 (RAMI 4.0)

RAMI 4.0 is an SOA proposed by the German Platform Industrie 4.0 especially for smart manufacturing and CPS. This model consists of a three-dimensional map combining a six-layer architecture (namely asset, integration, communication, information, functional, and business) with the product life circle axis (namely development, maintenance usage, production, and maintenance usage) and the factory hierarchy axis (namely product, field device, control device, station, work centers, enterprise, and connected world).

RAMI 4.0 mainly serves as guidance for entrepreneurial and technical concerns in industry internet. RAMI 4.0 does not propose a detailed technical implementation but rather recommends standards for each layer with a focus on the manufacturing domain. Architecture alignment and cooperation between RAMI 4.0 and other similar frameworks (such as IIRA) are available.

10.3.7 ThingsBoard

ThingsBoard is another open source platform for data collection, processing and visualization for IoT solutions. It enables the developer to customize rich real-time IoT dashboards for data visualization and device remote control. The ThingsBoard Rule Engine allows user to create complex rule chains in order to process data and build event-based workflows that suit different use cases.

ThingsBoard Inc. is a Ukraine-based US corporation founded in 2016. The ThingsBoard IoT platform has gained popularity over the past few years. It supports connectivity via MQTT, CoAP, and HTTP. Integrations with OPC UA server, the SigFox backend, and the LoRaWAN backend are also available to convert payloads into the ThingsBoard format. Devices connecting to AWS IoT broker, IBM Waston IoT broker, and Azure Hub can also be accessed through ThingsBorad. ThingsBorad has been successfully applied in fleet tracking, smart metering, smart farming, and the smart energy domain.

10.3.8 ThingSpeak

ThingSpeak is an IoT analytic platform for data aggregation, data analysis, and data visualization from MathWorks. Its main features are advanced data analysis and visualization directly using MATLAB. ThingSpeak allows devices to update and receive update via MQTT API or REST APIs.

10.3.9 ThingWorx

ThingWorx is an IIoT platform designed by PTC Inc. for rapidly development of IoT solutions with adequate capability and flexibility. The ThingWorx platform offers a complete set of IIoT functionalities including connecting, building, analysis, management, and experience. ThingWorx proposed a data model defining three entities (including Things, Thing Template, and Thing Shapes) and four components (including Properties, Services, Events, and Subscriptions) to describe connected devices.

To connect devices with ThingWorx, the major connectivity methods are a REST API and Edge Micro Server. The ThingWorx Edge Micro Server is available as a binary executable for Linux and Windows. It establishes an always on bidirectional connection with the ThingWorx platform. For IoT devices that cannot run Edge Micro Server, there are MQTT and CoAP protocol adapters to communicate with native protocol devices and ThingsWorx. To integrate with existing infrastructures, ThingWorx offers IoT connectors to connect devices using AWS or Azure cloud. As an industry oriented IIoT platform, ThingWorx offers a suite of 150+ industrial device drivers to connect with multiple types of industrial equipment via Windows clients.

Notably, ThingWorx offers three pre-built manufacturing applications to help improve operational efficiency and productivity. These applications are role-based: Controls Advisor offers seamlessly connectivity with PLCs and assets via the OPC server; Asset Advisor provides real-time monitoring of asset status and health to improve maintenance efficiency; and Operator Advisor helps increase workforce productivity.

10.4 FIWARE Generic Enabler (FIWARE GE)

FIWARE is a project sponsored by the European Commission with ICT industry to accelerate the deployment of smart solutions in various domains as a part of their Future Internet programme.

As mentioned in Section 10.3.2, the core feature of FIWARE is context management. The Context Broker is the core and only mandatory component for developing any "Powered by FIWARE" solutions. Around the core context management, there is a rich suite of complementary FIWARE Generic Enabler (GEs) that can be added to build smart solutions, as shown in Figure 10.5. For example, in the catalogue of context processing, analysis, and visualization using, FIWARE GE Cosmos supports big data context analysis, Kurento supports real-time processing of media streams, Knowage offers business intelligence and data visualization, and FogFlow [8] can be used for building IoT edge computing networks. In the catalogue of context data/API management, publication and monetization, GEs such as Keyrock, Wilma, and AuthZForce PDP/PAP offers add-on security to a smart solution. FIWARE offers interfaces to connect to IoT devices, robotics, and third-party systems to gather context information or trigger actuations. For example, the IDAS GEs offers a wide range of IoT-agents with interfaces to the most used IoT protocols. Fast Real Time Publish-Subscribe (RTPS) is an incubated GE that helps interface with robotic systems.

The following subsections give details about the main components and key concepts of FIWARE GEs.

10.4.1 Core Context Management GE

To support smart solutions, the FIWARE provides means of produce, collect, publish and consume context information. The FIWARE core context management is based on OMA Next Generation Service Interface (OMA NGSI) specifications using NGSI-9 and NGSI-10 interfaces. The NGSI-10 interface is used for exchanging entities and attributes. The NGSI-9 interface is used for exchanging availability information about the entities and attributes.

The context information is characterized by entities with their attributes and the values of the attributes using the FIWARE context data model. FIWARE harmonized data models offer guidelines and predefined data models for several use cases (devices, alerts, point of interests, environment, key performance indicator, etc.). The FIWARE context data model is introduced in Section 10.4.2. Orion Context Broker (OCB) is an open source C++ implementation as part of FIWARE platform. OCB offers management of context information including updates, queries, registration and subscription. The Context Broker holds only the latest value of the entities and attributes. In order to store and get historical context information, other FIWARE GEs like QuantumLeap, Cygnus and Daraco can connect with OCB to generate context history and store historical data.

10.4.2   NGSI Context Data Model

The FIWARE NGSI context data model is defined in NGSIv2 Open API specifications. As summarized in Figure 10.6, NGSI data model consists of three major elements: entity, attribute, and metadata. Entities and attributes in NGSIv2 are represented by JSON Objects. An entity is the core element of NGSI context data model. An entity represents a physical or logical object (e.g., a sensor, a machine, a room, an alarm in a system, etc.). Each entity is uniquely identified by a combination of entity id and entity type. Entity type describes the type of the thing represented by the entity. For example, an entity with id "KistaObserved_001" could be of type "EnviromentObserved".

Context attributes describe the properties of a context entity. An entity can have multiple attributes. For example, "Temperature" and "Humidity" can be the attributes of the entity "KistaObserved_001". An attribute is characterized by its name, type, and value. The attribute type is the NGSI

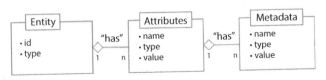

Figure 10.6 NGSIv2 data model conceptual diagram.

value type of the attribute value. NGSI has its own value type system for attribute values, so that NGSI value types are not the same as JSON types. Finally, attribute values contain the actual data of the attributes. Optional metadata can also be added to an attribute value when needed.

Context metadata describes the properties of the attribute. The context metadata is characterized by its name, type, and value similar to context attributes. Multiple metadata can be optionally included in the value part of an attribute. For example, the "Temperature" attribute can have "accuracy" and "timestamp" metadata within its value. The metadata type is a NGSI value of the type of the metadata value.

To further support linked context data, an extension of NGSIv2 called NGSI-LD is defined using JSON-LD by ETSI Context Information Management (CIM). It supports more complex context data management by using linked data. The UML representation of NGSIv2 data model is shown in Figure 10.7. A simple mapping script between NGSIv2 and NGSI-LD is offered by FIWARE Community.

The main elements of NGSI-LD are entity, property, and relationship. In the context of traditional NGSIv2, attributes and their value in NGSIv2 can been migrated to properties in NGSI-LD. Relationships establish associations between instances by linked data. The core class is entity. An entity can be the subject of properties and relationships while relationships and

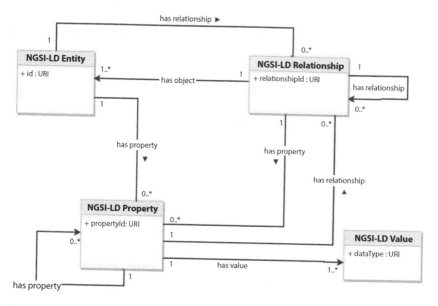

Figure 10.7 UML representation of NGSI-LD information model.

properties can be the subject of other relationships and properties (called "relationships-of relationships" or "properties-of-relationships" or "relationships-of-properties" or "properties-of properties"). All elements are identified with an ID and type by using Uniform Resource Identifiers (URIs).

10.4.3 IDAS IoT Agents

As mentioned in the previous section, one big challenge in IoT is to overcome the heterogeneity of devices talking different protocols. Instead of trying to solve the battle of protocols at the device level, FIWARE offers solutions which allow coexistence of standards. The simplest and most common FIWARE IoT use case scenario is represented in Figure 10.8. In this use case, the FIWARE Context Broker manages the context information. Applications and services can reach the Context Broker through its northbound interface using NGSI. On the southside of the Context Broker, different IDAS IoT Agents are connected using NGSI. These IoT Agents allow a group of devices to talk to the Context Broker while using their own native protocols, i.e., an IoT Agent translates an IoT specific protocol into or from the NGSI context information model. Currently, most widely used IoT protocols (such as HTTP, MQTT, and LoRaWAN) have ready to be used official FIWARE IoT agents. For unsupported protocols, costume agents can be built using a FIWARE IoT Agent Node.js module. By mapping different protocols into the NGSI context model, IoT agents offer interoperability without requiring the devices or gateways to support NGSI natively.

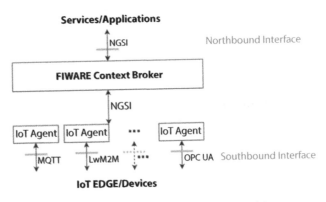

Figure 10.8 FIWARE IoT stack (Inspired by FIWARE Tour Guide).

In FIWARE, all IoT end nodes and resources are represented in the end as NGSI context entities and related attributes in the Context Broker. Third party users can access measurement data or send commands to devices via the Context Broker—regardless of the underlying devices or protocols. Figure 10.9 shows a sequence diagram of different interactions between IoT agents and the Context Broker. When a device connects to the IoT Agent,

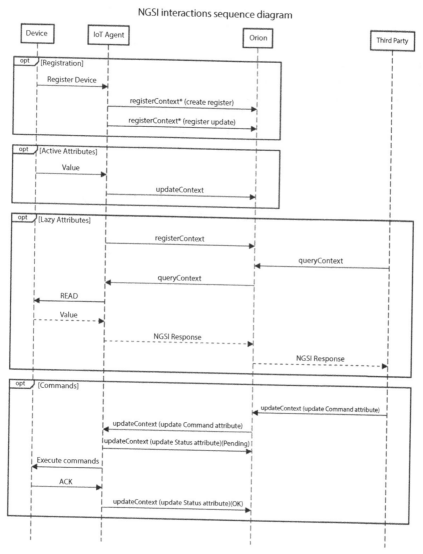

Figure 10.9 Device to NGSI mapping interactions.

it needs to be provisioned with the IoT agent. The IoT agent will register the device with the Context Broker. Measurements are readings from the sensors that can be grouped into active attributes and lazy attributes. Measurements are sent to the IoT Agent using the devices' native protocols and pass through the southbound to the Context Broker using the NGSI protocol. The transmission of active attributes is initiated by the device. The active attribute's value is sent to the IoT Agent and then updated to the Context Broker. Lazy attributes can be accessed by third-party users via a query from the northbound interface of the stack. Commands to actuate devices propagate from the north port of the Context Broker and flow south down to the north port of the IoT Agents using NGSI. Commands are translated to different protocols by IoT Agents and then sent to the device using the device's native protocols. Once the device performs the command, the device can send an acknowledgement (ACK) to the IoT Agent who will in turn update the device's status information in the Context Broker. Details of several IoT Agents used in this project will be illustrated in the following subsections.

10.4.3.1   IoT Agent-JSON

The IoT Agent for JSON based protocol provides the bridge between the Context Broker NGSI interface and JSON. It acts as a gateway for devise

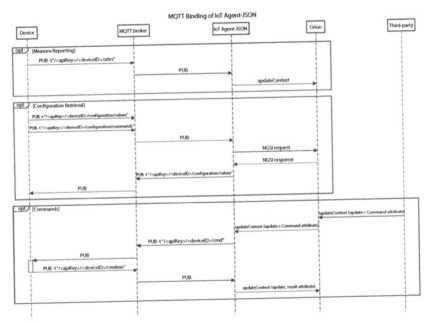

Figure 10.10 MQTT binding interactions of IoT Agent-JSON.

talking the JSON-based protocol (such as MQTT, HTTP and AMQP) and the NGSI Context Broker.

For communication using MQTT protocol, provision of the devices is needed in order to let the IoT Agent know which topic it should subscribe to. Each MQTT topic has the prefix following the form: /<apiKey>/<deviceID>/topicSpecificPart. Where the "apiKey" is an alphanumerical string used to group devices and "deviceID" is the ID identifies the device. The device id and API keys must be provisioned in the IoT Agent before sending any information. The "topicSpecificPart" is used where different topics are used to separate the different types of messages. For instance, MQTT interactions are grouped into three types: measure reporting, configuration retrieval, and commands. The MQTT interactions' sequence diagram is shown in Figure 10.10.

10.4.3.2   IoT Agent-OPC UA

As introduced in Section 10.2.2, OPC UA is a widely adopted by industry client–server protocol. On the factory floor, an OPC UA server is responsible for gathering data from machinery and making this data available to OPC UA clients. In the case of FIWARE, the IoT Agent-OPC UA acts as an OPC UA client and bridge between the OPC UA server and the Context Broker.

Before the IoT Agent-OPC UA can interact with the OPC UA server, it needs to become aware of the variables and methods that are available at the OPC UA server. Provisioning can be done by retrieving a configuration file via the REST API. The OPC UA variables will be mapped into NGSI active attributes and OPC UA methods will be configured as commands.

10.4.3.3   Context Provider

Apart from storing data in Orion's internal database, FIWARE context availability management can record entities and attributes sources via registration operation. The registration operation registers the context (entities and attributes) with context provider. A context provider is a URL that identifies the source of context data information. When Orion receives a context query or update with its targeted context unfindable locally. The Orion will look up its registration to check if there are any context providers registered for the targeted element. In other words, context provider should be registered before any context query or update request is made [33].

Figure 10.11 shows the requesting forwarding diagram of context provider. Firstly, the registration is made by a POST operation to /v2/registrations/specifying the context provider's URL, entity and attribute being

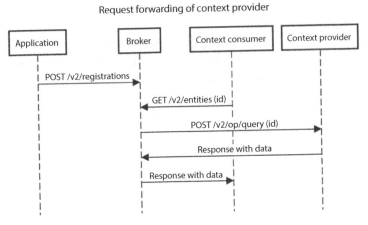

Figure 10.11 Request forwarding diagram of context provider.

provided. Then, the request forwarding is triggered by a GET request from context consumer. The Orion will forward a query via a POST /v2/op/ query to the context provider. The context provider will respond the Orion with payload. Lastly, The Orion will forward the response to the context consumer.

10.4.4   FIWARE for Smart Industry

With the efforts of FIWARE to breaking up the information silos and sim-plifying data management, FIWARE's reference architecture is expected to accelerate the digital transformation of manufacturing industries. Based on the existing industrial reference architectures (such as IIRA and RAMI 4.0), a FIWARE-powered smart industry reference architecture is pre-sented in Figure 10.12.

From a CPS shop floor, IDAS IoT Agents connect to sensors and machin-ery in the physical world. IoT Agents handle data via multiple IoT and industry protocols (such as MQTT, LwM2M, OPC-UA, oneM2M, etc.). Fast RTPS works as middleware in robot operating systems 2 (ROS2) and offers interface for robotic systems [9]. There are also other incubated sys-tem adapters that are under development that can offer additional connec-tivity alternatives from the physical shop floor to the information cloud. An example of such an alternative is FIROS which works as a translator between ROS and the cloud. It transforms ROS messages into NGSIv2 and vice versa [11].

The FIWARE OCB integrates the data coming from machinery, sensors, robotic systems, coordinate-measurement machine (CMM) systems with

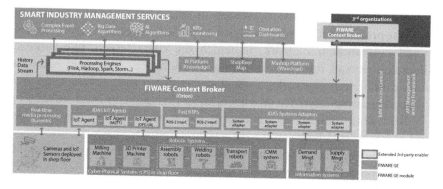

Figure 10.12 A reference architecture for smart industry powered by FIWARE.

management information from information systems; therefore, breaking the previous information silos. Historical data can be processed using processing engines (such as Flink, Hadoop, or Spark) and be fed to advanced AI, big data analysis, and complex event processing services to deliver more valuable insights. Knowage enables KPI monitoring and other business intelligence functions. Operational dashboards can be created using FIWARE GE WireCloud mashup platform. A FIWARE OCB can also integrate with another OCB or connect to third organizations' applications. To address security, access control ensures that the context data are only accessible by authorized parties. API management and business support frameworks audit the system.

10.5   Discussion

Previous work related to the project includes surveys focusing on interoperability and on IoT reference architectures. Interoperability solutions adopting FIWARE and IoT interoperability testing are also related to the topic area of this work.

A number of surveys of IIoT related standards and frameworks have been published. For example, Kuila *et al.* studied several popular and commercially used IoT frameworks and platforms. In 2015, Derhamy *et al.* surveyed 17 commercial IoT frameworks and compared them in terms of their architectural approaches and supporting protocols. A more in-depth survey of eight IoT frameworks by major players was presented by Ammar, with the emphasis on the security mechanisms employed. Reference architectures for interoperable manufacturing are discussed in [10], with a focus on interoperability challenges in smart factories. Fahmideh and Zowghi presented a detailed analysis on 63 IoT approaches using a proposed evaluation framework, in which the characteristic like context, lifecycle coverage, roles and modeling are addressed. To present relations among different frameworks, a visual methodology to structure, align and compare existing reference architectures in IIoT domain is introduced in [7]. This work presents a configurable visual view showing the relations and characteristics between the surveyed reference frameworks.

The following subsections introduce related work in industrial solutions that have been adopted by FIWARE and are suitable for IoT interoperability testing.

10.5.1 Solutions Adopting FIWARE

This subsection presents four related industrial solutions that have adopted FIWARE GE, with two solutions in the manufacturing domain, one in the agriculture domain, and the last one related to cross-domain interoperability.

MASAI is a middleware designed to support IoT data collection and pre-filtering in manufacturing environment. The approach is presented using FIWARE IoT Hub. The solution consists of two main components: FIWARE IoT hub and IoT gateway. Factory floor devices integrated with the IoT hub through an IoT gateway using MQTT. The data coming from the devices is then filtered and streamed to a cloud platform called Cloud Collaborative Manufacturing Networks (C2NET) using WebSocket. A use case with MASAI deployment is conducted in a laboratory with an assembly line. The case study verified the proposed approach enables the collection and monitoring of the factory floor data streams from the cloud platform. According to the roadmap on MASAI's factsheet, more manufacturing-oriented protocols (such as OPC UA) are being added to the MASAI.

Alonso *et al.* present an implementation of the Industrial Data Space (IDS) Association Reference Architecture using the FIWARE GE. The core component of the proposed solution is an IDS Connecter, which is implemented by a conjunction of OPC UA IoT Agents and FIWARE OCB. The OPC UA IoT Agents map between the objects from the OPC UA servers on the shop floor and the domain specific data model defined by NGSI. A zero-defect manufacturing use case is deployed for analysis and the required data is retrieved from the milling machines and CMMs. The results showed improvements via a quality control service on produced objects, and a predictive maintenance system on the milling machine.

The olution ensures confidentiality and authenticity of the exchanged data by using encryption, identity management, and access control.

To explore the challenges in IoT enabled precision agriculture, Martinez *et al.* designed a FIWARE-based farm management system as a use case scenario. A comprehensive testbed was implemented to test the performance of the FIWARE platform in the context of supporting background agriculture applications. The testbed represents the most important part of the use case, with virtual IoT nodes acting as context generating nodes, FIWARE OCB and Cygnus acting as the IoT middleware connecting to the Cosmos big data analysis, and a sample application querying context from Cosmos. Latency and throughput of Orion were evaluated and showed positive result of FIWARE supporting scalability in agriculture domain.

In supporting decision making, a platform for early wildfire detection was designed by Kalatzis *et al.* It realizes cross-domain and cross-platform organizational interoperability by utilizing data from various different sources (such as sensors, cameras, weather forecasts, and twitter). It introduces an interoperability IoT2Edge agent between the underlying platforms and server. The IoT2Edge agent translates the data derived from different platforms into a NGSI-LD context information model. Next the NGSI-LD data is sent to the server through an NGSI API and stored in the IoT2Edge server. The IoT2Edge server mainly consists of FIWARE OCB, FIWARE Cygnus, and decision-making algorithms. Intelligent decision making to estimate the wildfire's danger level is based on the semantic reasoning over the collected data. The system succeeded in detecting an actual wildfire incident in Greece (on 23 July 2018).

10.5.2   IoT Interoperability Testing

Testing and evaluation of IoT systems has always been a challenge. Among the testing efforts in IoT domain, the following works were identified to be most relevant to address IoT interoperability.

ETSI has conducted a series of plug test events to validate standards in IoT domains. According to the ETSI specification, interoperability testing aims to prove the end-to-end functionality of at least two communicating systems. The testing method is referred to as passive interoperability testing, which means only observing the behavior of the system under test at the interface that offer only normal user control. Datta *et al.* proposed an approach for semantic interoperability testing between IoT systems. In their study, two scenarios regarding semantic interoperability testing are defined: interoperability tests between two systems and interoperability tests at data level.

With regard to testing a specific IoT platform—such as FIWARE, the performance of FIWARE has been tested using functional testing and stress testing during its quality assurance activities. Aaujo *et al.* evaluated performance of FIWARE deployment considering vertical and horizontal scalability. A conformance testing of FIWARE was conducted by Ahmad *et al.* who adopted model-based testing in IoT systems.

While the ETSI approach in interoperability testing can be used to validate the interoperability of protocols and standards, when testing IoT platforms and middleware, efforts have mainly focused on functional and performance testing, with a few tests addressing interoperability.

10.6   Conclusion

Regarding the incompatibility issues in IIoT, interoperability can be classified into technical, syntactical, semantic, and organizational levels. There have been many efforts and attempts realize greater interoperability by pursuing standardization of technologies, using gateways or middleware, adopting semantic web technologies, developing compatible platforms, etc. We studied nine industrial frameworks as a sample of the current IIoT ecosystems. Among these nine frameworks we found that most IoT platforms address interoperability by adding support for more communication technologies and protocols. Some platforms (such as ThingWorx and FIWARE) define data models to support semantic interoperability. Most platforms are domain-based with only a few pursuing cross-domains organizational interoperability. The IoT domain and industrial domain are still mostly isolated. The conclusion is that we are still at an early stage of IIoT interoperability; therefore, it is vital for standardization organizations and major industrial players to work together to increase the interoperability of existing solutions rather than proposing numerous new (isolated) platforms. Additionally, it is important for developers to take interoperability into consideration when developing IIoT applications.

Based on the knowledge gained from the solutions that have been studied during this project, FIWARE was identified as a potential platform to support IIoT interoperability. In the specific scenario used for our case study, the FIWARE OCB offers core context management for the proposed smart factory scenario while FIWARE IoT Agents serve as interoperability providers for IoT devices. The MQTT and OPC UA protocols were chosen and tested as representatives of the IoT domain and the industrial domain. IoT Agent JSON and IoT Agent OPC UA map MQTT messages and OPC UA messages into the NGSI v2 data model and interact with the OCB.

Among our proposed nine key scenarios for testing interoperability of FIWARE GEs, our testbed meets the requirements in eight out of these nine key scenarios. The results show that FIWARE GEs have the potential to support interoperability for Industry 4.0.

References

1. Raptis, T.P., Passarella, A., Conti, M.J.I.A., Data Management in Industry 4.0: State of the Art and Open Challenges. *IEEE Access*, 7, 97052–97093, 2019.
2. Zhong, R.Y., Xu, X., Klotz, E., Newman, S.T., Intelligent Manufacturing in the Context of Industry 4.0: A Review. *Engineering*, 3, 5, 616–630, 10/01/2017. https://doi.org/10.1016/J.ENG.2017.05.015.
3. Greer, C., Burns, M.J., Wollman, D.A., Griffor, E.R., *Cyber-physical systems and Internet of Things, Special Publication (NIST SP)—1900-202*, 2019. https://nvlpubs.nist.gov/nistpubs/SpecialPublications/NIST.SP.1900-202.pdf
4. Yaqoob, I. *et al.*, Internet of Things Architecture: Recent Advances, Taxonomy, Requirements, and Open Challenges. *IEEE Wirel. Commun.*, 24, 3, 10–16, 2017.
5. Noura, M., Atiquzzaman, M., Gaedke, M.J., Interoperability in Internet of Things: Taxonomies and Open Challenges. *Mob. Netw. Appl.*, 24, 3, 796–809, June 01, 2019.
6. Lelli, F., Interoperability of the Time of Industry 4.0 and the Internet of Things. *Future Internet*, 11, 2, 36, 2019.
7. Derhamy, H., Rönnholm, J., Delsing, J., Eliasson, J., Deventer, J.V., Protocol interoperability of OPC UA in service-oriented architectures, in: *2017 IEEE 15th International Conference on Industrial Informatics (INDIN)*, pp. 44–50, 24–26 July 2017.
8. Han, B., Cao, X., Shi, H., Modeling the throughput of IEEE 802.15.4 based wireless networks under interference, in: *2017 32nd Youth Academic Annual Conference of Chinese Association of Automation (YAC)*, pp. 1014–1019, 19–21 May 2017.
9. *IEEE Standard for Low-Rate Wireless Networks. IEEE Std 802.15.4-2015 (Revision of IEEE Std 802.15.4-2011)*, pp. 1–709, Apr. 2016. http://www.jatit.org/volumes/Vol99No15/13Vol99No15.pdf
10. Kim, S.H., Chong, P.K., Kim, T., Performance Study of Routing Protocols in ZigBee Wireless Mesh Networks. 95, 2, 1829–1853, July 01 2017.
11. Radmand, P., Talevski, A., Petersen, S., Carlsen, S., Comparison of industrial WSN standards, in: *4th IEEE International Conference on Digital Ecosystems and Technologies*, pp. 632–637, 13–16 April 2010.
12. Adame, T., Bel, A., Bellalta, B., Barcelo, J., Gonzalez, J., Oliver, M., Capacity Analysis of IEEE 802.11ah WLANs for M2M Communications, in: *Multiple*

Access Communications, pp. 139–155, Springer International Publishing, Cham, 2013.

13. Gomez, C., Oller, J., Paradells, J., Overview and Evaluation of Bluetooth Low Energy: An Emerging Low-Power Wireless Technology. *Sensors (Basel)*, 12, 9, 11734–11753, 2012.

14. Rama, Y. and Özpmar, M.A., A Comparison of Long-Range Licensed and Unlicensed LPWAN Technologies According to Their Geolocation Services and Commercial Opportunities, in: *2018 18th Mediterranean Microwave Symposium (MMS)*, pp. 398–403, 31 Oct.–2 Nov. 2018.

15. Deering, S. and Hinden, R., *RFC 2460: Internet protocol, version 6 (IPv6) specification*, December, 1998. https://datatracker.ietf.org/doc/html/rfc2460

16. MQTT Version 5.0., Edited by Andrew Banks, Ed Briggs, Ken Borgendale, and Rahul Gupta. 25 December 2017. OASIS Committee Specification 01. http://docs.oasisopen.org/mqtt/mqtt/v5.0/cs01/mqtt-v5.0-cs01.html. Latest version: http://docs.oasisopen.org/mqtt/mqtt/v5.0/mqtt-v5.0.html.

17. Shelby, Z., Hartke, K., Bormann, C., *The Constrained Application Protocol (CoAP), Internet Request for Comments*, vol. RFC 7252, Jun. 2014. https://www.scirp.org/(S(351jmbntvnsjt1aadkposzje))/reference/ReferencesPapers.aspx?ReferenceID=1598461

18. Saint-Andre, P., *Extensible Messaging and Presence Protocol (XMPP): Core, Internet Request for Comments*, vol. RFC 6120, Mar. 2011.

19. Winter, E.T. *et al.*, *RPL: IPv6 Routing Protocol for Low-Power and Lossy Networks, Internet Request for Comments*, vol. RFC 6550, Mar. 2012. https://www.rfc-editor.org/info/rfc6550

20. Hartig, O. and Pérez, J., Semantics and complexity of GraphQL, in: *Proceedings of the 2018 World Wide Web Conference*, pp. 1155–1164, 2018.

21. Monostori, L. *et al.*, Cyber-physical systems in manufacturing. *CIRP Ann.*, 65, 2, 621–641, 01/01/2016. 2016. https://doi.org/10.1016/j.cirp.2016.06.005.

22. Xu, X., From cloud computing to cloud manufacturing. *Robot. Comput. Integr. Manuf.*, 28, 1, 75–86, 02/01/2012. https://doi.org/10.1016/j.rcim.2011.07.002.

23. Gao, R. *et al.*, Cloud-enabled prognosis for manufacturing. *CIRP Ann.*, 64, 2, 749–772, 01/01/2015 2015. https://doi.org/10.1016/j.cirp.2015.05.011.

24. Schmidt, B. and Wang, L., Cloud-enhanced predictive maintenance. *Int. J. Adv. Manuf. Technol.*, 99, 1, 513, 10/01/2018.

25. Mourtzis, D. and Vlachou, E., A cloud-based cyber-physical system for adaptive shop floor scheduling and condition-based maintenance. *J. Manuf. Syst.*, vol, 179–198, 04/01/2018. 2018. https://doi.org/10.1016/j.jmsy.2018.05.008.

26. Chen, B., Wan, J., Celesti, A., Li, D., Abbas, H., Zhang, Q., Edge Computing in IoT Based Manufacturing. *IEEE Commun. Mag.*, 56, 9, 103–109, 2018.

27. Fonseca, J.M.C., Marquez, F.G., Jacobs, T. (Eds.), *FIWARE-NGSI v2 Specification*, (accessed Sep. 9, 2019). http://fiware-ges.github.io/orion/api/v2/stable/

28. Context Information Management (CIM); NGSI-LD API. 2001. Retrieved 11 February 2022, from https:// www.etsi.org/deliver/etsi_gs/ CIM/001_099/009/01.01.01_60/gs_CIM009v 010101p.pdf.

29. *KAA-Enterprise IoT Platform for Exceptional Cloud Experience*, https://www. kaaproject.org/ (accessed Jun. 15, 2019). https://kaaproject.github.io/

30. Schweichhart, K., *Reference architectural model Industrie 4.0 (rami 4.0), An introduction*, vol. 40, 2016, [Online]. Available: https://www.plattform-i40.de, https://ec.europa.eu/futurium/en/system/files/ged/a2-schweichhart-reference_architectural_model_industrie_4.0_rami_4.0.pdf

31. *ThingsBoard Open-source IoT Platform*, thingsboard.io (accessed Jul. 15, 2019). https://thingsboard.io/

32. *ThingSpeak for IoT Projects*, thingspeak.com (accessed Jul. 15, 2020). https:// thingsboard.io/

33. P.E.I. Solutions, *Platform technology: ThingWorx*, https://www.thingworx. com/ (accessed Jul. 13, 2019). https://developer.thingworx.com/en

34. Jha, S., Kumar, R., Chatterjee, J.M., Khari, M., Collaborative handshaking approaches between internet of computing and internet of things towards a smart world: A review from 2009-2017. *Telecommun. Syst.*, 70, 4, 617–634, 2019.

35. Yadav, M. and Chatterjee, J.M., Study of Privacy Issues in Internet of Things. *Global J. Appl. Data Sci. Internet Things*, 2, 2, 31–40, 2018.

11

Investigation of Holistic Approaches for Privacy Aware Design of Cyber-Physical Systems

Manas Kumar Yogi[1]*, A.S.N. Chakravarthy[2] and Jyotir Moy Chatterjee[3]

[1]*Computer Science and Engineering, Pragati Engineering College (Autonomous), Surampalem, India*
[2]*Computer Science & Engineering, JNTUK Kakinada, India*
[3]*IT, Lord Buddha Education Foundation, Kathmandu, Nepal*

Abstract

It is imagined that future cyber-physical systems will give a more helpful living and work space. Nonetheless, such systems need unavoidably to gather furthermore, measure privacy-touchy data. That implies the advantages accompany potential privacy spillage hazards. These days, this privacy issue gets more consideration as a legitimate necessity of the users who participate in a CPS ecosystem. In this postulation, privacy-by-plan approaches are examined where privacy improvement is figured it out through considering privacy in the physical layer plan. We have presented a comprehensive study regarding the current challenges in the field of CPS privacy. We throw light towards the design principles which are not focussed by majority of the CPS designers due to their non-exposure to such tactics. This chapter will act as a readymade guide to researchers who want to know how to lay foundations towards a privacy aware CPS architecture.

Keywords: Authentication, privacy, security, smart, identity

*Corresponding author: manas.yogi@gmail.com

Uzzal Sharma, Parma Nand, Jyotir Moy Chatterjee, Vishal Jain, Noor Zaman Jhanjhi and R. Sujatha (eds.)
Cyber-Physical Systems: Foundations and Techniques, (257–272) © 2022 Scrivener Publishing LLC

11.1   Introduction

A cyber-physical framework (CPS) comprises of two significant segments: a physical measure and a cyber-framework. The physical interaction, which can be a characteristic marvel or a man-made physical framework, is observed and constrained by the cyber framework, which regularly is an organized arrangement of a few small gadgets with detecting, calculation, and correspondence capacities. There have been countless proposed CPS applications, like smart house, smart grid, e-Health, assisted living, and so forth. They are imagined to shape a smart climate which will significantly profit the clients. A common CPS frequently gathers a colossal measure of privacy-delicate data for information examination and dynamic. The data empowers the framework to settle on smart choices through complex calculations. In any case, a privacy spillage might actually occur in any stage(s) of information assortment, information transmission, information preparing, or information stockpiling. Data security laws advocate an approved information beneficiary to hold and handle just the information totally fundamental for the fruition of its obligations just as restricting the admittance to individual information to those expecting to showcase the handling [1]. To this end, GDPR advocates the privacy-by-design approach which can "intrinsically" protect privacy through the incorporation of information assurance from the beginning of the designing of systems instead of an expansion thereafter [2, 4]. Contingent upon the physical-layer tasks, privacy-by-design approaches can additionally be classified into various classes. As of now, most privacy-by-design moves toward center around the information transmission stage, which compares to detecting and correspondence in the physical layer of a CPS. The examination on the wire-tap channel determines the mystery limit. Based on the hypothesis of wire-tap channel, individuals have created privacy plans, for example, fake commotion and helpful sticking [3]. As of late, secure information pressure in source coding additionally draws in much consideration.

11.2   Popular Privacy Design Recommendations

11.2.1   Dynamic Authorization

Dynamic authorization is an innovation where authorization and access rights to an association's organization, applications, information, or other delicate resources are conceded dynamically progressively utilizing trait based standards and strategies. With customary Role-Based Access Control (RBAC), or rundown based authorization frameworks, heads need to continually screen and re-evaluate changes in client status, reassign and renounce jobs, or even screen and reassign consents on singular documents or records [5]. With dynamic authorization, admittance to information is allowed or denied continuously by strategy as indicated by factors, like the most recent client status, information arrangements, and climate data. A dynamic authorization framework with ABAC fundamentally smoothes out the administration cycle [6]. It eliminates the need to exclusively direct thousands or even countless access-control records as well as job and job tasks consistently. Furthermore, associations don't have to convey costly and complex character administration arrangements. With ABAC, many jobs can be supplanted by only a couple arrangements. These arrangements are overseen midway across every delicate application and frameworks, giving a solitary sheet of glass over the "who, what, where, when, and why." Centralized administration makes it simple to add or refresh approaches and rapidly convey them across the endeavour. Authorization arrangements are overseen remotely from the secured application (otherwise known as "Externalized Authorization Management"), so they can be altered without requiring code changes or application vacation [7]. This empowers associations to respond rapidly to changes in business or administrative conditions, enormously expanding deftness and adaptability, and upgrading generally speaking information assurance. Dynamic authorization with ABAC additionally gives focal observing and following of client action and information access furnishing consistence and security officials with knowledge into client conduct and dubious exercises [8].

11.2.2 End to End Security

This mechanism protection assists you with keeping away from misrepresentation and information theft [9]. With the right defensive measures, you can build your general wellbeing while at the same time dealing with your PC with web association.

11.2.3 Enrollment and Authentication APIs

Since API is a significant element with an outside asset that has the capacity of tolerating and reacting to secured asset demands by clients and customers, they should be prepared to guarantee that applications and customers attempting to get to information are valid, so they can continue to approve full access when character is affirmed. The cycles of affirming the character of clients attempting to get to assets on the worker and this is the thing that is known as API verification. API Key authentication is a strategy that was designed to conquer the shortcomings of shared qualifications which was a major issue in HTTP Basic authentication [10]. The API key is typically a long series of numbers and letters that you either remember for the solicitation header or solicitation URL. At the point when the customer validates the API key, the worker stamps their character and permits them to get to information. API merchants may furnish you with a public and private key contingent upon your necessities, where the previous can be utilized to restrict clients to specific capacities, and the last behaves like a secret key that permits you full access.

11.2.4   Distributed Authorization

Somewhat recently, many exploration efforts on access control have been never really stored, share and send information while guaranteeing its trustworthiness, legitimacy and realness. Incorporated regulator issues might be tended to by adjusting an answer dependent on a Distributed Ledger Technologies for the confirmation of access authorizations to an entrance control instrument [11]. In any case, when information volumes and sharing develops as quick as in online social networks or smart cities, it becomes hard to oversee access control and manage individual information. A potential methodology is safely store access control arrangements on Distributed Ledger Technologies, whereby the candidate can be made mindful of their consents to get to their own information. Specifically, CPS fashioners can utilize the utilization of a Secret Sharing plan to divide individual information in pieces among network hubs, anyway their creative arrangement is costly and not GDPR consistent because of the storing of individual information on the Distributed Ledger Technologies.

In CPS plan for protection, the authorization administration is responsible for enforcing the entrance rights that are indicated in the smart agreements ACLs [12]. At the point when this help is worked by a solitary focal supplier, trust should be given to this one, since the keys are kept in one spot as it were. Expecting that this supplier can be straightforward however inquisitive, security might be undermined, for example an online social network website sharing a client geo-location with his/her companions, if inquisitive, can admittance to this information. In this manner, we propose to decentralize the assistance to move the trust to the convention. For this situation, hubs in a network are viewed as semi-or un-trusted, yet an information protection/cryptographical instrument, incorporated into their execution convention, permit the entire framework to be trusted.

11.2.5 Decentralization Authentication

Numerous specialists say that a secret phrase based login is an unreliable way to deal with online communications and that multifaceted plans add erosion that decrease client selection and efficiency [13]. Acquiring guaranteed validation of an individual's personality while clinging to new information protection laws and guidelines presents a minefield of safety and client encounters gives that are expensive and incapable. Many organizations have effectively understood that two-factor verification is a blemished bandage. Things being what they are, are there more powerful options for online confirmation? A few associations inside the self-sovereign character (SSI) people group have consolidated to work together on the approval of decentralized personality ways to deal with the basic secret phrase based verification issue. ATB Financial, Evernym, IBM, the Sovrin Foundation and Workday have met up in a joint multi-stage work to consider and brood working instances of unquestionable qualifications for the motivations behind mindfulness and training [14].

11.2.6 Interoperable Privacy Profiles

As the name proposes, an Interoperable Privacy Profile is a design that is acknowledged across an undertaking or across numerous associations. To be "Interoperable," the profile follows a set administration measure that approves profile construction and commands its utilization to convey a particular mission or business need across the undertaking. The profile, once finished, follows a change the executives interaction, like that of a living archive, and should be discoverable across associations sharing a typical (mission or business) interest.

The Interoperable Privacy Profile contains three perspectives that are utilized to distinguish the mission or business need of the undertaking, alongside functional and specialized parts to accomplish that need. The Interoperable Privacy Profile sees are: Reference View, Technical Guidance View, and Implementation Instance View [15]. These perspectives are characterized as follows:

Reference View: Serves as the undeniable level conceptual model or reference for the profiled undertaking part. It incorporates fundamental credits, undertaking elements, and direction data. The reference see is execution autonomous, seller free, and in some cases innovation autonomous. The reference view ought to contain appropriate mission needs explanations, use cases and reference design.

Specialized Guidance View: A bunch of at least one base principles, and where appropriate, the meaning of picked classes, subsets, alternatives, and boundaries of those base guidelines important for setting up the practices of a specific capacity or undertaking segment. The specialized direction see is merchant autonomous and incorporates essential credits, endeavour substances, execution references, direction, and consistence data.

Execution Instance View: Portrays a particular example of an execution and characterizes discrete setups and boundaries for the given occasion. It incorporates fundamental ascribes, venture substances, consistence data, and explicit strategies and methods. The execution occasion view might possibly be merchant autonomous. This is the most itemized and explicit perspective on a profile.

11.3   Current Privacy Challenges in CPS

In most of the cases, limitations in CPS design knowledge results in poor or weaker privacy designs. Even though the companies deploying CPS might not gather personal data initially, after sometime it could be possible to track the data usage, if the communication is not secured through encryption [16]. The healthy design practise is to include both encryption and anonymization techniques rather than depending on only one of them. These two approaches act as multiple lines of defense against the attackers. Without authorization, the data becomes unreadable due to encryption. However, even if a corrupt user manages to decrypt the data, he will have to overcome the additional barrier of de-anonymizing the data in order to cause a privacy breach as the data is anonymized.

The following table shows some of the current challenges in the privacy preservation mechanisms.

Sl. no.	Approach	Challenges
1	Cryptography based methods, Blockchain based methods	Computational cost, Scalability, Communicational complexity
2	Statistical model, Perturbation based methods	Time consuming, Data utility reduces as perturbation increases, Maintaining balance between privacy and data correctness is difficult

(Continued)

(*Continued*)

| 3 | Authentication based control mechanisms | Increasing in processing time, storage need escalates, reduction in system reliability |
| 4 | Machine Learning, Deep learning methods | Complex to achieve data utility, high communication overhead, high effort in parameter setting |

11.4   Privacy Aware Design for CPS

Recommendation 1: Privacy first!
First thing first, privacy ought to be important for the extent of the arranging and advancement cycles. Make it a propensity to thoroughly consider how you need to manage privacy and information during the primary phase of the venture. Brief those inquiries during the underlying gathering or meetings to generate new ideas. Additionally, keep away from the utilization of dim examples however much as could be expected during the UI design. Indeed, those unobtrusive pre-stamped checkboxes arrangement/promotion thingy toward the finish of the installment structure are useful for transient advantages. In any case, the eventual outcome can be serious for your item's straightforwardness issue. More irate clients, more grumbling tickets.

Recommendation 2: Think like a Hacker
Attempt to list down a wide range of information that will be gathered. And afterward distinguish the potential manners by which the information could be abused or abused. Run a progression of assessments and assessment with your group to recognize those defects and potential section focuses.

Commonly, most hackers have two kinds of outlook: explorative and manipulative. Put on the comparable attitude when dealing with your inner assessment meetings. Investigate and recognize however much weaknesses as could reasonably be expected from the beginning to stay away from significant security mishaps.

Recommendation 3: Collect as little information as possible
At whatever point your administrations are going to do some information assortment, disclose to the clients in layman words. Reveal to them which specific information you are going to gather and how are you going to manage them. No languages. Keep it basic. A model, feature the writings

under the sign-up CTA that you will send them news and updates to their inboxes. Try not to shock them!

Approximately 90% of application clients show that having clear data about how applications will access or utilize their own information is "very" or "fairly" imperative to them when choosing to download an application.

From the guideline perspective, a very much designed item watches out for gather 'barely enough' information from the clients. Ensure that the gathered information is not put away for more than proposed timeframe. Nonetheless, on the off chance that you should store those information for seemingly forever, you need to design cautiously on the most proficient method to store them safely to abstain from spilling or abusing.

Recommendation 4: Protect the Information

Separated information assortment, we additionally need to zero in on encryption. A large portion of our information is put away on the web or 'in a cloud'. Nonetheless, a great many people don't understand that putting away information in a cloud is really similar to putting away them in another person's PCs in somewhere else.

In this manner, make a point to scramble your information accurately prior to putting away them on the web. Obviously, we are not looking at wrapping your entire pieces of information like air pocket wrapping a house. As a standard practice, apply the 80/20 Pareto principle. Which level of information is really delicate? Recognize them and plan the encryption in like manner.

Recommendation 5: Respect Identity

The quintessence of privacy is about decision. Ensure that the client can handle over their online personality (anonymous or genuine name). They ought to likewise have the option to choose by themselves however much as could be expected how much information (names, age and so forth) ought to be uncovered or be covered up.

An exemplary terrible model is when web-based media Google+ reported that it didn't let clients to pick their own social character, which caused a shock on the web. From the design viewpoint, clients ought to have the option to refresh their privacy settings through clear UI design. Try not to shroud them somewhere down in the screens. Keep in mind, permitting pseudonymity or secrecy is additionally a decent method to shield clients from genuine outcomes like provocations and separation.

11.5   Limitations

Limitations for following Recommendation 1:
Our study indicated that CPS designers don't consider privacy as a top of the line resident in their application designs. This legitimizes our choice to foster a privacy aware design system to control the manner of thinking of programmers. We accept that this outlook of gathering as much information as potential should be altered towards a privacy attitude where just the most fundamental information things are accumulated and handled. Another study flagged that it is adequate to gather information with no control saying that 'If it's totally anonymized, and it's simply business information about who's come and come out.' This outlook is additionally not steady of PbD and makes extra issues like asset wastage (e.g., for capacity, information cleaning, information handling and so on) Further, anonymizing is a danger moderation approach, not a danger disposal approach. Anonymization additionally could prompt privacy infringement because of unlawful de-anonymization draws near. We heard comparable perspectives concerning information stockpiling too.

Limitations for following Recommendation 2:
Most of the CPS designers think from a business point of view. Developing mindset of a hacker is difficult for them. Developing misuse cases becomes a challenge for them. The CPS designers have a superficial viewpoint regarding privacy. For instance, few designers do not want to include privacy preserving techniques thinking that his design actions would jeopardise the device outcomes which may hinder the usage experience. For example if we consider a medical CPS, the designers may be wary to apply category-based aggregation as it may cause reduction in precision in a medical context.'

Limitations for following Recommendation 3:
While ensuring CPSs unique information utilizing privacy saving models, finding the initial origins of cyber assaults [17] needs anomaly-based detection components that produce high bogus caution rates. This issue is identified with achieving the high dependability versus privacy of a framework on the grounds that most existing privacy-saving models add clamor and plans for completely anonymizing and keeping their characters get yet corrupt the location exactness of anomaly-based detection components. It is critical to foster exceptionally proficient privacy-protecting anomaly-distinguishing strategies that can defend CPSs information and recognize new assault information without unveiling any touchy data across their networks.

Limitations for following Recommendation 4:
Perceiving which information to stow away and which information to uncover in order to expand the security level remaining parts a consistently developing test, the analysts cancel its exchange between information utility and Privacy. Most security saving systems, similar to anonymization, k-lack of clarity and differential protection, depends on specific kind of heterogeneity of the data, either pre or post computation. Various CPS designers assume the general setting where a user wishes to convey a lot of assessments to an inspector support (for instance an idea structure), while keeping data that is related with these assessments private. On one hand, the examiner is a real gatherer for these assessments, from which he desires to construe some utility. Of course, the relationship of these assessments with the customer's private data empowers the analyst to misguidedly infer private information.

Limitations for following Recommendation 5:
Few CPS designers have already proposed cloud-based validation plot utilizing a modular exponential strategy initially encodes a label's data with respect to interchanges among IoV and radar. At that point, the obscurity of the tag is created as a productive method of guaranteeing information privacy by shielding its data from vindictive activities. Contrasted and different conventions, it shows that it is successful and solid as far as having a lower computational overhead and less correspondence associations. Some confirmation work is based on access control, for example, a self-versatile access control strategy for safely seeing patients records in both ordinary and crisis cases is proposed, with a de-duplication technique used to save the capacity of indistinguishable clinical documents. Initially, the clinical information is scrambled by an entrance strategy and afterward the technique applied based on a break-glass control one. The test results show that this procedure is productive and functional however that the time it burns-through increments with the spans of the characteristics.

11.6 Converting Risks of Applying AI Into Advantages

Artificial intelligence (AI) can possibly tackle numerous normal business challenges—from rapidly recognizing a couple of problematic charges in huge number of solicitations to foreseeing customers' necessities and needs. Be that as it may, there might be a flipside to these advances. Protection concerns are springing up as organizations feed more and more shopper and vendor information into cutting edge, AI-fuelled algorithms to make new pieces of touchy information, unbeknownst to influenced customers and workers. The reach and variety of AI applications implies that the issues and dangers are complex. These are included in the following subsections.

11.6.1   Proof of Recognition and De-Anonymization

Simulated intelligence applications can be used to recognize and thusly track individuals across different contraptions, in their homes, at work, and out in the open spaces. For example, while singular data is routinely (pseudo-)anonymized inside datasets, AI can be used to de-anonymize this data. Facial affirmation is another means by which individuals can be followed and perceived, which can change suspicions for lack of clarity out in the open space.

11.6.2   Segregation, Shamefulness, Mistakes

Identification using AI mechanisms, profiling, and robotized dynamic may in like manner brief inappropriate, oppressive, or uneven outcomes. People can be misclassified, misidentified, or judged conversely, and such mistakes or tendencies may excessively impact certain social affairs of people.

11.6.3   Haziness and Bias of Profiling

In certain situations, the modest utilizations of AI can be dark to people, regulators, or even the creators of the actual framework, making it hard to challenge or question results. While there are specific responses for dealing with the interpretability and furthermore the ability to survey of specific structures for different accomplices, a key test remains where this is crazy, and the outcome in a general sense influences people's lives.

11.6.4   Abuse Arising From Information

Hardly any people are consistently unable to totally get what sorts and how much data their contraptions, organizations, and stages make, association, or offer. As we bring keen and related devices into our homes, work environments, public spaces, and even bodies, the need quite far on data misuse ends up being continuously crushing. In this scene, vocations of AI for purposes like profiling, or to follow and recognize people across contraptions and shockingly transparently spaces, improve this deviation.

The new development, use, investigation, and improvement of AI ought to be reliant upon the base essential of with respect to, progressing, and getting worldwide fundamental opportunities standards. Different sorts of AI and different spaces of use raise express upright and administrative normal opportunities issues. To ensure that they safeguard individuals from the risks acted by AI like well as address the normal gathering and social harms, existing laws ought to be reviewed, and if fundamental braced, to address the effects of new and emerging threats to rights, including setting up clear cutoff focuses, securities and oversight and obligation instruments.

11.6.5   Tips for CPS Designers Including AI in the CPS Ecosystem

Urge the board to isolate AI from investigation of other innovation dangers to separate the privatized information the innovation makes and any dangers that the information can be compromised.

Ensure security conventions are trailed by vendors long get-togethers for administrations are agreed upon. Urge the board to keep standard timetables to ensure innovation accomplices are staying faithful to their commitments to secure individual information.

Push the board to consent to the toughest arrangement of security guidelines, regardless of whether the organization isn't right now in the EU or different business sectors with broad prerequisites. That way, if the organization ventures into those spaces, it will not be an enormous weight to retrofit security conventions.

Circle back to innovation contractors to ensure security conventions are being followed. On the off chance that an AI apparatus created by a vendor should erase incidental information, request check that those cancellations occur. The dependable guideline of protection law master Imran Ahmad, a Toronto-based attorney with Blake, Cassels and Graydon who has some expertise in innovation and network safety issues, is to "trust yet check" that settled upon security rehearses are being followed.

A new part of AI research called adversarial learning tries to further develop AI technologies so they're less vulnerable to such avoidance assaults. For instance, we have done some underlying exploration on the most proficient method to make it harder for malware, which could be utilized to disregard an individual's privacy, to avoid discovery. One technique we concocted was to add uncertainty to the AI models so the assailants can't precisely anticipate what the model will do. Will it examine for a certain information arrangement? Or will it run the sandbox? Preferably, a pernicious piece of programming will not know and will accidentally uncover its intentions.

Another way we can utilize AI to further develop privacy is by examining the weaknesses of profound neural networks. No algorithm is awesome, and these models are powerless in light of the fact that they are frequently extremely touchy to little changes in the information they are perusing. For instance, analysts have shown that a Post-it note added to a stop sign can deceive an AI model into intuition it is seeing a speed limit sign all things being equal. Unpretentious adjustments like that exploit the manner in which models are trained to decrease error. Those error-decrease methods open a weakness that permits assailants to track down the littlest changes that will trick the model.

These weaknesses can be utilized to further develop privacy by adding clamor to individual information. For instance, specialists from the Max Planck Institute for Informatics in Germany have planned shrewd approaches to modify Flickr pictures to thwart facial acknowledgment programming. The changes are amazingly inconspicuous, to such an extent that they're imperceptible by the natural eye.

The third way that AI can assist with relieving privacy issues is by protecting information privacy when the models are being assembled. One promising improvement is called federated learning, which Google utilizes in its Gboard smart console to anticipate which word to type straightaway. Federated learning fabricates a last profound neural network from information stored on various gadgets, like cell phones, instead of one focal information repository. The vital advantage of federated learning is that the original information never leaves the nearby gadgets. Along these lines privacy is secured somewhat. It's anything but an ideal arrangement, however, in light of the fact that while the nearby gadgets complete a portion of the calculations, they don't complete them. The transitional outcomes could uncover a few information about the gadget and its client.

Federated learning offers a brief look at a future where AI is more deferential of privacy. We are cheerful that proceeded with examination into AI will discover more ways it very well may be essential for the arrangement as opposed to a cause of issues.

11.7 Conclusion and Future Scope

Most of the privacy design issues can be faced by using patterns. The patterns provide the users with intrinsic privacy features which should not be bypassed at any cost. Obviously, if these are bypassed during design phase privacy attribute of the overall system weakens. Also, when the companies related to CPS design perform acquisition of user consent, it should not become an excuse for poor design of privacy within the system. Privacy patterns will be very much the dominant force in coming future with respect to CPS design. The objective of the designers should be minimum data collection to complete the operation of the device. We conclude that in future a hybrid design approach will be a primitive of privacy aware design for CPS. Due to the complex nature of CPS architecture and heterogeneous nature of sensor data involved in a CPS, privacy threat agnostic principles will lead to a better system design.

New strategies may address a portion of the privacy issues innate in AI, however they're in their earliest stages and not without their shortcomings. Federated learning trains algorithms across decentralized edge gadgets without trading their information tests, yet it's hard to assess and helpless before variances in force, calculation, and web. Differential privacy, which uncovered information about an informational index while retaining information about the people, endures plunges in exactness brought about by infused clamour. With respect to homomorphic encryption—a form of encryption that permits calculation on scrambled information—it's to some degree moderate and computationally requesting. All things considered; analysts accept every one of the three methodologies are positive developments.

References

1. Rajesh, N., Sujatha, K., Lawrence, A.A., Survey on privacy preserving data mining techniques using recent algorithms. *Int. J. Comput. Appl.*, 133, 7, 30–33, Jan. 2016.

2. Giraldo, J., Sarkar, E., Cardenas, A.A., Maniatakos, M., Kantarcioglu, M., Security and privacy in cyber-physical systems: A survey of surveys. *IEEE Des. Test*, 34, 4, 7–17, Aug. 2017.

3. Fan, K., Jiang, W., Luo, Q., Li, H., Yang, Y., Cloud-based RFID mutual authentication scheme for efficient privacy preserving in IoV. *J. Franklin Inst.*, 358, 1, 193–209, Jan. 2021.

4. Yang, Y., Zheng, X., Guo, W., Liu, X., Chang, V., Privacy preserving smart IoT-based healthcare big data storage and selfadaptive access control system. *Inf. Sci.*, 479, 567–592, Apr. 2019.

5. Wang, J., Cai, Z., Li, Y., Yang, D., Li, J., Gao, H., Protecting query privacy with differentially private k-anonymity in location-based services. *Pers. Ubiquit. Comput.*, 22, 3, 453–469, Jun. 2018.

6. Sangogboye, F.C., Jia, R., Hong, T., Spanos, C., Kjaergaard, M.B., A framework for privacy-preserving data publishing with enhanced utility for cyber-physical systems. *ACM Trans. Sens. Netw.*, 14, 3–4, 1–22, Dec. 2018.

7. Min, Z., Yang, G., Sangaiah, A.K., Bai, S., Liu, G., A privacy protection-oriented parallel fully homomorphic encryption algorithm in cyber physical systems. *EURASIP J. Wirel. Commun. Netw.*, 2019, 1, 15, Dec. 2019.

8. Marano, S., Matta, V., Willett, P.K., Distributed detection with censoring sensors under physical layer secrecy. *IEEE Trans. Signal Process.*, 57, 5, 1976–1986, 2009.

9. Mhanna, M. and Piantanida, P., On secure distributed hypothesis testing, in: *Proceedings of ISIT 2015*, pp. 1605–1609, 2015.

10. Molina-Markham, A., Shenoy, P., Fu, K., Cecchet, E., Irwin, D., Private memoirs of a smart meter, in: *Proceedings of the 2nd ACM Workshop on Embedded Sensing Systems for Energy-Efficiency in Building*, pp. 61–66, 2010.

11. Nadendla, V., *Secure distributed detection in wireless sensor networks via encryption of sensor decision*, Master's thesis, Louisiana State University, 2009.

12. Nadendla, V.S.S., Chen, H., Varshney, P.K., Secure distributed detection in the presence of eavesdroppers, in: *Proceedings of ASILOMAR 2010*, pp. 1437–1441, 2010.

13. Nielsen, F., An information-geometric characterization of Chernoff information. *IEEE Signal Process. Lett.*, 20, 3, 269–272, 2013.

14. Nikaidô, H., On von Neumann's minimax theorem. *Pac. J. Math.*, 4, 1, 65–72, 1954.

15. Schmidt, S., Krahn, H., Fischer, S., Wätjen, D., A security architecture for mobile wireless sensor networks, in: *Proceedings of the First European Conference on Security in Ad-hoc and Sensor Networks*, pp. 166–177, 2005.

16. Smallwood, R.D. and Sondik, E.J., The optimal control of partially observable Markov processes over a finite horizon. *Oper. Res.*, 21, 1071–1088, 1973.

17. Le, D.N., Kumar, R., Mishra, B.K., Chatterjee, J.M., Khari, M. (Eds.), *Cyber Security in Parallel and Distributed Computing: Concepts, Techniques, Applications and Case Studies*, John Wiley & Sons, Hoboken, NJ: John Wiley & Sons, Inc.; Beverly, MA: Scrivener Publishing LLC, 2019.

12

Exposing Security and Privacy Issues on Cyber-Physical Systems

Keshav Kaushik

*School of Computer Science, University of Petroleum and Energy Studies,
Dehradun, India*

Abstract

Cyber-Physical Systems (CPS), especially mobile CPS and the Internet of Things (IoT), have infiltrated every area of society. CPS combine sensor, processing, mechanization, and networking into physical things and infrastructure, letting them to communicate with one another and with the Internet. They may be utilized in a broad range of industries, including aviation, automobile, biochemical mechanisms, public infrastructure, electronic goods, electricity, amusement, pharmaceuticals, manufacturing, transportation, and so on. Because of its important functions, the CPS draws a large number of cyber attackers who can pose severe security risks and cause a system failure. Furthermore, because most CPS apps gather and handle sensitive data, failing to safeguard such data results in privacy violations. As a result, CPS programs must be run with suitable privacy and security measures to avoid any unintended consequences for applications and users. Embedded device and computers monitor and manage physical phenomena, which include feedback mechanisms that allow physical actions to impact computations and vice versa.

Keywords: CPS, IoT, embedded devices

12.1 Introduction to Cyber-Physical Systems (CPS)

The social and financial potential of such connections is considerably greater than previously anticipated, and huge investments are being made

---

Email: officialkeshavkaushik@gmail.com

Uzzal Sharma, Parma Nand, Jyotir Moy Chatterjee, Vishal Jain, Noor Zaman Jhanjhi and R. Sujatha (eds.)
Cyber-Physical Systems: Foundations and Techniques, (273–288) © 2022 Scrivener Publishing LLC

to accelerate innovation around the world. The CPS is based on integrated devices, which are processors and programs placed in objects that are not designed to calculate, such as vehicles, toys, hospital instruments, and scientific equipment. Recent advancements in communications, electronics, computers, and process control have paved the way for more integration and communication between physical and digital components, as well as people. With CPS, this becomes a real thing. CPS is a human-interactive networked system having cyber and physical elements. These technologies have the potential to have a significant influence on our daily lives. Considering enhanced computing capabilities in modern automobiles, the growing usage of smart gadgets in our homes, the relevance of automated processes in medical settings, or the capacity to operate demonstrated high from afar.

Notwithstanding all of the advantages of CPS and its ability to change people's lives, there are serious worries about its privacy. Maintaining CPS security comes with a slew of difficulties. Surveillance issues were raised, for instance, as a result of this approach of elements that may not have been intended or established with safety in mind, or as a result of the increased amount of attack possibilities that may be manipulated as a result of the connectivity of such a complicated structure. Confidentiality is becoming increasingly essential as the amount of information used to power these technologies grows. CPS frequently gathers large volumes of data to make informed choices and meet operational objectives. Intelligent CPSs are also vulnerable to privacy and security intrusions as a result of the flaws in current information and communication technology. Furthermore, as smart CPSs get more complicated, security problems will appear. Owing to the ever-changing cyber-physical world, attackers will be capable of launching increasingly complex assaults in the ahead. As a result, modern construction paradigms, system designs, and cryptographic protocols are required for enhanced security and privacy protection in smart CPSs. Through signal processing to analyze information, CPS covers a wide variety of academic areas. The core architecture for CPS, encompassing intelligent devices and network characteristics in connection to the TCP/IP stack, is briefly reviewed in this article [1]. As a result, numerous dangers, attack types with associated subcategories, and potential repercussions are explored, as well as a study of alternative ways to dealing with current concerns. Additionally, threat modeling techniques were included in the scope of this project. Also examined are the demands and prerequisites for security CPS. As a result, the focus of this article is on explaining various components of the CPS in terms of protection and stability concerns. Virtualization software as an essential tool for abstractions plays a vital part in CPS since it reflects the activities of the real world onto the cyber domain. In this respect, the paper discusses the problems connected with mobility and virtualization; as a result, the article discusses three primary forms of virtualization, namely connection, gadget, and software virtualization.

Despite the use of CPSs, the privacy and security risks connected with these systems have grown. Attackers are using silent assaults to get accessibility to CPSs' confidential information. Various privacy-preserving methods, such as cryptography and k-anonymity, have been proposed in the past to keep CPS data safer. Unfortunately, due to advancements in CPS structure, these approaches will require some changes. Conversely, differential privacy has shown to be an effective method for protecting CPS online privacy. The authors [2] offer a complete overview of differentially private methods for CPSs in this study. The authors looked at how differential privacy is used and implemented in four key CPS application areas, namely, power systems, transportation infrastructure, medical systems, and the manufacturing IoT. With the number of applications for Blockchain (BC) [3] technology CPS is growing at an exponential rate. Nevertheless, due to the intricacy involved, defining durable and accurate smart contracts (SCs) for these smart applications is a difficult process. Current manufacturing, technological, and business operations are being modernized by SC. It is self-executing, self-verifiable, and integrated within the BC, obviating the need for trustworthy third-party platforms and, as a result, saving both administrative and operational expenses. It also increases system performance while lowering security threats. SCs, on the other hand, are enthusiastic about Industry 4.0's new technological changes.

CPS requires cybersecurity [4] and it imperils safety that can be implemented by hazard analysis, losses, and safety constraints. CPS also requires improved design tools that enable the design methodology. The design methodology is used to support scalability and complexity management, specification, analysis and modeling, and do verification and validation. CPS has applications in various fields like—robotics, military, energy, healthcare, infrastructure, consumer, communication, transportation, etc. Moreover, CPS is a generic intelligent feedback system that is real-time, adaptive, and predictive and has distributed network with the power of actuation and wireless sensing. There are various essential components of CPS as shown in Figure 12.1. These CPS essential components are described below:

- Internet of Things of Sensors—The IoT refers to a network of physical items, sometimes known as "objects," that are

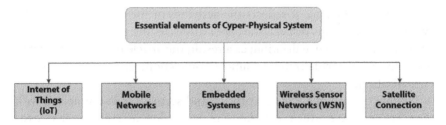

Figure 12.1 Essential elements of CPS.

integrated with sensing devices, applications, and other techniques that are used to communicate and exchange information between devices and organizations over the Internet. Both CPS and IoT relate to current trends in combining digital skills, such as network connectivity, with physical devices and systems. The lack of clear differentiating measures and the consolidation of terminologies point to a growing agreement on CPS and IoT ideas' similarity. Through the integration of the different organizations' academic, creativity, and standards activities, this confluence provides chances for development.

- Mobile Networks—Cellular networks are another name for mobile networks. They're composed of "cells," [5] which are generally hexagonal pieces of terrain with at minimum one transmitter cell tower and employ a variety of radio transmissions. According to the desires and requirements produced by the usage of mobile apps, mobile network congestion is substantially rising. The mobile networks play a crucial role in the architecture of CPS.

- Embedded Systems—A CPS [6] is a system that combines computing with physical processes. Conventional methods are monitored and controlled by embedded systems and servers, which generally include feedback mechanisms where physical activities impact calculations and vice versa. CPS is about the junction, not the unification, of the physical and the cyber as an intellectual exercise. Understanding the cyber and physical individual components is insufficient. Rather, we must comprehend their interactions. In basic terms, cyber-physical systems refer to the entire network, including both hardware and virtual elements. Just the primary brain of the computer, wherein your instructions are executed, is referred to as an embedded device.

- Wireless Sensor Networks (WSN)—WSN [7] are a significant component in CPS because of their minimal sophistication and resilience. In a dispersed controlled environment, integrating a wireless sensor network into a cyber-physical system delivers enormous benefits. Nevertheless, the CPS's complex structure and WSN make it vulnerable to both internal and external attacks. These risks may result in network economic or architectural damages.

- Satellite Communication—The operational circumstances [8] in an inclusive environment pose a geographical challenge for CPS in geo area, and the human computer interaction will be critical. A shift in our attitude about GIS might lead to the development of new value-added geospatial data applications. It will necessitate new data exchange, analytics, protection, and security methods and systems, among other things. The authors [9] have created a panorama of available communication modeling products and approaches, and then offer an infrastructure for engaging with the entire CPS model.

12.2 Cyber-Attacks and Security in CPS

To execute sophisticated control and automation activities, our civilization is heavily dependent on the effective coupling of physical and digital technologies. Designing [10] such cyber-physical systems to assure their effectiveness, safety, and reliability is an extremely important study topic. Computational and physiological assets are tightly intertwined in many real-world systems: embedded systems and telecommunication systems regulate physical actuators that function in the outside globe and obtain information from sensors, resulting in a smart control loop competent of adjustment, independence, and increased efficiency. CPS is a term that is used to describe such organizations. Due to wide range of applications, CPS possesses the need for cybersecurity. Pertaining to cybersecurity domain, the CPS are very much prone to intrusion detection, privacy, malicious attacks and resilience.

Computer engineering science [11] have historically treated security and safety as separate issues. The addition of computer aspects to CPSs has opened a completely new world of possible difficulties that conventional engineers are not usually aware of. Software engineers and/or technologists, on the other hand, have generally thought of security, as an information or communications security issue that should be addressed. Improvements in CPSs and the Internet of Things necessitate a coordinated approach to security and safety. This article [12] establishes a safety/security detection mechanism for CPSs and IoT systems, as well as examines new approaches for improving CPS and IoT scheme security and safety. People faced additional problems because of the establishment of CPS. Assuring the cybersecurity of CPS is among the most difficult issues in a wide range of cyber-attack countermeasures. The purpose of this study is to examine and categorize current research publications on CPS security. CPS philosophical concerns are discussed. Their impact on many elements of people's life is examined. The functioning of the CPS is explained. The major challenges and answers in estimating the impacts of cyber-attacks, modelling and detection of cyber-attacks, and developing security architecture are discussed. The most common forms of assaults and threats to CPS are examined.

CPS has created preparation for future customized healthcare because of its significant leap ahead. Such technologies, nevertheless, are vulnerable to cyber-attacks. The security problems of CPS should be carefully examined and handled in order to offer patients with a safe and trustworthy medical experience. As a result, this article kicks off a debate on CPS security. Security concerns with its key components, such as wireless body area networks, cloud technology, and 5G, are highlighted. The significant impact of virtualization to secure communication is also examined in this chapter [13]. To control and analyse physical phenomena, CPSs combine communication and computation characteristics. Communication networks are frequently used to specific methodology, motors, and devices, which are typically built on Programmable Logic Controllers (PLC). The usage of communications infrastructure makes the CPS more vulnerable to assaults that might put it in dangerous situations. In this work [14], we present a defensive approach for centralized management networks that avoids impairments caused by cyber assaults in the sensor and/or actuator communication methods without altering the behavior of the closed environment when it is not invaded.

IoT devices collect data from their surroundings, do calculations on it, and then retain or communicate the information to another device with comparable characteristics. Numerous trust and security problems develop because of this communication mechanism, which must be addressed immediately. Certain trust and security problems might pose a danger to the IoT infrastructure; therefore, they must be addressed using the most up-to-date design, methodology, and technologies. This article [15] aims to illustrate some of the most significant challenges to IoT security and trust, as well as how current design addresses them. There are various cyber-attacks possible on the CPSs. Most of them are shown in Figure 12.2. The cyber-attacks related to CPS are categorized based on the various components of CPS. Cyber-attacks like GPS spoofing, false radar signals, failure of equipment, illegal access, and hardware tampering are related to the sensors that are the part of CPS. Attacks on actuators comprises of power attacks, installation on spyware, bounded attacks, software tampering and compromised signals.

Communication systems are also vulnerable to the majority of cyber-attacks, most of them are—data theft, spoofing of data packets, eavesdropping, Sybil attacks, and software malfunctioning. The Feedback systems form the integral part of CPS and they are vulnerable to fake feedback, attack on integrity, and disruption of control. Selective Forwarding [16], Packet Impersonation attack, Protocol Rewinding, Sybil, and other telecommunication assaults can be used to interrupt resource distribution among nodes in favor of virus that violates system package routing. Any manipulation of the data may result in problems in subsequent processing needs. If an adversary can only collect and send genuine data packets,

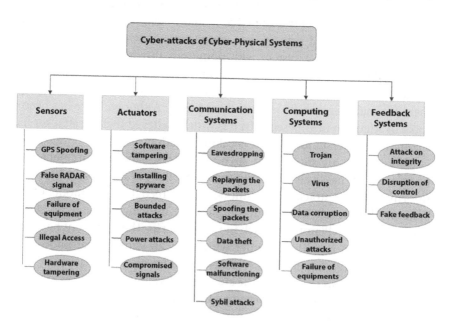

Figure 12.2 Cyber-attacks of CPS.

then recording some "regular" data and playing it, back to evade detection is a viable attack strategy. The creation of protocols to create connections between disturbance producers and listening devices between and within CPS is required for secure communication. Numerous e-businesses and retail establishments are turning to IoT-based technologies for their sales, advertising, efficiency, and marketing as technology progresses. Such IoT-based products are extremely beneficial to both the company and the client. Those approaches, nevertheless, are subject to a variety of privacy and security problems. The increase of cyber risks in IoT, the corporate perspective of IoT for E-Business & Commerce Security, developments in e-business and retail as a result of IoT, and the movement of malicious attackers linked to security and privacy issues in e-business and retail were all described in this article [17].

The interplay between cyber realm and physical sphere components and processes may be used to improve the cyber-physical system's safety. To accomplish so, we must first examine multiple cyber and physical domain information flows and use model capabilities to define the relationship between them. The authors [18] provided a concept of cross-domain safety for cyber-physical systems in this research, as well as a vulnerability assessment methodology that can be used to generate innovative cross-domain attack scenarios, attack detection techniques, and so on. The manner humans live now and in the future will be radically altered by technological advancements in decentralized CPS. A multi-agent CPS, from the standpoint of security and privacy, is a connection of sensors, actuators, and compute nodes, i.e., a system with numerous threat vectors and hidden vulnerabilities originating from both computer and direct assaults. In this work [19], we propose that a fundamental change in application development for multi-agent CPS is urgently required. Although there has been a spike in attention in CPS security, it is widely believed that the attacker has a complete understanding of physical information systems.

This study [20] shows that such an unreasonable requirement may be relaxed: by passively watching the controller parameters and sensory information, the attacker may still be able to recognize the model of the system. The assault with input–output data information may be classified as a Known-Plaintext Attack in this scenario. The opponent has been given sufficient conditions under which he can gain special knowledge about the underlying physical systems. To address security issues in CPS, only a few tools were created. The study on this subject is in growing market in order to enhance knowledge and provide lot additional security mechanisms for the CPS. In this work [21], we explore existing risks to CPSs, suggest a categorization and grid for these vulnerabilities, and use a quantitative method to do a basic statistical analysis of the obtained data. We discovered that four key contributors to the threat classification of CPSs are the kind of threat, effect, purpose, and event types. In this article [22], we use a unified framework to analyze and standardize existing research on CPS safety. We pursue the well-known classification system of dangers, security flaws, threats, and control mechanisms from a safety standpoint; from a CPS elements point of view, we concentrate on cyber, physical, and cyber-physical elements; and from a CPS systems approach, we investigate general CPS characteristics as well as reflective structures, such as smart metering and healthcare CPS. The paradigm can be both generic and particular, capturing any information needed in a CPS program.

12.3   Privacy in CPS

Vital infrastructure, smart facilities, and industrial control systems all rely heavily on CPS. Because they lack sufficient security mechanisms, they are more susceptible and unstable than traditional computer systems, posing a new threat to the control system. In situations of risk, CPS personal data is essential and delicate, and its disclosure would allow an adversary to corrupt manufacturing systems, raising the danger of human injury and boosting the possible loss of assets. The authors [23] have presented a new risk vector for CPS in which an attacker may remotely and quickly extract critical control and data programs from CPS without requiring any identification. CPS relies on a wide range of discrete and varied sensors, which may jeopardize the confidentiality of these new technologies' consumers.

Challenges [24] on privacy are usually passive in nature, and may need gaining access to private information or inferring particular information from the public data. Following the identification of a CPS's flaws, defenses must be developed to restrict or impede adversary access. The defenses are divided into three categories. Security methods like as identification, access restrictions, security rules, and network segmentation are used to prevent the attack. Despite the importance of preventative methods, attackers with sufficient money, time, and dedication can still defeat the CPS network and execute effective assaults. Anomaly behavior and assaults in the network are detected using detection techniques. Since most CPS operate in real time, a security protocol may be required to intervene immediately in order to minimize identified threats. Proactive reaction refers to the measures taken after an attack has been discovered, with the goal of reducing the assault's effect and, if feasible, restoring the system. We concentrate on those that are conducted online in response to the identification of an assault and are largely automated.

Transportation Cyber-Physical Systems (TCPS) [25] have progressed in tandem with the global transportation sector. The fast spread of TCPS presents us with a wealth of information and limitless opportunities for analysing and comprehending the complicated underlying mechanism that regulates the new intelligence environment. TCPS also opens up a slew of new application possibilities, including vehicle safety, energy economy, pollution reduction, and intelligent repair. Nevertheless, when using TCPS's services and convenience, users, cars, and even the networks themselves may lose anonymity during data transfer and analysis. In a general sense, this chapter summarizes the state-of-the-art study results on TCPS. Firstly, the authors have mentioned the standard TCPS paradigm and its basic data transmission method. Secondly, the authors provided a bird's-eye perspective of the current literature on the difficulties and privacy protection measures when it comes to TCPS privacy issues. Finally, the authors discussed the most current difficulties in TCPS as well as possible solutions to privacy concerns.

This article [26] gives a high-level overview of new control-theoretic methods to CPS privacy and security. It approaches the topic from a risk-based perspective and creates a model structure that allows us to present and connect many of the latest contributions to the field. The authors focused on the notion of risk in terms of CPS under cyber-attacks, with a specific focus on characterisation of known attacks and assessment of likelihood and impact for CPS. The risk management process is then utilized to provide an assessment of the region and to map various contributions to three key components of the framework. The protection of CPSs is critical for protecting sensitive data and identifying cyber-attacks. For securing actual information and detecting cyber-attacks, creating a comprehensive privacy-preserving anomaly detection technique necessitates physical and cyber data about devices, such as Supervisory Control and Data Acquisition (SCADA). This study [27] proposed PPAD-CPS, a novel privacy-preserving outlier detection methodology for protecting sensitive information and detecting hostile findings in power systems and associated network traffic.

The authors initially suggested a safe and smart framework for increasing data privacy in this paper [28]. Next, the authors showed a novel privacy-preserving collaborative learning mechanism and proposed a two-phase data breach mitigation system that includes intelligent data conversion and cooperative data leakage identification. The success of our suggested system is demonstrated by numerical findings based on a real-world dataset, which indicate that our scheme can achieve high precision, economy, and safety. CPS are part of the next era of integrated ICT systems, which are more prevalent in our daily lives. The most difficult challenge in the CPS area is ensuring cybersecurity against cyber-attacks. The purpose of this article [29] is to examine threats and assaults in different CPS domains, as well as to explore defensive strategies for avoiding assaults. In the research of the challenges and solutions in the estimate of cyber-attack repercussions, attack modeling, and proposed security implementation, several security research have been contrasted.

The most recent homomorphic cryptographic techniques only handle a restricted set of data types, rendering them challenging to use in a real-world setting. The authors [30] presented a concurrent completely homomorphic encryption method that allows floating-point values to overcome this restriction. The suggested technique not only broadens the data types allowed by current fully homomorphic encryption techniques, but it also takes use of the features of multi-nodes in a public cloud to perform parallel cryptography through group-wise cipher text calculations. ALPHA [31], an anonymous orthogonal code-based privacy-preserving method for CPSs, is presented in this paper. The CPS is a fundamental component of today's power grid, aggregating power usage from connected phones while maintaining customer information private, unidentified, and unidentifiable. An Anonymous Orthogonal Code-Based Privacy Preserving Scheme for Industrial Cyber-Physical Systems (ALPHA) is a proposed scheme that uses orthogonal bit codes and a systematized method to confirm and handle user information confidentiality and untraceability while minimizing computational and communication overhead expenses.

In distributed software settings, this article [32] offers a combination of intent access controls with an obscurity approach for privacy-preserving policies and mechanisms that illustrate policy conflicting issues. This integrated strategy will secure specific private information while also allowing data to be shared with authorized parties for legitimate purposes. We utilized a heuristic algorithm to a privacy accessing management system in which the private need is to fulfil the k-anonymity, and we evaluated data with k-anonymity to produce a specific amount of concealment that preserves the utility of information. In a distributed environment [33] with spread spectrum receivers, the authors offered a private information waveform design technique supported by artificial noise (AN) to improve communication concealment. Initially, the authors looked at the scenario when the eavesdropper has complete channel state knowledge (CSI). To maximize the attainable secrecy performance, the authors optimize the AF factor for transmitting the information bearing signal as well as the

AN autocorrelation. Completing a succession of semidefinite programmes yields the best solution. Furthermore, using an incomplete eavesdropper's CSI, a more realistic case is examined.

12.4   Conclusion & Future Trends in CPS Security

CPS are cyber-physical systems that engage in a feedback mechanism with the assistance of human interference, engagement, and usage. As the foundation for developing and future intelligent applications, these technologies will strengthen our vital infrastructure and have the capability to have a substantial influence on our everyday lives. The growing usage of CPS, on the other side, introduces new dangers that might have serious implications for consumers. Because security issues in this field have become a worldwide issue, developing strong, safe, and effective CPS is a major research topic. Security concerns are not modern, but technological advancements need the development of innovative ways to safeguard data from unintended effects. New risks and cyber-attacks will continue to be influenced, necessitating the development of new techniques to safeguard CPS. This article [34] examines security concerns at several stages of the CPS architecture, as well as threat assessment and CPS security approaches. Ultimately, the problems, prospective study topics, and potential solutions are given and debated.

CPS often entails a network of interconnected technologies that can constantly monitor real-world objects and activities. They are similar to IoT systems, with the exception that CPS concentrates on the interplay of mechanical, communication, and computing operations. Because of their integration with IoT, a new CPS component, the Internet of Cyber-Physical Things, has emerged (IoCPT). The rapid and substantial evolution of CPS has an impact on many parts of people's lives and allows for a larger range of services and solutions, such as e-Health, smart homes, and e-Commerce. Interlinking the virtual and physical realms, on the other hand, introduces new security threats. As a result, CPS security has piqued the interest of both academics and businesses. The essential elements of CPS, as well as the associated applications, technology, and regulations, are covered in this article [35]. Furthermore, CPS unpatched vulnerabilities, risks, and assaults are examined, as well as important concerns and difficulties. In particular, current security methods are given and assessed, with their primary shortcomings identified. Ultimately, based on the lessons acquired during this extensive study, numerous comments and suggestions are made.

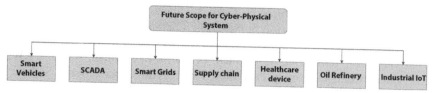

Figure 12.3 Future scope for CPS.

CPS has its wide range of applications and is evolving day-by-day. A connectivity of embedded devices that communicate with tangible outputs and inputs is referred to as a CPS. In other respects, CPS is made up of a collection of linked systems that can observe and modify real-world IoT objects and activities. Sensors, integrators, and actuators are the three primary core components of the CPS. CPS systems may also detect and adapt to their surroundings, allowing them to influence and manipulate the physical universe. Figure 12.3 shows the future scope of CPS in various domains. Domains like smart vehicles—electronic devices, unmanned vehicles, come under the future scope of CPS. Moreover, advanced areas like SCADA, smart grids, supply chain, healthcare devices, oil refineries and industrial IoT comes under the purview of CPS.

Mobile CPS might serve as a fundamental approach for the construction of automotive communication networks, enhancing user privacy and security in changing vehicular communication situations. The authors initially differentiate mobile CPS from regular CPS in this study [36]. After that, the authors went through their three new application aspects: vehicular networking technologies, healthcare systems, and mobile learning. Following that, the authors highlighted four major mobile CPS research issues: safety, power consumption, mobile dynamic environment, and system reliability.

This chapter has highlighted the various aspects of security and privacy in the CPS. The cyber-attacks on CPS are also highlighted in this chapter. Moreover, the future aspects and research areas related to CPS are also mentioned in this chapter.

References

1. Nazarenko, A.A. and Safdar, G.A., Survey on security and privacy issues in cyber physical systems. *AIMS Electron. Electr. Eng.*, 3, 2, 111–143, Apr. 2019.

2. Hassan, M.U., Rehmani, M.H., Chen, J., Differential Privacy Techniques for Cyber Physical Systems: A Survey. *IEEE Commun. Surv. Tutor.*, 22, 1, 746–789, Jan. 2020.

3. Gupta, R., Tanwar, S., Al-Turjman, F., Italiya, P., Nauman, A., Kim, S.W., Smart Contract Privacy Protection Using AI in Cyber-Physical Systems: Tools, Techniques and Challenges. *IEEE Access*, 8, 24746–24772, 2020.

4. Lee, E.A., Cyber-Physical Systems - a Concept Map, 2012. https://ptolemy.berkeley.edu/projects/cps/ (accessed Aug. 31, 2021).

5. Viswanathan, P., Understanding How a Mobile Network Works, May 26, 2020. https://www.lifewire.com/how-does-a-mobile-network-work-2373338 (accessed Sep. 01, 2021).

6. Dhandha, A., What is the difference between embedded system vs cyber physical system? - Quora, 2018. https://www.quora.com/What-is-the-difference-between-embedded-system-vs-cyber-physical-system?share=1 (accessed Sep. 01, 2021).

7. Ali, S., Al Balushi, T., Nadir, Z., Hussain, O.K., WSN Security Mechanisms for CPS. *Stud. Comput. Intell.*, 768, 65–87, 2018.

8. Yan, W. and Sakairi, T., Geo CPS: Spatial challenges and opportunities for CPS in the geographic dimension. *J. Urban Manage.*, 8, 3, 331–341, Dec. 2019.

9. Deschamps, H., Tauran, B., Cardoso, J., Siron, P., Distributing Cyber-Physical Systems Simulation: The Satellite Constellation Case, 2017.

10. Zanero, S., Cyber-Physical Systems. *Comput. (Long. Beach. Calif.)*, 50, 4, 14–16, 2017.

11. Wolf, M. and Serpanos, D., Safety and security in cyber-physical systems and internet-of-things systems. *Proc. IEEE*, vol. 106, pp. 9–20, Jan. 2018.

12. Alguliyev, R., Imamverdiyev, Y., Sukhostat, L., Cyber-physical systems and their security issues. *Comput. Ind.*, 100, 212–223, Sep. 2018.

13. Saleem, K., Tan, Z., Buchanan, W., Security for Cyber-Physical Systems in Healthcare, in: *Heal. 4.0 How Virtualization Big Data are Revolutionizing Healthc*, pp. 233–251, Jan. 2017.

14. Lima, P.M., Carvalho, L.K., Moreira, M.V., Detectable and Undetectable Network Attack Security of Cyber-physical Systems, in: *IFAC-PapersOnLine*, vol. 51, pp. 179–185, Jan. 2018.

15. Kaushik, K. and Singh, K., Security and trust in iot communications: Role and impact, in: *Advances in Intelligent Systems and Computing*, vol. 989, pp. 791–798, 2020.

16. Krotofil, M. and Gollmann, D., The process matters: Ensuring data veracity in Cyber-physical systems. *ASIACCS 2015 - Proc. 10th ACM Symp. Information, Comput. Commun. Secur*, pp. 133–144, Apr. 2015.

17. Kaushik, K. and Dahiya, S., Security and privacy in iot based e-business and retail. *Proc. 2018 Int. Conf. Syst. Model. Adv. Res. Trends, SMART 2018*, pp. 78–81, Nov. 2018.

18. Chhetri, S.R., Wan, J., Al Faruque, M.A., Cross-domain security of cyber-physical systems. *Proc. Asia South Pacific Des. Autom. Conf. ASP-DAC*, pp. 200–205, Feb. 2017.

19. Bonakdarpour, B., Deshmukh, J.V., Pajic, M., Opportunities and Challenges in Monitoring Cyber-Physical Systems Security. *Lect. Notes Comput. Sci. (including Subser. Lect. Notes Artif. Intell. Lect. Notes Bioinformatics)*, 11247 LNCS, 9–18, Nov. 2018.

20. Yuan, Y. and Mo, Y., Security for cyber-physical systems: Secure control against known-plaintext attack. *Sci. China Technol. Sci. 2020*, 63, 9, 1637–1646, Jul. 2020.

21. Al-Mhiqani, M.N. *et al.*, Cyber-security incidents: A review cases in cyber-physical systems. *Int. J. Adv. Comput. Sci. Appl.*, 9, 1, 499–508, 2018.

22. Humayed, A., Lin, J., Li, F., Luo, B., Cyber-Physical Systems Security - A Survey. *IEEE Internet Things J.*, 4, 6, 1802–1831, Dec. 2017.

23. Yang, K., Lin, X., Sun, L., CShield: Enabling code privacy for Cyber–Physical systems. *Futur. Gener. Comput. Syst.*, 125, 564–574, Dec. 2021.

24. Giraldo, J., Sarkar, E., Cardenas, A.A., Maniatakos, M., Kantarcioglu, M., Security and Privacy in Cyber-Physical Systems: A Survey of Surveys. *IEEE Des. Test*, 34, 4, 7–17, Aug. 2017.

25. Han, M., Duan, Z., Li, Y., Privacy Issues for Transportation Cyber Physical Systems, in: *SpringerBriefs Comput. Sci.*, vol. 0, pp. 67–86, 2017.

26. Chong, M.S., Sandberg, H., Teixeira, A.M.H., A tutorial introduction to security and privacy for cyber-physical systems. *2019 18th Eur. Control Conf. ECC 2019*, pp. 968–978, Jun. 2019.

27. Keshk, M., Sitnikova, E., Moustafa, N., Hu, J., Khalil, I., An Integrated Framework for Privacy-Preserving Based Anomaly Detection for Cyber-Physical Systems. *IEEE Trans. Sustain. Comput.*, 6, 1, 66–79, Mar. 2019.

28. Lu, Y., Huang, X., Dai, Y., Maharjan, S., Zhang, Y., Federated Learning for Data Privacy Preservation in Vehicular Cyber-Physical Systems. *IEEE Netw.*, 34, 3, 50–56, May 2020.

29. Thaseen, S., Cherukuri, A.K., Ahmad, A., Improving Security and Privacy in Cyber-Physical Systems, in: *Cybersecurity Priv. Cyber-Physical Syst*, pp. 3–43, Jun. 2019.

30. Min, Z., Yang, G., Sangaiah, A.K., Bai, S., Liu, G., A privacy protection-oriented parallel fully homomorphic encryption algorithm in cyber physical systems. *EURASIP J. Wirel. Commun. Netw. 2019*, 1, 1–14, Jan. 2019.

31. Ali, W., Din, I.U., Almogren, A., Kumar, N., ALPHA: An Anonymous Orthogonal Code-Based Privacy Preserving Scheme for Industrial Cyber-Physical Systems. *IEEE Trans. Ind. Inform.*, 17, 11, 7716–7724, Nov. 2021.

32. Sharma, T., Bambenek, J.C., Bashir, M., Preserving Privacy in Cyber-physical-social systems: An Anonymity and Access Control Approach, Jan. 2020. Accessed: Sep. 01, 2021. [Online]. Available: https://www.ideals.illinois.edu/handle/2142/106049.

33. Xu, Q., Ren, P., Song, H., Du, Q., Security-Aware Waveforms for Enhancing Wireless Communications Privacy in Cyber-Physical Systems via Multipath Receptions. *IEEE Internet Things J.*, 4, 6, 1924–1933, Dec. 2017.

34. Ashibani, Y. and Mahmoud, Q.H., Cyber physical systems security: Analysis, challenges and solutions. *Comput. Secur.*, 68, 81–97, Jul. 2017.

35. Yaacoub, J.P.A., Salman, O., Noura, H.N., Kaaniche, N., Chehab, A., Malli, M., Cyber-physical systems security: Limitations, issues and future trends. *Microprocess. Microsyst.*, 77, 103201, Sep. 2020.

36. Guo, Y., Hu, X., Hu, B., Cheng, J., Zhou, M., Kwok, R.Y.K., Mobile Cyber Physical Systems: Current Challenges and Future Networking Applications. *IEEE Access*, 6, 12360–12368, Dec. 2017.

13
Applications of Cyber-Physical Systems

Amandeep Kaur[1]* and Jyotir Moy Chatterjee[2]

[1]Department of Computer Engineering, Punjabi University, Patiala, India
[2]Department of IT, Lord Buddha Education Foundation, Kathmandu, Nepal

Abstract

Cyber-Physical System (CPS) has recently gained intense popularity in the digital world. It has defined a new generation of digital system that mainly focuses on complex interconnectedness and amalgamation of virtual and physical worlds. CPS comprises of highly integrated computation, communication, control, and physical elements. The idea of Industry 4.0 has further surged the demand of CPS as one of the important components. So, in order to understand CPS more precisely, this study presents a detailed survey of the varied CPS application areas with more focus on features/architecture and related work. There are numerous interdisciplinary areas pertaining to CPS but this article is limited to Healthcare, Education, Agriculture, Energy Management, Smart Transportation, Smart Manufacturing and Smart Buildings. The other interesting CPS application areas are Military, Robotics, Decision Making, Process Control, Diagnostics, Aeronautics, and Civil Infrastructure Monitoring.

Keywords: Cyber-physical systems, application areas of cyber-physical systems, CPS applications, Industry 4.0, smart manufacturing, smart buildings, healthcare

13.1 Introduction

Cyber-Physical Systems (CPSs) refer to integration of computational systems with the physical world objects. CPS provides collaboration of physical and virtual environments that requires additional computational power, computing resources, communication channels and storage for

---

*Corresponding author: amandeepk@ieee.org

Uzzal Sharma, Parma Nand, Jyotir Moy Chatterjee, Vishal Jain, Noor Zaman Jhanjhi and R. Sujatha (eds.)
Cyber-Physical Systems: Foundations and Techniques, (289–310) © 2022 Scrivener Publishing LLC

monitoring and controlling the physical world entities. CPS represents a wave of advanced digital systems, that exhibit following functionalities:

(1) Establishing advanced connectivity that would confirm real-time acquisition of data from the physical world and interpretation of information by virtual environment.
(2) Constructing a virtual environment with intelligent data management, analytics and computational abilities. The use of CPS aims to increase the implementation of large-scale systems by improving the adaptability, autonomy, efficiency, functionality, reliability, safety, and usability of such systems [13].

At high level of abstraction, CPS has six major building blocks, as shown in Figure 13.1, consisting of physical entities (sensors, actuators, embedded and/or physical systems) and cyber entities that ensure effective communication, control and computation over the cyber world [11, 27].

These, physical and virtual components are deeply coupled to be able to operate on different temporal and spatial dimensions, while exhibiting numerous and unique behavioral methodologies and interact with each other in ways that change with context [16].

Although CPS related research started way back in 2006 [20] when this term was first coined in the National Workshop on Cyber-physical Systems. But, with the commencement of Industry 4.0 i.e. the fourth industrial

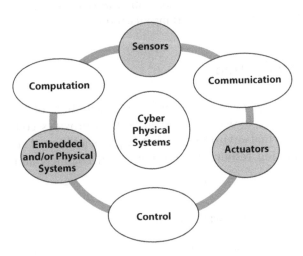

Figure 13.1 Building blocks of cyber-physical systems.

revolution, CPS has attracted researchers in a different perspective in which CPS has been defined as one of the key technologies of Industry 4.0.

13.2   Applications of Cyber-Physical Systems

Cyber-physical systems (CPSs) have attracted a lot of attention these days and considered to be a prominent technology. Many researchers have explored and presented studies related to collaboration of CPS with varied domains. CPS application domain covers varied areas including agriculture, energy, education, healthcare, manufacturing, transportation, military, smart environment, etc. In this section we will discuss some CPS applications with focus on architecture, features and related works.

13.2.1   Healthcare

CPS has been found to be a strong competitor for the technologies used to develop healthcare applications including on-site and off-site patient care. CPS provides ability to monitor patients remotely and give feedback despite of patient's location. Extensive research is carried out for the medical sensors [30, 51] deployed in healthcare sector. These advanced sensors aid in remote patients' data collection. This collected data is further sent to a gateway through wireless communication for safe storage and timely availability for the physicians.

Primarily, healthcare CPS, also known as Medical CPS (MCPS), research focuses on intelligent sensor embedded systems for real time patient health observation, telemedicine systems that help in providing medical services remotely and autonomous robots to coordinate with patient's physical activities [5]. As per author [13], MCPS are extensively being used in hospitals and other medical care services to provide high quality and ceaseless medical aid to patients, but there are numerous challenges being faced from safety view point [35].

In [22], authors have presented a classification of CPS perspectives based on the service being provided with following categories:

1) *Application*—CPS in healthcare offers varied applications/ services related to deployment in hospitals, assisted living, and elderly care. Depending upon the services being offered by MCPS, the elements of architecture vary. For instance, in hospitals where the medical aid is readily available, the intensive care unit (ICU) and Operation Theater (OT)

require more complex and safety-critical CPS architecture. In a controlled environment, a networked closed-loop CPS is suggested that works by involving medical professionals in the working to ensure patient safety and effective workflows. On the contrary, in the assisted living environment, health monitoring without intervening the patient's normal living routine is desirable. The MCPS for such environments would be very useful in providing support and care both in elderly living and individual homes [22].

2) *Framework*—The framework of a CPS is delineated by three major components namely, infrastructure, data requirement and composition. From the infrastructure viewpoint, CPS architecture can be server based or cloud based. Server based infrastructure is considered more appropriate for small architecture whereas cloud-based offers more scalability and accessibility and are more economical [58]. CPS architectures also depend on the type of data to be used. In healthcare, we deal with variety of data ranging from simple textual data like temperature, blood pressure to complex data like MRI images, CT scans, etc. [63] stated that depending on applications, the data gathering techniques and data transmission procedures vary. In addition, CPS architecture also needs to incorporate the computational and communicational requirements of the service.

3) *Sensing ability*—The primary functionality of every CPS is sensing. The biomedical sensors collect data from patients as input and fed to controllers for further processing and use. The major elements governing sensing ability of CPS are types of sensors (homogenous and/or heterogeneous), sensing methodology (active or passive) and sensor parameters (single or multiple) to be used during patient data collection.

4) *Data management*—Another important perspective for CPS architectures is the management of data collected in the data acquisition phase which involves data integration, storage and processing. Data integration involves collection of data from sensors and its processing to obtain vital information. This process reduces the amount of information to be shared over communicational channels. The data is then stored in the real-time database for its timely availability [17]. Data processing can be performed in distributed manner, in base

station or in cloud. The most crucial part of a MCPS is real time processing of data [32].

5) *Computation*—Computational processes in MCPS are executed for two major parameters: modeling (identification of necessary methodology to implement) and monitoring (observing patients from anywhere and at any time). Therefore, physicians need to access the required patient data accurately and timely [22].

6) *Communicational channels*—In MCPS, the communicational channels involves collection of patient data through sensors and delivering it over the cloud [23]. Recent developments in image processing as mentioned in [4] have presented ways for extracting and compressing images to be shared over communicational channels with higher efficiency.

7) *Security*—It is of utmost importance to ensure the security of patient data for any kind of unethical access and theft. So, MCPS architecture must inculcate high security features.

8) *Control*—To bring effectiveness in dealing with emergency patients and calling the appropriate medical physician, the Medical CPSs must be aided with control and actuation resulting in appropriate decision making.

13.2.1.1   Related Work

A number of research studies have proposed different CPS architectures in healthcare sector with their respective features and limitations.

[44] delineated an MCPS that facilitates physicians for diagnosing local and remote residents. It is based on cloud computing and facilitates physicians in collection, evaluation and diagnosis patient's data. The operability of this system is highly dependent on high speed internet connectivity which is quite difficult to be ensured in remote areas.

[46] investigated the technique for an efficient retrieval of the dental images from the databases in real time. Image attributes were used to recover and depict these images. The process includes identification of images and then classification into different teeth categories. The system has been found to be robust and provides accurate results. However, the implementation of this system requires a huge teeth model database.

In [39], authors have developed a system to be implemented in the operating room through integration of information technology and cybernetics. The CPS developed consisted of a robotic nurse that would provide assistance to surgeons during surgeries by passing surgical instruments. In addition, it would also keep a count of surgical instruments used as a personal health record.

To aid physicians in their routine tasks, [3] proposed a system that provides electronic checklist. This system was also built with the feature to interconnection with other devices and software applications. The major features offered by this system consisted of supporting medical staff in intensive care units to prepare medication for patients, data gathering, and other routine activities. Although this system offers multiple advanced features like time and profile based analysis of patients, patient care monitoring, etc., this system is not found yet to be applicable to all medical domains.

The research study in [57] is based on detection of varied falling postures. A particular falling posture is depicted by measuring the variation in numerical values between the body contact on ground and the body on rest at a specific time interval. It also identifies different types of daily activities such as jumping, walking, jogging, sitting, standing, movement on a staircase, etc.

[28] presented a study based on analysis of posture for predicting the recovery period post hip replacement surgery. The proposed system is an interconnection of seven sensors installed at some specific locations near surgery part. System detects the hip position and evaluates the load applied on the affected area by collecting information sent through these sensors. Furthermore, it also raises an alarm to notify the physicians in case of any unfavorable conditions.

The authors in [34] developed a system that collects data from wearable devices in order to monitor the medical profile of the people. The system is meant to capture audio and video signals to initiate early response to accidents.

[60] is a research article based on wireless bio-sensor network system, developed to predict heartbeat rate, pulse rate and oxygen saturation in the patient's body. The implementation is based on spatial contextual data collected from environmental parameters like temperature, and precipitation. This system also offered an interactive interface for medical professionals to help them monitor important signs from patients.

[40] proposed MCPS for collecting and accessing real time data through sensor networks. The major components of the proposed architecture were medical sensors for data collection, monitoring facility, cloud storage and a healthcare official for regulating security policies.

13.2.2 Education

On one side, where corona lockdown has hit the economy of the world badly but on the other side drastic rise in E-learning has been experienced. The need of Virtual learning Environments have gained popularity during this time of crisis. Furthermore, the collaboration of physical environments and virtual learning environments proposed as an Educational Cyber-Physical Systems (ECPSs) has also attracted researchers.

Based on related studies, it has been observed that an ECPS paradigm must follow a set of mandatory requirements to provide effective communicational channels to help students and faculty interact in a better way. Moreover, administrative, assessment and pedagogical tools for managing learning process effectively as also desirable.

The essential components of an ECPS are:

- *Virtual elements:* This is required to enhance student involvement in learning process. Different virtual elements can be images, videos, project based learning, demonstrations, etc.
- *Interfacing:* involving students in virtual activities through the physical modules.
- *Physical modules:* physical resources for providing interactions among students.
- *Feedback modules:* monitoring student progression.
- *Networking capabilities:* sharing of data and information among students and faculty [48].

13.2.2.1 Related Works

The idea of collaborating CPSs with Education has gained popularity over the years and various researchers have contributed in this experimentation along with case studies. One of the studies focused on describing the use of Quartz language along with Averest toolset to implement cyber-physical system for educational purposes. The methodology was implemented for a post graduation course and focused on evaluation through practical work assignments given to students [7].

In another study, a smart laboratory was created through a cyber-physical system which included procedures related to habit based control, less audible communications and statistical analysis [36, 37].

The authors in [24] and [15] delineated their ideology related to offering cyber-physical systems as a mandatory course with theory and practical in the curriculum of undergraduate students. The idea is to provide an insight to students about the relevance and need of cyber-physical systems.

Student engagement for evaluation and testing of CPS has also been encouraged by different researchers. In one of the studies, a programming model was developed that encouraged students to implement and test CPS control programs. Students modeled and programmed a CPS application through a web page. As a case study, students applied the proposed model in an embedded system design lab work [45].

13.2.3   Agriculture

Through technologies such as precision agriculture, smart water management, and efficient food circulation, CPS research can enhance gross food productivity and availability, thereby playing a vital role in agricultural development. Sustained monitoring of the environment and its consequences on crops is used in agriculture to attain optimal output. Furthermore, contemporary tools and technologies can integrate information technology and agricultural science to boost crop output in a way that is both economically and environmentally sustainable.

A CPS built and used to agriculture, the Agricultural Cyber-Physics System (ACPS), may collect crucial information on climate, soil, and crops in a high-granularity and timely manner to achieve a more accurate agricultural management system. ACPS may also continually monitor various resources, including as irrigation, humidity, plant health, and so on, using sensors in order to maintain ideal environmental values using actuators and devices.

A typical ACPS system is composed of:

- *Sensors*—Sensors are installed physically in different regions across the fields for monitoring environmental variables like temperature, pressure, humidity and so on. Further, data collection occurs and distributed across the network.
- *Network*—Data is sent from the receiving node to the control center using network communication equipment.
- *Control center*—The data collected by the sensor nodes is evaluated by the remote control center, to determine the directives of target agricultural facility.
- *Farming tasks*—Agricultural activities like fertilizing, irrigating, spraying insecticides, and so on are controlled remotely [2].

13.2.3.1   Related Work

In [53], authors shared a cost effective greenhouse observation system for scientific farming by observing different atmospheric properties such as temperature, humidity and illuminance.

Irrigation schedules can be improved based on soil water monitoring. There have been a variety of methodologies used to study geographical variance of irrigation water amount. For this purpose, [1] experimented by installing sensors with in the areas to monitor the amount of irrigation water required. It is observed that electrical conductivity of soil and field elevation parameters can be used to distinguish the field areas as per different levels of water requirements.

Researchers in [55] used soil moisture data derived from sensors put in the field, along with crop reflectance measurements, to calculate wheat yield potential and nitrogen fertilizer rate is required.

Profitability of fruit farming is always a concern for modern agriculture systems. An autonomous infield monitoring system was created by [29] to efficiently collect long-term and current environmental variations in a fruit field, with the goal of improving integrated pest management program. Using WSNs, a remote observatory system was developed to provide precision farming services that can collect large-scale, long-distance and long-term infield data.

Based on multitemporal and multispectral satellite photos [10] provided a procedure for estimating groundwater required for irrigation. The procedure starts by classifying the crop, then this data is entered into the CPS, along with an accurate estimation of the crop's water needs, and rectified as per farming exercises in the area.

Smart Pest Control system has been developed by [43] for efficient monitoring of rats in the fields to avoid crop loss. Using this approach, one can save a ton of money to be spent on pest control, agricultural waste, and pollution.

On the basis of CPS architecture and design technologies consisting of four levels, namely physical, network, decision and application layer, [47] developed a precision agriculture observatory system to capture the vegetation status of potato crop. In order to boost agricultural output, farmers can use the proposed system to track the evolution of particular metrics of interest and make suitable decisions.

13.2.4   Energy Management

Cyber-Physical Energy Systems (CPESs) are special embedded systems that manage physical and virtual variables such as battery life, power flow, computational process and network limits that constitute basic requirements for the bulk of existing energy systems [65]. Most of the current energy systems are large and distributed to adhere with new challenges and futuristic energy demands. Moreover, these systems should be flexible, efficient, sustainable, reliable, and secure. Because of this, Cyber-Physical Energy Systems (CPESs) have been deemed to be a suitable option for adaptive performance. CPES can achieve this level of performance by incorporating virtual technologies to monitor, communicate and control the growing physical systems in a systematic manner [42].

Listed below are the desirable characteristics of a CPES:

- *Reliability:* These systems should not compromise with system failures and environmental changes.
- *Autonomies:* Unexpected situations and subsystem breakdowns must be accommodated by CPES's robustness. It should be self-adapting and self-repairing in the event of a problem, i.e. it should be self-reliant.
- *Integrated:* By using network connectivity or embedded real-time systems, CPES should be able to integrate compute and physical energy processes;
- *Networked:* In distributed systems, CPES makes use of networks. These internal networks include wired/wireless networks, Wireless LAN, Bluetooth, and other technologies to accommodate variety of devices and services.

Smart Grids (SGs) are emerging as the next-generation electrical power grid, capable of adaptive and optimal power generation, distribution, and consumption. They intend to intelligently integrate the behaviors and actions of all stakeholders in the energy supply chain in order to efficiently deliver sustainable, economic, and secure electric energy, as well as to ensure economical and environmentally sustainable use. The seamless integration and interaction of power network infrastructure as physical systems and information sensing, processing, intelligence, and control as cyber systems is critical to the success of SGs. Furthermore, the emerging new technology platform known as cyber–physical energy systems (CPESs) and cyber–physical power systems (CPSSs) is the perfect solution to address the specific integration and interaction issues in SGs, focusing on effective and efficient interaction and integration of physical and cyber systems. Adopting CPS technologies in SGs will improve their operational efficiency, responsiveness to prosumers, economic viability, and environmental sustainability [64].

13.2.4.1 Related Work

[56] created a cyber-physical power system application that can collect real time power consumption statistics and shared the need of autonomous electric vehicles and charging stations in the smart grid. The energy management framework presented also observed reduction in energy consumption, allowing for more efficient power supply and distribution.

[38] developed a distributed model cyber-physical power systems that are vulnerable to data attacks. They mentioned dynamic state estimators based on a 9-bus power system for optimum control of large scale distributed systems.

[42] presented a cyber-physical smart grid model based on an incremental approach across micro grid. CPS components, as well as cyber and physical networks that indicate linkages, are incorporated into this schematic model. The cyber and physical components of these CPS modules were combined. In the cyber world, each physical component has a virtual counterpart. Microsource (DG) and loads, on the other hand, are present in each microgrid component. Microsources are controlled by a micro source controller, and each load is controlled by a local controller. In the cyber realm, these controllers have a matching component. The communication network is used to communicate between the local controllers and the Micro grid Central Controller. At the physical layer, energy is exchanged. Authors have also recommended future study topics such as de-centralized load management, closed loop voltage control, and small signal stabilization applied to smart grids.

[18] described the innovative INSPIRE co-simulation environment for both power and ICT systems, which is intended for assessing smart grid applications. The study evaluated the substantial influence of ICT scenarios on the performance of CPES applications for identifying a critical power system condition and recovering from the disturbed state by executing suitable countermeasures.

The goal of [50] is to comprehensively describe the interaction models and accompanying solution approaches in current CPPS research. The interactive characteristics of CPPSs are explored, as well as their modeling methods, which are thoroughly evaluated and described from the visual, mechanism, probability, and simulation perspectives. Furthermore, the applicability and features of these models that are appropriate for certain study topics are explored. Various CPSS-related problem-solving techniques are also examined and addressed.

Authors proposed the idea of Energy Internet Cyber-Physical Systems (EI-CPS) in this research study [14]. Different morphological characteristics have been studied, such as dynamic property of multi energy flow, efficient and fast information processing capability, and coupling between energy and information flow, as well as technical challenges encountered in the implementation of EI-CPS.

13.2.5   Smart Transportation

Intelligent transportation aims to provide better transport services to society by enhancing public safety, reducing wait time, better traffic management, avoid congestion of traffic, etc. through sophisticated sensing, communication, computing, and control techniques. Researchers aim to achieve zero traffic death rate through implementation of autonomous vehicles.

Intelligent cars have improved their skills in highly and even completely autonomous driving. Before shifting to completely autonomous driving, it's crucial to study driving so that an improved vehicle performance and traffic throughput could be achieved.

Smart transportation cyber-physical systems, also known as Cyber-physical vehicle systems (CPVS) or Vehicular cyber-physical systems (VCPS), are made up of the following subsystems:

- *Controller*—The cyber world
- *Physical vehicle plant*
- *Driver*
- *Human Intervention*
- *Environment.*

The behavior and final performance of the vehicle are determined by these strongly linked components. The co-design process in CPVS enables us to fully explore the system's potential by optimizing physical architecture and parameters in collaboration with the controller [31]. We must examine the "Human" of an autonomous car in addition to the cyber and physical worlds. In addition, the interaction effects of the vehicle plant, controlling factors and driving styles should be thoroughly studied [41].

The design optimization of a CPVS, by considering process duration, actuator properties, energy consumption, and controller workload, was explored in [8].

The co-design of a typical CPVS utilizing platform-based design approach has been addressed in [41], which comprises of an autonomous vehicle with multiple driving behaviors. The study aimed to identify best design variable values to optimize the performance of system while fulfilling a number of restrictions.

13.2.5.1   Related Work

In the area of transportation engineering, traffic measurement is one of the core functionalities as mentioned in [66]. The study discussed the implementation of road CPS for autonomous traffic data collection by counting the number of vehicles moving across different physical locations.

In addition to general circuitry in a cyber-physical system, CPVS includes wireless and satellite monitoring techniques to handle complicated traffic flows, assure safety, and expand situational awareness. CPS research related to autonomous vehicles also tends to enhance communication between vehicles and infrastructures [33].

Computer vision algorithms based on convolutional neural networks (CNN) are utilized to automate the detection and re-identification of trucks utilizing traffic cameras in order to correlate vehicle weights to bridge responses [26].

[62] investigates the characteristics of cyber-physical vehicle system such as heterogeneity and distributedness, and then proposed a model with extended hybrid automata in CPVS. Finally, an experimental study based on the proposed model has been discussed for vehicle speed control system.

13.2.6   Smart Manufacturing

Because of factors such as mass production, local and international marketing, economic expansion, and so on, smart manufacturing has become an emerging area.

Nowadays, it is widely acknowledged that the primary difficulties in the design of production systems are flexibility, modularity, and reconfigurability. Smart manufacturing involves integration of software and hardware techniques to enhance efficiency in the manufacturing [21]. Another term that is commonly used to describe next-generation smart manufacturing is "smart factory". CPS is a critical technology for understanding Smart Manufacturing.

One of the results of the Industrie 4.0 initiative is Smart Manufacturing. Industry 4.0 is a strategic project launched by Germany that provides a significant potential for future production [25]. The goal of Industrie 4.0 is to be a trailblazer in future production. The Smart Manufacturing Leadership Coalition (SMLC), a non-profit organization, was founded in the United States comprising of manufacturing suppliers, practitioners, and consortia, as well as technology firms, educational institutions and government labs for achieving future smart manufacturing [52].

This fourth industrial revolution has impacted a wide range of industries, including manufacturing, education, and the military. There are four key elements at the heart of Industry 4.0 that make it the most powerful revolution in history. The Internet of Things (IoT), Internet of Services (IoS), Smart Factory, and Cyber-Physical Systems are the main aspects. According to the authors, Smart Factory is a component of Smart Manufacturing and hence a key feature of Industry 4.0. The architecture of Cyber-Physical Manufacturing Systems (CPMS) proposed by [61] comprises of following modules:

- *System Input*—includes customer product requirements, man power, raw materials, funds, etc.
- *Internet of Services*—to handle virtual service related activities connectivity, interoperatability, virtualization, cloud computing, web service, etc.
- *Internet of Things*—sensors and actuators, etc.
- *Cyber-Physical System*—for integrating physical and virtual environments as per defined standards for data exchange, processing, and communications.
- *Internet of Content and Knowledge*—for efficient processing of data to be transformed into useful information during manufacturing process.
- *Interconnection*—how all components are collaborating among themselves.
- *Factory*—place representing physical manufacturing of products where process is controlled by all other components as per interconnection in manufacturing process.
- *Output*—manufactured goods, products, services.

13.2.6.1   Related Work

To deal with changes in the industrial environment, the author suggested a paradigm and technology for building a Cyber-Physical Manufacturing System (CPMS). These CPMSs are biologically inspired engineered systems that exhibit the behavior of being self-adjusting and auto-recovering as well as highly responsive to changing manufacturing demands. The architecture of CPMS is mainly based on Internet of Things (IoT) paradigm comprising of wireless and sensor networks [54].

In [12], authors discussed a logical structure of CPS based smart factory integrated with different technologies like Big data, Digital twin, virtualization and cloud computing. The model presented is way similar to the notion of Industry 4.0 that involves the integration of leading edge technologies to provide better manufacturing solutions. It has also been discovered that the combination of these technologies would also result in an engineered system that would exhibit properties like self-adjusting, self-learning, inferring, etc.

[59] introduced Cyber-Physical Product Service System (CPSS) and its application to industry examples. They asserted that by using CPSS industry can easily understand the change in requirements with respect to service, hardware and software and ultimately would offer better adaptability to changing manufacturing demands.

[6] presented a model of automated warehouse based on cyber-physical system to achieve higher flexibility.

13.2.7   Smart Buildings: Smart Cities and Smart Houses

The growing popularity of CPS-based infrastructure makes the concept of smart buildings a reality. The process of making buildings smart mainly consists of installing a distributed CPS to control and automate different basic building processes like heating, cooling, ventilation, lighting, managing security systems, etc. Smart/Intelligent Building is often mentioned in context to the next-generation building. Moreover, these are required to comprehend the notions of smart grid, smart city and smart homes [21].

Smart city refers to a next-generation urban infrastructure that accounts for smart integration of services including Energy distribution, Medical facilities, Security, Transportation, Environmental monitoring, Business management, and Social Interactions.

One of the important constituents of smart cities are smart homes that too require smart integration of CPS elements to control physical and virtual environment within a house.

The ultimate goal of smart infrastructure, comprising of intelligent buildings, smart houses and smart cities, is to provide ease in lives of residents. Smart infrastructure will also contribute in public protection through implementation of smart transport [13].

13.2.7.1   Related Work

[9] identifies the characteristics of some important definitions of smart cities, explains some lessons learned from this in CPS, and explains some basic research agendas. The author proposed smart cities as a new CPS paradigm that includes strict system requirements to ensure personal information protection, flexibility, environmental considerations and processing large amounts of information.

Different smart house models have been presented by researchers including the Gator Tech Smart House, Duke University Smart House, Smart Home by Iowa State University, and National Institute of Information and Communications Technology (NICT) Ubiquitous Home, etc. [19].

[49] discussed a user-friendly model of a smart house equipped with mobile based control center which was designed to facilitate all types of users with ubiquitous access to control complex components of CPS represented by sensors, actuators, process and robots.

[36] presented the notion of applying CPS for laboratory automation. With the technological advancements, the laboratories' works have also been revolutionized with inclusion of new equipment setups and services consisting of regularizing environmental conditions, analyzing incidents and other abnormalities, etc.

13.3   Conclusion

The Cyber-Physical Systems (CPSs) has gained popularity over the time to be a good fit for academic research and industry oriented tasks. It has emerged as a best design standard present and future digital systems in collaboration with real world. In fact, the notion of Industry 4.0 has increased the popularity of CPS and made researchers think about the implementation of CPS from different dimensions. CPS has been put forth as one of the main components of Industry 4.0.

The idea behind CPS is not merely focused on the integration of physical and cyber world rather additionally, demands for sophisticated data gathering and management, computation and analysis of the information flow between physical and virtual environment. In addition, CPS are expected to exhibit other desirable properties including, adjustability, efficiency, reliability, security and usability.

In this review, the importance of CPS from interdisciplinary view point has been presented. The major building blocks of the CPS have also been mentioned. Although CPS is a wide research area, it spans over varied interdisciplinary applications in different dimensions. Therefore, each application requires the analysis of related system architecture, features, requirements, reasoning competencies and integration with advanced technologies. Although there are numerous application areas pertaining to implementation of CPS but in this study we have focused majorly on Healthcare, Education, Agriculture, Energy Management, Smart Transportation, Smart Manufacturing and Smart Buildings. The elaborative study about these areas includes features, CPS architecture and related works for each application area. The other interesting CPS application areas are Military, Robotics, Decision Making, Process Control, Diagnostics, Aeronautics, Civil Infrastructure Monitoring, etc. After studying few of the CPS application areas, it has been realized that each of them can be further investigated as a separate research area as it included distinct and multiple sub applications.

References

1. Adamchuk, V., II, Pan, L., Marx, D.B., Martin, D.L., Locating soil monitoring sites using spatial analysis of multilayer data, in: *Proceedings of 19th World Congress of Soil Science*, pp. 1–6, 2010.
2. An, W., Wu, D., Ci, S., Luo, H., Adamchuk, V., Xu, Z., Agriculture cyber-physical systems, in: *Cyber-physical systems*, pp. 399–417, Academic Press, Boston, 2017.
3. Avrunin, G.S., Clarke, L.A., Osterweil, L.J., Rausch, T., Smart checklists for human-intensive medical systems, in: *IEEE/IFIP International Conference on Dependable Systems and Networks Workshops (DSN 2012)*, IEEE, pp. 1–6, 2012.
4. Aziz, S.M. and Pham, D.M., Energy efficient image transmission in wireless multimedia sensor networks. *IEEE Commun. Lett.*, 17, 6, 1084–1087, 2013.
5. Banerjee, A., Gupta, S.K.S., Fainekos, G., Varsamopoulos, G., Towards modeling and analysis of cyber-physical medical systems, in: *Proceedings of the 4th International Symposium on Applied Sciences in Biomedical and Communication Technologies*, pp. 1–5, 2011.

6. Basile, F., Chiacchio, P., Coppola, J., Gerbasio, D., Automated warehouse systems: A cyber-physical system perspective, in: *2015 IEEE 20th Conference on Emerging Technologies & Factory Automation (ETFA)*, IEEE, pp. 1–4, 2015.

7. Bauer, K. and Schneider, K., Teaching cyber-physical systems: A programming approach, in: *Proceedings of the Workshop on Embedded and Cyber-Physical Systems Education*, pp. 1–8, 2012.

8. Bradley, J.M. and Atkins, E.M., Optimization and control of cyber-physical vehicle systems. *Sensors*, 15, 9, 23020–23049, 2015.

9. Cassandras, C.G., Smart cities as cyber-physical social systems. *Eng. J.*, 2, 2, 156–158, 2016.

10. Castaño, S., Sanz, D., Gómez-Alday, J.J., Methodology for quantifying groundwater abstractions for agriculture via remote sensing and GIS. *Water Resour. Manage.*, 24, 4, 795–814, 2010.

11. Chattopadhyay, A., Prakash, A., Shafique, M., Secure Cyber-Physical Systems: Current trends, tools and open research problems, in: *Design, Automation & Test in Europe Conference & Exhibition (DATE), 2017*, IEEE, pp. 1104–1109, 2017.

12. Chen, G., Wang, P., Feng, B., Li, Y., Liu, D., The framework design of smart factory in discrete manufacturing industry based on cyber-physical system. *Int. J. Comput. Integr. Manuf.*, 33, 1, 79–101, 2020.

13. Chen, H., Applications of cyber-physical system: a literature review. *J. Ind. Inf. Integr.*, 2, 03, 1750012, 2017.

14. Chen, Z., Zhang, Y., Cai, Z., Li, L., Liu, P., Characteristics and technical challenges in energy Internet cyber-physical system, in: *2016 IEEE PES Innovative Smart Grid Technologies Conference Europe (ISGT-Europe)*, IEEE, pp. 1–5, 2016.

15. Cheng, A.M.K., An undergraduate cyber-physical systems course, in: *Proceedings of the 4th ACM SIGBED International Workshop on Design, Modeling, and Evaluation of Cyber-Physical Systems*, pp. 31–34, 2014.

16. Cyber Physical Systems, Program Solicitation, National Science Foundation, Directorate for Computer & Information Science & Engineering, accessed on August 30, 2021. https://www.nsf.gov/pubs/2010/nsf10515/nsf10515.htm, 2010.

17. Rodrigues, J.J.P.C. and Sene, M., Real-time data management on wireless sensor networks: A survey. *J. Netw. Comput. Appl.*, 35, 3, 1013–1021, 2012.

18. Georg, H., Müller, S.C., Rehtanz, C., Wietfeld, C., Analyzing cyber-physical energy systems: The INSPIRE cosimulation of power and ICT systems using HLA. *IEEE Trans. Industr. Inform.*, 10, 4, 2364–2373, 2014.

19. Hoseini, G., Hosein, A., Dahlan, N.D., Berardi, U., Hoseini, A.G., Nastaran, M., The essence of future smart houses: From embedding ICT to adapting to sustainability principles. *Renew. Sust. Energ.*, 24, 593–607, 2013. https://doi.org/10.1016/j.rser.2013.02.032.

20. Gill, H., NSF perspective and status on cyber-physical systems, in: *National Workshop on Cyber-physical Systems*, Austin, TX, 2006.

21. Gunes, V., Peter, S., Givargis, T., Vahid, F., A survey on concepts, applications, and challenges in cyber-physical systems. *KSII Trans. Internet Inf. (TIIS)*, 8, 12, 4242–4268, 2014.

22. Haque, S.A., Aziz, S.M., Rahman, M., Review of cyber-physical system in healthcare. *Int. J. Distrib. Sens. Netw.*, 10, 4, 217415, 2014.

23. Hassan, M.M., Lin, K., Yue, X., Wan, J., A multimedia healthcare data sharing approach through cloud-based body area network. *Future Gener. Comput. Syst.*, 66, 48–58, 2017.

24. Helps, Richard, G., Pack, S.J., Cyber-physical system concepts for IT students, in: *Proceedings of the 14th annual ACM SIGITE conference on Information technology education*, pp. 7–12, 2013.

25. Henning, K., Wahlster, W., Helbig, J., Recommendations for implementing the strategic initiative INDUSTRIE 4.0, Final Report of the Industrie 4.0 Working Group, acatech -- National Academy of Science and Engineering, München, April 2013.

26. Hou, R., Jeong, S., Lynch, J.P., Law, K.H., Cyber-physical system architecture for automating the mapping of truck loads to bridge behavior using computer vision in connected highway corridors. *Transp. Res. Part C Emerg. Technol.*, 111, 547–571, 2020. https://doi.org/10.1016/j.trc.2019.11.024.

27. Hu, L., Xie, N., Kuang, Z., Zhao, K., Review of Cyber-Physical System Architecture. *2012 IEEE 15th International Symposium on Object/Component/Service-Oriented Real-Time Distributed Computing Workshops*, pp. 25–30, 2012.

28. Iso-Ketola, P., Karinsalo, T., Vanhala, J., HipGuard: A wearable measurement system for patients recovering from a hip operation, in: *2008 Second International Conference on Pervasive Computing Technologies for Healthcar*, IEEE, pp. 196–199, 2008.

29. Jiang, J., Lin, T., Yang, E., Tseng, C., Chen, C., Yen, C., Zheng, X. *et al.*, Application of a web-based remote agro-ecological monitoring system for observing spatial distribution and dynamics of Bactrocera dorsalis in fruit orchards. *Precis. Agric.*, 14, 3, 323–342, 2013.

30. Jovanov, E., Milenkovic, A., Otto, C., De Groen, P.C., A wireless body area network of intelligent motion sensors for computer assisted physical rehabilitation. *J. Neoroeng. Rehabil.*, 2, 1, 1–10, 2005.

31. Justin, M. and Atkins, E.M., Cyber–physical optimization for unmanned aircraft systems. *J. Aerosp. Inf. Syst.*, 11, 1, 48–60, 2014.

32. Kang, W., *Adaptive real-time data management for Cyber-Physical Systems*, University of Virginia, USA, 2009.

33. Kim, K. and Kumar, P.R., An overview and some challenges in cyber-physical systems. *J. Indian Inst. Sci.*, 93, 3, 341–352, 2013.

34. Konstantas, D. and Herzog, R., Continuous monitoring of vital constants for mobile users: the MobiHealth approach, in: *Proceedings of the 25th Annual International Conference of the IEEE Engineering in Medicine and Biology Society (IEEE Cat. No. 03CH37439)*, vol. 4, IEEE, pp. 3728–3731, 2003.

35. Lee, I., Sokolsky, O., Chen, S., Hatcliff, J., Jee, E., Kim, B., King, A. *et al.*, Challenges and research directions in medical cyber–physical systems, in: *Proceedings of the IEEE*, vol. 100, pp. 75–90, 2011.

36. Lei, C., Liang, H., Man, K.L., Building a smart laboratory environment at a university via a cyber-physical system, in: *Proceedings of 2013 IEEE International Conference on Teaching, Assessment and Learning for Engineering (TALE)*, IEEE, pp. 243–247, 2013.

37. Lei, C., Man, K.L., Liang, H., Lim, E.G., Wan, K., Building an intelligent laboratory environment via a cyber-physical system. *Int. J. Distrib. Sens.*, 9, 12, 109014, 2013.

38. Li, Y., Wu, J., Li, S., State estimation for distributed cyber-physical power systems under data attacks. *Int. J. Model. Identif. Control.*, 26, 4, 317–323, 2016.

39. Li, Y., Jacob, M., Akingba, G., Wachs, J.P., A cyber-physical management system for delivering and monitoring surgical instruments in the OR. *Surg. Innov.*, 20, 4, 377–384, 2013.

40. Lounis, A., Hadjidj, A., Bouabdallah, A., Challal, Y., Secure and scalable cloud-based architecture for e-health wireless sensor networks, in: *2012 21st International Conference on Computer Communications and Networks (ICCCN)*, IEEE, pp. 1–7, 2012.

41. Chen, L., Xing, Y., Zhang, J., Cao, D., Cyber-Physical Vehicle Systems: Methodology and Applications, in: *Synthesis Lectures on Advances in Automotive Technologies*, vol. 4, pp. 1–85, 2020.

42. Macana, C.A., Quijano, N., Mojica-Nava, E., A survey on cyber physical energy systems and their applications on smart grids. *2011 IEEE PES conference on innovative smart grid technologies Latin America (ISGT LA)*, IEEE, pp. 1–7, 2011.

43. Mehdipour, F., Smart field monitoring: An application of cyber-physical systems in agriculture (work in progress), in: *2014 IIAI 3rd International Conference on Advanced Applied Informatics*, IEEE, pp. 181–184, 2014.

44. Miah, S.J., Hasan, J., Gammack, J.G., On-cloud healthcare clinic: an e-health consultancy approach for remote communities in a developing country. *Telemat. Inform.*, 34, 1, 311–322, 2017.

45. Peter, S., Momtaz, F., Givargis, T., From the browser to the remote physical lab: Programming cyber-physical systems, in: *2015 IEEE Frontiers in Education Conference (FIE)*, IEEE, pp. 1–7, 2015.

46. Pilevar, A.H., DISR: Dental image segmentation and retrieval. *J. Med. Signals. Sens.*, 2, 1, 42, 2012.

47. Rad, C.R., Hancu, O., Takacs, I.A., Olteanu, G., Smart monitoring of potato crop: a cyber-physical system architecture model in the field of precision agriculture. *Agriculture and Agricultural Science Procedia*, vol. 6, pp. 73–79, 2015.

48. Santos, R., Devincenzi, S., Botelho, S., Bichet, M., A model for implementation of educational cyber physical systems. *Rev. Spacious*, 39, 10, 36–54, 2018.

49. Seiger, R., Lemme, D., Struwe, S., Schlegel, T., An interactive mobile control center for cyber-physical systems, in: *Proceedings of the 2016 ACM International Joint Conference on Pervasive and Ubiquitous Computing: Adjunct*, pp. 193–196, 2016.

50. Shi, L., Dai, Q., Ni, Y., Cyber–physical interactions in power systems: A review of models, methods, and applications, in: *Electric Power Systems Research*, vol. 163, pp. 396–412, 2018.

51. Shnayder, V., Chen, B., Lorincz, K., Fulford-Jones, T.R.F., Welsh, M., Sensor networks for medical care. *Proceedings of the 3rd International Conference on Embedded Networked Sensor Systems*, 2005.

52. Implementing 21st Century Smart Manufacturing, in: *Workshop Summary Report*, SMLC - Smart Manufacturing Leadership Coalition, Washington, D.C, 2011.

53. Srbinovska, M., Gavrovski, C., Dimcev, V., Krkoleva, A., Borozan, V., Environmental parameters monitoring in precision agriculture using wireless sensor networks. *J. Clean. Prod.*, 88, 297–307, 2015.

54. Tran, N.H., Park, H.S., Nguyen, Q.V., Hoang, T.D., Development of a smart cyber-physical manufacturing system in the industry 4.0 context. *Appl. Sci.*, 9, 16, 3325, 2019.

55. Walsh, A.R., Olga, S., Klatt, A.R., Solie, J.B., Godsey, C.B., Raun, W.R., Use of soil moisture data for refined GreenSeekersensor based nitrogen recommendations in winter wheat (Triticum aestivum L.). *Precis. Agric.*, 14, 3, 343–356, 2013.

56. Wan, J., Yan, H., Li, D., Zhou, K., Zeng, L., Cyber-physical systems for optimal energy management scheme of autonomous electric vehicle. *J. Comput.*, 56, 8, 947–956, 2013.

57. Wang, C.C., Chiang, C.Y., Lin, P.Y., Chou, Y.C., Kuo, I.T., Huang, C.N., Chan, C.T., Development of a fall detecting system for the elderly residents. *In 2008 2nd international conference on bioinformatics and biomedical engineering*, IEEE, pp. 1359–1362, 2008.

58. Wang, J., Abid, H., Lee, S., Shu, L., Xia, F., A secured healthcare application architecture for cyber-physical systems, *Control Engineering and Applied Informatics*, 13, 3, 101–108, 2011. arXiv preprint arXiv:1201.0213.

59. Wiesner, S., Marilungo, E., Thoben, K.D., Cyber-physical product-service systems–challenges for requirements engineering. *Int. J. Autom. Technol.*, 11, 1, 17–28, 2017.

60. Wood, A.D., Stankovic, J.A., Virone, G., Selavo, L., He, Z., Cao, Q., Doan, T., Wu, Y., Fang, L., Stoleru, R., Context-aware wireless sensor networks for assisted living and residential monitoring. *IEEE J. Netw.*, 22, 4, 26–33, 2008.

61. Yao, X., Zhou, J., Lin, Y., Li, Y., Yu, H., Liu, Y., Smart manufacturing based on cyber-physical systems and beyond. *J. Intell. Manuf.*, 30, 8, 2805–2817, 2019.

62. Li, Y.J., Chen, M.C., Zhang, G.Q., Shao, Y., Feng, F., Xi, H., A model for vehicular cyber-physical system based on extended hybrid automaton,

in: *2013 8th International Conference on Computer Science & Education*, IEEE, pp. 1305–1308, 2013.

63. Yilmaz, T., Munoz, M., Foster, R.N., Hao, Y., Wearable wireless sensors for healthcare applications, in: *2013 International Workshop on Antenna Technology (iWAT)*, IEEE, pp. 376–379, 2013.

64. Yu, X. and Xue, Y., Smart grids: A cyber–physical systems perspective. *Proceedings of the IEEE*, vol. 104, pp. 1058–1070, 2016.

65. Zhang, F., Shi, Z., Wolf., W., A dynamic battery model for co-design in cyber-physical systems, in: *2009 29th IEEE International Conference on Distributed Computing Systems Workshops*, IEEE, pp. 51–56, 2009.

66. Privacy-preserving point-to-point transportation traffic measurement through bit array masking in intelligent cyber-physical road systems, in: *2013 IEEE International Conference on Green Computing and Communications and IEEE Internet of Things and IEEE Cyber, Physical and Social Computing*, IEEE, pp. 826–833, 2013.

Index

Printed and bound by CPI Group (UK) Ltd, Croydon, CR0 4YY

27/10/2024

14580126-0002